Those were the golden days

By

Gloriana Selvanathan

Published 2014 by arima publishing

www.arimapublishing.com

ISBN 978 1 84549 628 9
© Gloriana Selvanathan 2014

Printed and bound in the United Kingdom

Typeset in Garamond

Swirl is an imprint of arima publishing.

arima publishing
ASK House, Northgate Avenue
Bury St Edmunds, Suffolk IP32 6BB
t: (+44) 01284 700321

www.arimapublishing.com

About the author

Gloriana Selvanathan hails from Sri Lanka and lives in Berlin, for the past 29 years. Her first book *4th Dimension of Love*, was published in 2005. This is her second book. She is the International Coordinator for International Film Festivals and Jury for the same festivals. Her life in Berlin, revolves around the film world. She worked in television, produced Documentary films and has her own school for English language, speech and drama in Berlin.

This book is dedicated to

My noble father Mr.S.V.Gunanayagam

and

My wonderful mother Gnanamani Gunanayagm

Who brought us up with love, care and affection

Foreword

It is strange how in a moment of crisis the mind whips back to childhood. My mind refused to drift away from the radiance of memory. Once I was discussing my childhood to that of the present generation in the language school, and found the interest in their eyes deepening. Students were eagerly listening to my satisfying, blissful, challenging, adventurous, depressing, and horrifying, discontented, intrigued, indignant, stubborn, provocative, Idyll, prudent and many other qualities reflected in my childhood. For many of them it was something that existed only in fiction and fairytale. There were torrent of questions from them, which made me to think if there was so much interest, then I should talk about it not only relating the incidents in bits and pieces, but to express the whole episode of my childhood, like a Banyan tree with roots, main branches, with fruits, green leaves and dried leaves so that one could see the complete picture. This book is the result of such feeling.

I was a dreamer full of theories never put to test when I was a child. Perplexity to fantasy endeavored to induce me to act strangely in the most awkward situation. Forgotten memories down past all those nerve cells, dark alleys leading to my brain box and revived my old instincts. I had tried a decent observance for the etiquette of speaking no ill of the dead. Surely my childhood was eventful, awesome and hilarious but it was never dull. We knew good food, good people and excellent upbringing.

Those were the days, sustainability and social justice could be combined. I had often thought how lucky that we were not brought up in a tasteless home or disagreeable parents. Remarkable parents are uncommon. The glories of those days are gone but the memory is still embedded in each cell and the nerves are throbbing with the full force of its application.

Later in life when we faced the grief, the disgust, the gaffe and regret, the illusion of escape that mattered. For me often the golden memory of my childhood was that escape. Beautiful were the days that are gone. When I sit with people, who talked simplistic nonsense my thoughts would fly backwards to the meaningful and noble teachings of my parents, which I still remember but could not bring them all into practice, due to the artificial life we have imposed on ourselves, willingly or not. I want my children and other young people, who have left my country and lost part of their heritage and culture, to know that they come from a background, which they can be proud of.

When I asked about various locations that I remembered about my town, I was informed that they were either changed or did not exist. My vivid memories should not be buried with me. It should be a reconnaissance. I have tried my best to give the exact picture, but cannot over rule some flaws. In that case I would sincerely acknowledge it was not intentional.

I have attached the maximum number of photographs I could get, to add colour to my story, thinking something is better than nothing although some of them are very old and poor in quality. I apologize for that.

My purpose of this book is to bring happiness for those who lived in my period to overcome the nostalgia they have, which could only rewind the memories but not bring the possibility of seeing that ever again, neither the people nor the places whereas for the others to know that those things really happened and the places really existed that they could at least visualize them as a utopia and wonder. I hope in either way I satisfy the readers. This book is never intended for the intellectuals but for the common people and young people who could read and understand simple language and enjoy. I sign this book on the 16th of March the 87th wedding anniversary of my parents, for whom I extend the greatest respect and thank you, for the marvelous life they had given to me and my siblings during our childhood. Therefore my parents deserve this tribute.

I really wish this book will become a bridge between all our friends and those, who knew my parents.

Gloriana.Gunarubini Selvanathan. 16th March 2014.

(Nee Gunanayagam) Berlin.

Chapter 1

My little town

The town Point Pedro in the northern most part of Sri Lanka was the town I was born and bred. It is a coastal town but something special. Due to the salty sea breeze, there were different plants in different areas. Waving casuarinas lining the road green heads reaching far into the blue or the vibrant colours of Bougainvilleas and Hibiscus or the slender coconut palms bent and stretched or the zyrophetic cactus and creepers with red and purple flowers decorated the road sides of the coast. The dark tarred roads occasionally marred by the white patches of holes due to wears and tares met by the sandy lanes meant only for pedestrians and bikes, were common occurrences. Conglomeration of shanty clay huts alternated with the white washed houses of the rich people, interspaced with the occasional crumbling ware houses, were typical sights in the area. Towards the middle of the town, rare combination of open space occasionally filled with shrubs and bushes but mostly habitable, existed together with the houses and buildings. My part of the town captured your imagination with its curving white beaches and brilliant tropical colours with its cheerful friendly populace. In the monsoon seasons the sun shot glistening rays among the early mists from the sea. In the afternoons the morning coolness from the sea was gone and the air lay like halting in the hot sun. Heat was not exactly broken but certainly bent enough to still hurt. The high humidity was lessened, when the clouds drifted in cotton wool patches lending light and shadow. In the nights when there was no moon, the stars were brilliant dome, no moon to dim their sparkle. The long slow roll of the sea, out there under the moonlight, showing the phosphorous shimmering over the curling head of bow wave was my everlasting memory

Point Pedro was and is the northern most point of Sri Lanka. Actually its name in Tamil "Paruthithurai" has been used from time that cannot be traced. The translation of it is "Cotton Harbour". The origin of this name may be the ancient practice of exporting cotton to India done by the special section of people "*Samankarar*" which means ship people. The western name Point Pedro was given during the colonial time. A Dutch sailor travelling along the coast of Northern Sri Lanka found this town as the Northern most point of the Island and the town was named after him. Actually the name was "Pethuru Thurai" means "Pethuru Harbour". But later being the Northern most point it became

Point Pedro. This was the only reason given by my father for the town's name. When I asked him how was that possible that people change the original name, he told me another good example. There is a bridge in South India which is called Barber's Bridge. Nobody knew why that bridge was called by that name, because there was no connection to barbers and the bridge what so ever. Then Dr. Sethuppilai, a great scholar in one of his books explained how the name came. The bridge was named after one of the British person Lord Hamden during the Colonial time. During the course of time the name changed in the tongues of the locals as "Ambatten Bridge". "Ambatton" means "Barber" in Tamil. Therefore they translated it as Barber's Bridge". Similarly there were different stories for the name of my town. The Sinhalese name "Pethuru Thoduwa" has the same meaning as the western name.

To understand the things about my visits, habits, various incidents and activities you should know where those places were situated. My house was situated at the meeting point of two streets. Beach road on the left and right and the First cross street which ended in Beach road. Most of the people who lived around us were educated Christians and Hindus. But the local people were mostly associated with the sea, either fisher folks, who earned their wages by selling fish or cargo boat owners. They all had the greatest respect for my parents and everyone knew who I was. On the left side of our house was the colleague of my father, who taught at the same Boy's College. He had a daughter by his first marriage and a son by the second marriage. The son was a classmate of my third brother but he played more with me than with my brother, when we were children.

Our neighbour built a new house opposite to our house because he had to give the old house, which was next to our house, as a dowry to his daughter. They moved to the new house. He named the new house as "Green Nook". The house was a mix of hotel lounge and executive suite and painted in all shades of green. The floor changed levels restlessly. The enormous windows gave limitless but lonely views. The balcony ran three sides ending to a pent house.

His former house was empty except for his occasional visits. Mostly that house was locked. But the outer gate was only fastened by a rope. There were two mango trees and usually they bore a lot of mangoes. It was quite tempting especially for children like me. I had seen the street boys plucking them and running before my neighbour could catch them. Not willingly given was forcibly taken. My neighbour never thought of giving them willingly. In the school it was a habit the girls bring raw mango salt and chilli powder to eat. It was a special thrill to break the raw mango on the floor into pieces and to share it with friends with salt and chilli powder. One fine day during the lunch break I was at home and thought of plucking the mango from our neighbour. I just entered the premises and pulled two mangoes and came out of the gate. At that moment my neighbour came with his bald head shining in the afternoon sun and shouted at me. A storm of sweat had broken on my face without warning. Out of fear I dropped the mangoes and ran home. But my siblings coming out of the house saw that, and before I could enter the house, the news had gone to my father. Well he called me to come to the back yard and with fear I followed him. I saw anger evident on his face. He pulled a stork of the coconut. The stick swished and I saw the swift shadow on the sand and a sharp shocking burning of its work. He left in anger after warning me not to repeat it. After the punishment, when we came to the front yard my father saw that the two mangoes were at the corner of the veranda. My father said I should take and return them to my neighbour in the new house. Helplessly I took them, but feeling embarrassed to face my neighbour I went to his house and kept them in their living room entrance, and came back. That night, thinking I was sleeping, my father was telling my mother "That fool of a man, he should have given the mangoes himself instead of threatening a small child". Sleep seemed the only attractive proposition available. I went to sleep with my mind racing and slept fitfully haunted by dreams. I realised what a wonderful father I had. I felt so ashamed that I never ever did the same thing again. Once bitten twice shy. The cost of error may never be recovered. This memory was nagging me like a pain in the tooth that flares up suddenly and dies again.

Next to Green nook residents, was his neighbour Sivanantham who made big sets for the local traditional street musicals, called "*Koothu*". Then there was a small grocery shop owned by a Tamil man Rasa and his wife's family. There was a big house like a fortress owned by a big boat owner Thanigasalam, then a small lane. Here lived some families specially Ariyamalar, a friend of my sister. Next to that a bare land and then a family house of a teacher with four boys.

Followed by that, another of those hopper shops again a bare land in which later they built twin houses, and finally at the end of the road was the Government dispensary for the local people, shifted to another building a few blocks away later. When we were small all three of us, that is my two brothers and me had to take purgatives to clean our stomach. The purgative was available only at the government dispensary at the junction. The compounder working at the dispensary was the same one, who served at our private doctor. We always had the priority to go quicker to the apothecary in charge of the dispensary. While waiting to be called we saw the ones that really ought to be in bed and visited by a doctor at home are obliged to stagger down to the medical centre and spread their viruses round the waiting room. The purgative itself was quite bitter therefore we were allowed to chew a small part of the *beeda*, the sweetened betel, just to get over the nauseating feeling. We were not supposed to swallow but me and my third brother Chelva enjoyed by swallowing it. Sometimes if we delayed our return suddenly our stomachs churned and we ran at marathon speed to avoid the public delivery of purging on the street. No food would be given to us till we had five or ten motions. Only then we got the food. Quite an experience.

My play mate Rasaluxumi's house was the second house on the left. Next to that lived a couple in a small hut with their grown up son who was a fisherman. There ended the residents and the big beach started. On the opposite side was the house of another colleague of my father Mr.Rajaratnam, who passed away and his widow with her two daughters lived there. She was quite decent but a spit fire in anger. My father helped her in all her needs and whenever she came home she used to say "First god and second Gunanayagam master" (my father). She respected him so much. She had four daughters and one son; two of them were married and settled in the capital. The third and the fourth lived with her. The third daughter entered the university, so the youngest lived with her mother learning short hand typing. She was about eight years elder to me. Whenever her mother wanted to go out in the evenings she would ask my mother to send me to stay with her daughter. So that she was not alone. We would sit in the front veranda till her mother returned. So I called her Akka or sister and she used to relate short stories she had read in the magazines. She was a very good narrator. I enjoyed hearing them. They had a servant called Tharmi. He was from the Sinhalese community and did all the housework and the cooking for them. Sometimes another girl Latchumi in the neighbourhood also went to help them. Because they had this servant, they used to leave him alone in the house and go on holidays.

One day I was playing alone behind the kitchen with my small pots and pans. I saw Latchumi running and coming, telling me 'Tharmi is hanging on the rafter".

Then the whole neighbourhood was alerted. I was not allowed to go outside but we sat on the veranda and watched what was happening. The police was informed and owners were informed by telegram. The next day the eldest son-in-law came down. There was no suicide note and any suspicion of murder was over ruled. There was a post-mortem, and the horror of which I did not understand at that time. They found out that he had taken some kind of drug, Ganja to be precise, and under this influence had hung himself. By the time the coroner came and finished the post-mortem report it was late in the evening. The body should be buried. There was no one who volunteered to help, so the scavenger was called. Usually they have a cart and the body was put on this. My father, together with the son-in-law of the lady, went and supervised the burial. By the time my father came back it was nine o'clock in the evening.

The neighbours of this lady were a mother and daughter who were of great help for us in emergency. The mother was the former Matron of the girl's high school hostel Accasi and the daughter Amirtham, a teacher at the Girls' school and a classmate of my mother. They were plainly unwilling to get mixed up in any serious thing other than social functions and church activities. The piece of land next to their house was bare and a family lived, whose son later became a wrestler. But long after that there was a new house built by the owner of the land. The second cross street ran parallel to the house. Across the street there were small huts then a house of my father's old student.

The old post office building with its high walls was really a land mark for my town. There were empty lands near the post office and later people built houses. Opposite to the post office the beach stretched for about a mile. That was such a big and clean beach with white sand that people from various parts of the town sat there and simply enjoyed the fresh air and the sea breeze. Sometimes even when the air was still you wanted to fill the lungs with fresh air when visiting the beach. By day light or by moon light it was one of the most appalling places. That beach played a big role in my childhood.

The beach, sea and I were inseparable. The cool wind tasting salty in my mouth was an incredible pleasure for me. Although we had the beach behind our house it was more of a private place. Most of the residents visited the open beach opposite the old post office. There was a neon lamp and a radio for the public, which was removed in the later stage. People from all over Point Pedro came there in the evenings and on Sundays it was really crowded. There was one

Malayali man who sold sweets for the children. He would just croon, "Bombay Nice *Thumbumitas*¹". We never thought of the hygienic aspect. They were mild pink and gaudy pink in colour but only the thrill of buying those sweets did matter. It stuck to your mouth and face and making your lips dark pink. You could chew them and it seemed to me you could never lose the taste of it. When I was very young I was not allowed to go there alone. Either I go with my father or with my brothers. But when I was five, my grandfather's brother Chellaiah carried me to the beach when he came on vacation and stayed with us for quite a long time. When you visited the beach in the afternoons, which I often did, you would be sweating beneath the blaze of the sun. It felt good to have the feet into the warm sand. Playing in the sea getting wet and then rolling in the white sand to get dry, were some of the things I enjoyed doing, knowing well, if I were to be seen I would be warned. In December the wind was bitter and stung the skin. The sea turned from greenish blue to bluish grey. The waves had angry moods. I would sit for hours watching the changing colours of the sea making sure to elude possible surveillance. I was enthralled by the beauty.

Next to the post office was the residence of the post master. As far as I could remember the post masters who lived in Point Pedro during my childhood were close friends of my father or family. Then further down was the lawyer's house. The house belonged to a rich man but later divided into two. That costal road led to the big community of Catholics, their church the nunnery and the graveyard. There was a catholic primary school. Just a few meters before the grave yard the Hindu cemetery for cremation was situated. Almost at the end of the street about one mile from our house was the light house. Then it was only beach while the road bent in another direction. The sea in this part of the beach was not protected by reefs like what we had behind our house. It was open to the Park Straight and Indian Ocean. There were two big houses near the Light House one of which had sixteen rooms built by our local GP and the other belonged to the Director of education Mr. Arulnandhy, whose daughter was a classmate of my second sister and another one became my English teacher. At the corner lived another widow Mrs. Kandiah from our church with her two children. The son was my third brother's classmate. The daughter had long hair and studied in one of the popular schools in Jaffna and came home only for weekends or for the holidays. There was another house just opposite the light

¹ Sugar puffs

14

house where another widow Mrs. Richard lived who had one daughter and three sons. She was a teacher at the Boys' College in my town. The road was tarmac but deserted and one of the charmless areas in my town.

When my eldest brother came on vacation, he would go to the big beach with his friends in a bike. It was a quiet beach near the light house. He used to take me in his bike and allow me to play in the sand or sometimes collect shells, but he always kept an eye on me. Once while talking and sieving the sand with his hands he found a heavy gold ring. When he came home he gave it to my mother and said "Make a pair of bangles for *Kunchu*[2]". I can vividly remember the *"Thirumbi paar"* bangle design our goldsmith made which I wore proudly. I think that was my first gold bangle.

The Point Pedro Light House, a painting by my niece Sister Eunice after I left the country

On the right of our house we had a woman I remember, who had a big mouth and people were scared to talk with her. Very often there were street fights. Our next door neighbour was a fat woman Raki and she had a daughter. She was old but ageless, gaunt, plain spoken and hard. She could stand up to three of the

---

[2] My pet name

15

toughest, shrewdest people and get every penny she thought her hog was worth. Her brother, who was rich and did fish business, visited her wearing gold rings and chains. I had never seen her husband although she had boyfriends occasionally. The last one was a young man. Very often there would be fights and he would beat her, but after few days they would be together. She had a big mouth and if anyone tried to cross her boarder that would be the end. She would come to the streets and slash them into pieces verbally with every degrading, indecent language that even you hearing them, would be ashamed. Whatever said about her morals she was a devoted catholic, who attended the services regularly every Sunday. Once on a Christmas Eve I and my eldest brother were standing out on the street waiting for the carol party, she was in a hurry muttering something and my brother asked if anything mattered she replied, "Oh my god! Christ child is going to be born and I am late". She believed that.

There was a woman living in the backyard of Raki. She was a thin woman whose skin was the colour of roasted coffee bean and her hair still faintly crinkly with prominent squint eyes. My father said "How funny that this woman is named Swan". With all that she had a man who was very much in love with her. My father said "beauty is in the eyes of the beholder".

Our house was at a junction with three roads meeting. Therefore there were no houses opposite our house. But on the opposite side we had a small grocery shop owned by a Sinhalese man nicknamed Brumpy. He had small children with whom I played. Our small pocket money was mostly spent in this shop. During those days we used to buy a pound of sugar for 25 cents, a pound of salt was 1 cent, and a pound of bread was 20cents. Coming to the right side of my house, after our immediate neighbour, there were small thatched houses one of which had a small opening where we could buy the local Hoppers and "Dhosas". In the mornings and evenings they would make those foods and there would be a big crowd waiting in the street. My town was popular for local food, which carried the town's name. Another interesting and important quality of the town was we had the best food. The dhosas, hoppers and vadais prepared in a very special way were spicy and tasty. I don't think anyone in our town missed that. In particular roads and lanes we had thatched windows through which we could buy the famous hoppers and *dosas* and *vaddais* sold by popular cooks. People came from different parts of the town and even from the outskirts of the town to buy this food. Highly educated and people of higher status waited patiently to buy those snacks. There were popular old women who were house hold names only because of those special preparations made by them.

Further down was a catholic family, whose grandmother was the known auctioneer at the fish market and her grandson Arulanantham a classmate of my brother, who became a teacher later. Then the house of a clerical servant, who was a regular cards player at the beach, some more hopper shops then houses of people who worked in big cargo boats. The next was an up stair house owned by a teacher at the Boy's College. It had a story. The Sinhalese police officers lived there and once there was a death of an inspector's wife, who fell from the stairs and died. In a town like ours there was no limit for gossips. They spread a rumour that she was murdered. For some time it was not occupied but then a Muslim family lived there. In fact the youngest daughter was my class mate in the 6th grade.

There was an old Bakery a popular haunt of my third brother Chelva, then the house of the orange barley soda company owner. Once while he parked his van opposite our house, to supply soda to the shop, he gave me and my brother a bottle each, I simply could not consume the whole amount from the bottle. The next house was where we went and drew drinking water. Then started the store rooms and the office of the customs where we had a small but popular harbour. We always refer that area as "Jetty". On one side of the road was the sea therefore the road was a bit higher and opposite to the sea we had government quarters for the customs officers. When my parents' good friend Mr. Alwihare and his family were living in those quarters I used to have a stopover and had something to drink. A place I could use my English. There were steps in various places opposite the road to go to the beach.

The road on the left led to the photo studio. Kugan Studio was very popular not only in our town but also in other towns. Well established. Everybody knew it was the only studio for miles. In those days the camera was not equipped with electronic flashlights. And each time after using the flash bulbs the photographer removed it and threw the bulb and used a new one. Many times I had seen the street lads running and collecting them. Photos were taken at a slow speed if they were called for any public functions. It was a trend to go to the studio and take memorable photos. All ID photos and passport photos, wedding group photos and bride and bride groom photos were taken at the studio. There would be a small make up room with local face powder, a used comb and a smeared mirror for emergency. Taking a photograph with this gentle man was rather interesting. He used a particular word "isay" to call the people and soon it became his identity and sometimes the nick name. He would rule off individual decisions and command his customers to do what he said. No instruction of the customer was taken seriously by him. He would take as he wished. The customers had to say for what purpose the photo was. That's all. I would not deny that he had some brilliant shots otherwise he would not have become so popular. When we went to the studio he had a different camera system. The camera was set with a long black cloth hanging behind that. He would insert his head and adjust the position then peep out and remove the cover in front with the hand. Here no flash was used because the main podium would be illuminated with high voltage bulbs and switched on quickly just before the photo was taken. Once a year during Christmas he was called by my parents to take a family photo. He had a thriving business.

A few blocks away were the houses of my second sister's classmates Rasathy and Sithamparapillai and then a big Hindu temple, big market and the central bus terminal. Turning to the left of the studio there was a banyan tree which was converted into a small temple. The owner of this temple Annaviar had festivals for that particular goddess Kali. Every year during the *Navarathiri*[3] festival they had fire walking. We had to pass this place when we went to school. When I was very small I used to be afraid of this place, especially when they beat the drums. The fire bed was prepared across the street so that the devotees, after walking on the fire, went and fell into the sea, from where they were taken by the family. I remember seeing that only once and I had nightmares after that.

Closer to the temple separated by a small pathway was the store house. Next to that were the customs officers' quarters and the Magistrate's bungalow. Between these two there was a lane by which you could go to the back entrance of the Boy's College. There was an upstairs building which served as the hostel for the lady teachers of the College. This was called "Turret" by the British. Adjacent to that facing the sea was the Magistrate's residence, a huge premise with a driveway for the car. The next building was the Rest House where visitors and distinguished guests who visited Point Pedro stayed. Following the rest house was the office of the municipal council which started as the town council. This

---

[3] Nine days celebration for the three Hindu goddesses

was first opened by the Governor General Sir. John Kothalawelle. Next was the cross road which led to the Boy's College main entrance and opposite to that was our Methodist church. There was quite a big drainage along this road. Parallel to the drainage was the Girls' School which faced the sea. The Boys' College was surrounded by the Police station, the Courts and a huge Hindu temple with offices for the lawyers.

The Girls' School had a bigger area with the hostel for the students, the teachers' hostel, the Principal's Bungalow on one side and the class rooms, the hall and the playground on the other side. The hostel and the play ground for the boys 'college were about a few hundred meters away from the main college. We had the parsonage next to the college.

Our house was at the end of the first cross street. My parents named our house as "Bethany". The first cross street had residents from Singapore opposite to their house a theatre was built which turned into a store house. That house of the Singapore residents was one of my haunting places. Usually in every house they had coconut trees but other fruit trees were scattered in different houses. As children we searched for fruits that the adults did not eat. Some of them were typical fruits in our county and had only a local name. At the backyard of the Singapore resident's house, they had a tree called "*Ilanthai*". They were small fruits resembling apples. They are sour and sometimes a little bit sweet. The fun of collecting these fruits was more than eating them. They recommend that we had to wash and eat them because they fell on the ground. While collecting the fruits I often saw the creepy crawlies which never affected me. One could not over rule the presence of small worms inside those fruits and I would not deny some worms had a journey through my intestine. If they are delicacies for the Chinese and the Africans, why not for me? As far as I was concerned eating on the way was the most interesting thing because I could select the best fruits and eat and bring the rest to my brothers.

There was the famous motor garage Laxumi Motors owned by my husband's father from whom my husband inherited later. There were residents of various categories between our house and the garage. One of them belonged to an old lady Rasanayaki. One of her daughters was in the capital, the other one was in Singapore. Because she lived alone, there was no one to guide her about the curfew time when Marshal Law existed during the riots. So one day she came out of her house at 4 o clock in the morning to get milk from one of her neighbours. At that time the army came patrolling and she put her hands up and said in English "Please do not shoot me, I live in this road" And then she entered our house. And of course the army personals knew it was a mistake. But the fear of being shot kept the people inside.

An upstairs house next to Rasanayaki aunt's house was another place I visited when life was boring. Well, that was the adventure of plucking another variety of fruit called *"Nelli"*. There was a native physician and his grey haired wife in that house. Usually children did not dare to go there but I was an exception. As I stood near the entrance of the house, I would say in a loud voice, "Gunanayagam master's daughter is here to get some Nelli fruits". The woman would open the gate and the man would only stare at me. Boldly I would walk to the tree. When I collected more than my hand full I lifted my dress and put them there and walked on the road holding the dress high above my knees. I knew where to use my father's name as magic words.

There were two other houses a little away from the garage belonging to a boat owner Rasa then the Central Theatre the cinema hall. Central Theatre had a very big well with good drinking water that people were allowed to go and draw water during the day time. In fact part of the building was built above the well. Because our well water was salty, being near the sea, I was asked to accompany our servant girl to draw water from there. I was about nine or ten when this happened. I made it a point to go and get the water closer to the starting time of the film. The gates were closed at seven o'clock but the films started at 6.30.Due to the warm weather they let open the first two entrance doors so that the audience had better ventilation. Very often I and the servant girl would watch part of the film through one of the open doors of the cinema hall pretending to be drawing water. Sometimes when the watcher saw us watching, he came closer then we escaped spilling half the water down. Quite a thrilling experience it was.

Opposite to cinema hall there was the fish market. There were two barber salons a cycle repair shop and ended with the big market on one side and the central bus terminals on the other. These details I give because most of the locations played a role in my childhood one way or the other. That's why I remember them exactly.

Point Pedro market was very famous. It covered a big area and had everything possible in the name of fruits and vegetables. You could be happily wandering through the disarray of papaws and mangoes and bananas heaps over the cracked concrete floor watched over by vendors who squatted comfortably in the dust behind the piles. Sellers from the nearby villages started their journey at dawn. Some people came even from a distance of fourteen fifteen miles. It was open on the sides only with a roof. They also had thatched roofs during the rainy seasons. The vendors spread pieces of sacks and put their buys. You could buy wholesale which would be taken to smaller markets or retail sale for individual customers. Mostly you could bargain the price but you must be prepared to hear all kinds of swearing and filthy words, when you dared to ask for an extremely low bargain. Torrents of vulgar words float in the air, mostly uttered by women. I had never heard of those words or seen them in any of the dictionaries but people seemed to understand and react accordingly. Most of them had a fixed domain that the customers knew where to buy what. Women without blouses and with bare shoulders are typical villagers. All over clothes were worn as if they were inconvenience of hampering necessity. Farmers, merchants, quacks and hawkers appeared there and disappeared as the evening wasted away. It was a node of all areas. One could say that the women dominated the place. In fact Sunday silence never reigned in the market.

On one side we had the pavement shops with bangles, clips, local cosmetics and toys owned by migrated Indians or Muslims. Occasionally there were textiles spread on the floor for the vendors who could not leave their places for a long time. There would be local food served for the sellers. The women who sold the food always had a small branch of a tree to chase the flies sitting on the food. I think the people must have had an excellent immune system. Very often I and my third brother were sent to buy emergency commodities like chillies or onions or curry leaves, while cooking was in progress especially when the servants were not at hand. Then we also tasted some of the fruits or snacks. We were given a small bribe or asked to take the balance to do those errands. The market closed by seven or half past seven. For years and years I remember one tall, dark man with his hair tied as a knot at the back, with bare body, having a face like shale slope furrowed with gullies, selling Bengal grams prepared with chillies, onions, curry leaves and mustered. The aroma was so good and strong it invaded the market. He would give occasional shouts calling the name of the snack, which vibrated throughout the whole market. If he were to be seen in Europe, I am sure people would think he is a woman. The container, usually a woven basket called 'Kadagam', would be empty within an hour. My eldest brother liked it very much so sometimes I bought that and ate some of it while returning home. The aroma was so tempting.

The closing time was important for beggars and homeless. Half rotten fruits and other leftovers exchanged hands for the small services they did for the vendors. During rainy seasons it was a sight. We had dripping streets, slippery pavements and the traffic snarled. Most of the vendors had cotton sacks in a triangle shape over their heads to protect them from the rain that it looked like the modern rappers with their heads covered with hoods. Then it was tradition and now it is a modern trend. Wet goats and cows let loose by the owners and searched only when needed occupied the place together with the homeless people sharing a common waiting place. When the evening drew closer birds begun to be noisy and the pigeons made themselves prominent.

The town had a selection of shops of all categories. Surrounding the market were the shops. They varied from pent-hole shops to big established shops. Starting from the grosser shops on the east side one could come in a circle in the dusty road. After passing the sheds for the hiring cars you came across the narrow elongated furniture shop displaying the furniture to the pedestrians walking along the pavement, tempting them to look into the tall mirror at the entrance which was an advantage for the men to watch discreetly the women passing that way. A lane starting at the corner leading to *Odakarai,* divided into various tiny lanes which had seldom seen the sight of a car with the open aging drainage on one side, with a black boarder created by the everlasting stagnation of the water. The lane had one of the biggest upstairs houses owned by a rich man, and his son in law was interested in having public meetings at the beach successful or not. It had many by lanes in a complicated pattern that I was confused when I visited my class mates living there.

Turning to the right, at the corner was the CWE the government ration shop stinking with dry fish and Maldives fish kept openly in sacks for distribution. Frequently the queues curved like a sick snake with occasional street fights by the women, ended in the main road. There was a store house like a makeshift prison with only one or two people showing their bare bodies. Adjacent was the upstairs house with fire wood for sale and a cycle shop. Again a lane intercepted. Then the government ration store owned by the *"Chettiyar"*[4]. His nephew

---

[4] Group of people popular for trading

Jegathees was quite diplomatic when dealing with the customers. Close to that was our tailor's shop. Perumal tailor was originally from India settled in our town. He was tall and always had *betel*[5] in one of the cheeks and the traces of red stain in the tongue was quite visible. Most of my father's *Nationals*[6] were stitched by him. He was so popular and had great demand by the rich and the poor. During festival times like Dewali, Christmas and New Year, many others worked under his supervision sitting from before dawn until nearly mid night. His daughter was my classmate in the lower classes.

There was a junction with three roads intercepting. Then started the row of textile shops. The tea shop with meals served by the Malayalies and banana bunches hanging in different stages was actually out of place. The next two shops were very important for us. One was the official book shop where we bought our school things from books to pencils. On one side they had the school necessities and a small opening was there only to buy the Tamil periodical magazines from India and the news papers Local and Indian. All the customers must stand out in a slope and buy those manuals. Discreetly not staring, the owner would survey the people who waited.

The next corner shop Mani's cafe was my favourite. That was the only shop selling small booklets with the text of the film songs I was obsessed with. My pocket money was spent on this shop, mostly for those booklets and other mini comics in Tamil. The name cafe had nothing to do with selling tea, coffee or snacks. It was more or less books and sweets. Our first cross street was next to that and access to this shop was easy and discreet. It took about ten minutes to go to this shop and return so nobody missed me in the house. Only during meal times they would seek not otherwise. Moreover I was allowed to visit the friends and neighbours any time but my mother knew where to find me. At the age of 8 and 9 I knew all the text of the film songs and I remember them even now. My eldest brother had the talent to sing the interludes of the songs with *"Tantana"*[7] sounding like an instrument while I sang the melody.

Opposite the bus terminals were an array of shops. Two eating houses, a textile shop a fancy goods shop and the great and massive building of the Bank of

---

[5] A green leaf for chewing
[6] Traditional attire for men
[7] Word Used when there is no text but only a melody

Ceylon. Behind which there was a printing press. The main road bent leading to the Jaffna city. A few meters away was the Hindu Boys' School followed by houses of well known lawyers and my father's native physician, a primary school, a Hindu temple and the main office of the transport board, where the buses were parked, when not in use.

At the beginning of the main street were the gold smiths of various levels from the biggest jewellery shops to small gold smiths who did the patch work, squatting in one square meter cubicles, with fine fire in a pot and small instruments to work with. They belonged to a particular Tamil community but there were Muslims also in that trade. One daughter Kurasula of such Muslim gold smith was my class mate. There was another shop the Sri's Cafe a real eating house which was opened almost twenty four hours. Good food was served and most of the people who had to work early in the morning had their meals there. The counter had bunches of bananas, Beedas[8], and the special thing was the loud music and when I pass this shop I used to stop for a while and listen to the film songs. On the whole my town had Tamils, Sinhalese, Muslims, Malayalies and other Indian origins living harmoniously and serving each other. We never had any feeling of racial discrimination.

At the end of that street we had the one and the only medical practitioner who I remember was in his sixties or seventies. He was only an apothecary not an MBBS[9] but all the people believed that he had magical hands in curing the sick. My second sister said during the World War II when medicines were rare and expensive he was of great service to my family. My father had great faith in him. He had a driver cum compounder who accompanied the doctor in his house visits. I had seen them several times because of my poor health during my infancy. For every complaint I and presumably the other patients also were given a pink mixture which was bitter and a powdered medicine to be taken with water. I think more of the faith they had in him than the medicine he gave, people consulted him. The way he addressed me was special. It was an affectionate way of saying" you little rascal". His son became a doctor but the father was the favourite. They lived in the house attached to their practice. That was in the second cross street.

---

[8] A preparation of sweetened beetle leave used after meals
[9] State university degree

There were friends of ours as residents about whom I talk a lot in my later chapters. A lane leading to the market, then a Bakery belonging to a Tamil and opposite to that was the grave yard of the Methodist Church where all our family members were buried. Then there was a Hindu temple always flooded in winter, some local peoples' residents and ended in the public beach meeting the beach road.

Passing the second cross street was our town's Library. Occasionally my father went there and I went with him more of an outing than to read. I would scan through the books pretending to read till it was time for us to return. Sometimes I went there with my eldest brother in his bike just for the fun of it. When my father retired every day he visited the library to read the news papers and other books. At a particular time he would be always there and if he was needed for some matter or the other we knew where to find him.

This library played a bigger role for me when I was married. My husband had a rich business colleague and his sister had a daughter. She was 14 and used to walk to the school. A small made pretty girl. The father had a hard ware stores and they were rich in their own way. One day he got an anonymous letter demanding 10,000 rupees or his daughter would be kidnapped. That was the first of its kind in the town and the family got frightened. The uncle and my husband's friend came from the capital and the police was informed. They all met at my husband's workshop in order to avoid any suspicion for the kidnapper. The inspector of police was a Sinhalese and was a supporting actor in the local films. He made it into a big issue and planned to catch the perpetrators in a dramatic way. He strongly believed it was a plan of a dangerous gang. The letter said that the father should put a green light when he agreed and he should keep the money in a particular place inside this library. It was agreed that everything should go according to the plan except the inspector and another man would observe everything inside and outside the library.

Previous day the father lit green lights in his shop. The father took the money to the library as planned. As soon as he came out of the library he called and informed my husband's friend who was sitting in my husband's work shop where we had the telephone. This part of the story was narrated by the police officer who was actually on the spot because none of the relatives were allowed to be seen near the library. The man had a news paper before him but his whole attention was at the entrance. Then he saw a young boy in his puberty entering, looking rather nervously in all the directions. He slowly approached the spot where the money was kept. Then he took the packet with the money and walked outside. The police followed him for about one Kilometre hoping to find the main person behind the whole plan. The boy must have felt that something was wrong and started to run. This made the police alert and before the boy did something they caught him red handed with the money. He was taken to the police station and severely dealt that he spilled the beans. Deeply disturbed by the police the boy had spoken with a kind of laconic suspicion. They found out that the master plan was organised by an advanced level student living closer to the library. The police caught him and put him in the prison. Most surprising fact that emerged was, that the younger boy was the son of a driver who lived only a few houses away. That was the first kind of ransom incident which shocked the whole town. The first suggestion of being a terrorist act was proved wrong. The memory of the library became an everlasting memory.

In the middle of the area was the bus terminal where buses going in different directions throughout the district were halted. There were other private vehicles taking passengers who did not live on the main roads. Most of the clerical servants working in the head offices in Jaffna travelled from here. It was usual to see buses packed with passengers till the foot board, heads jutting out through every possible openings looking more of a human cargo transport vehicle rather than a public transport. We had a driver and a conductor who issued the tickets in each bus. The conductor had a special trick to travel on the foot board of the bus sometimes one leg hanging. To start and stop they used a whistle with different notes. But the famous method was to call in his loud voice "*Annai right*" which means OK brother.

There was only one special bus which looked different in form, and almost every day driven by the same driver, with a Hitler moustache. That was the mail bus which went to the post office to collect the mail and deliver to the mail train at Kodikamam railway station fourteen miles from Point Pedro. On its way the bus collected mails from other post offices. The mail train was the slowest of its kind by which one could reach the capital city. This bus passed our house on its way to the post office and passengers catching the train could waive their hands to stop the bus. There were no definite bus halts. Only this bus had a peculiar horn, that everybody knew the mail bus was going, and it was six in the evening. Usually when my grandfather or uncles came from distant areas they would catch that bus in front of our house. This had a special significance for us the children. It was while waiting to send them off we get what was called *Payana Kasu*, which means farewell money from them. Therefore we were all there punctually waiting eagerly for the tips. I collected that money to buy the cinema song books. Film songs were unofficially not welcomed at home especially when my grandfather and uncle who were priests were at home. My third brother Chelva was crazy after Tamil and English comics and magazines, and I for the film song books. My brother had a box where he kept his books but my hiding place was under the pillow or together with my school books. Sometimes he allowed me to have a look at them. I had my secret mischievous moments and read them in his absence of course without his permission. You could imagine why we needed this money and our punctuality for the send offs.

Along the first cross street closer to the market were the barber salons. Usually a barber came home to cut my father's hair but that was not often. Therefore I was sent with my brother for the hair cuts to one of those salons. They had high backed chairs facing tainted mirrors. The smell of cheap powder and sprays invaded the whole room which was three by two meters in area. There would be a black leather belt hanging on the wall for the barber to sharpen the blades of his knife. Big posters of the film stars were the only ornamental pieces. But we the children would be treated with a hair cutting machine. I was a bit frightened of that gadget, therefore I used to close my eyes, when the barber cut my hair. While going for the hair cut, both of us used to do a small shopping of buying the magazines or sweets.

After that we would walk back home. It was a superstition in the house, that one should not walk into the house with the hair on the dress. Yes, whatever said and done the barber happily left the remnants of hair on our clothes, knowing very well we were not allowed to go into the house directly from the salon. We shout at the top of our voice *"Amma* [10] we are back". Then water was warmed in the fire and brought to the well side for us to have the head bath. When my brothers grew older they directly went to the well and drew the cold water to have their bath. But when we were children it was done sometimes by my mother and sometimes by the servants. Of course the servants did a slip shot work and we were happy to escape with the minimum of pain. If mother came

---

[10] mother

then it was an ordeal. She brought the herb *"Seeakai* boiled with kummel seed which was supposed to have a cooling effect hot hot.

One should have a clear picture of our well side. The big well had a manually operated bucket attached to a very heavy beam of the Palmara tree loaded with weights at the bottom, to make the process of drawing the water with less effort. If my mother was at the well side, somebody either my second sister, brothers or the servants drew the water and filled the vessels or the tubs. There was a big cemented flat tub about half a foot high with an out let at the end, which was stuffed with a cloth stopper. But while getting in and out of this tub one could bring sand into it. A head bath with my mother was unbearable. Because she gave a real scrubbing, which was painful, and add to the misery the herbal mixture would flow into the eyes and irritate. It was cleaned only when she finished with the scrubbing because it was thought to be good for the eyes. The worst thing was when the soap fell down on the cement. Then the soap would have kissed the sand and taking that soap we were given a scrub. The smooth soap with the rough sand could be painful as ever. But there was no mercy till mother finished with us. Talcum powder was used to take away the dampness on the skin. We would be given fresh clothes after the bathe.

Chapter 2

The society and special places

In those days - that was in the 50s – we had no discrimination between Tamils and Sinhalese, and Sinhalese people worked in the government departments like in the Customs, the Excise Department and the Police force. There were bakeries owned by the Sinhalese, and they talked in Tamil. It was a very nice community. Because of the all island Christian schools for boys and girls, there was a big Christian community in the town. There were two schools one for the boys and one for the girls exclusively for the Hindus which developed later. Therefore my town became very popular, both in education, food and community life. My father used to say most of them who resided in the town were not originally from Point Pedro but settlers.

Electricity supply came from a big electricity plant opposite to the boys' hostel in the college road. There were lines men to take care of the repairs but the superintendent of this plant was a dark fat gentlemen travelling in an old model car. In fact the car was his trade mark. I can't remember the model of the car, might have been an Austin, but I only remember the door opened the other way round like the taxies in London. I saw this car often because he dropped his daughter to our school. At the beginning the street lamps were lighted manually by the lines men who rode a bike to accomplish their task. At six O'clock in the evening they start by carrying a long stick with a hook to switch on the street lights. With the setting of the sun everything suddenly assumed a uniform robe of shadows. Bunches of fruits could not be distinguished from the leaves that nourished them. Sometimes those lights were partly hidden by the tall trees and their branches. Nothing was as creepy as that light splashing making white look shining and everything else only a form and sometimes showing frightening shadows moving from normal leaves to horrifying shadows. I was frightened even to go to my neighbours' house or return home that I simply closed my eyes and ran. I had an unknown fear for those dark shadows. We had one lamp just in front of the house. Those street lamps were important because we never had traffic lights in the streets, and people driving the vehicles had those lamps as their guide lines. To my surprise seldom there was an accident

There were three Hindu temples active throughout the year and the fourth, a bit obscured. The temple on the main street was Lord Ganasha temple. There was a pond in the cross road, where they had the festival with lights, and brought the deity for a special festival held in the stone built stage, and the devotees came to worship from all over the area. This was a chance for the people who were not allowed to enter the inner part of the temple to see the god. There were strict caste systems those days. They also had another festival, where the god was taken in a chariot for the people to worship. The festival season remained for ten days, and each day was given to different prominent people, who took the responsibility of the expenses. There were special sheds erected for the devotees to have *jaggery[11]* water or butter milk free of charge. It was more like a fair, and hot peanuts, sweets and Bengal grams were sold. When I was a little girl, I used to go with my eldest brother Baba to watch the fun.

The second temple was in the courts road opposite to the courts. This temple was for the deity Ammen an incarnation of Kali. The Hindus believed any disease like chicken pox or measles were inflicted by her. They also had similar festivals but on the full moon day of the Tamil month April, which is fifteen days later than the English calendar called *Chithra Pournamy*, the god was decorated and taken to the towns limit and brought back to the temple with all its glory. We could watch that procession from our beach.

The third temple was opposite the library. That was the Sivan temple. They also had similar festivals but the speciality was the "*Sooran Por[12]*". That was the war between the god and a giant with incredible power, and one could not kill him immediately because each time his head fell down it came back to life. Only after several attempts the god could kill him. There were specialists who performed those acts and the public cheered every time the head fell down. It was quite remarkable how they handled both carts, which carried the statues. The fourth temple was behind our school and had their festivals too, but I knew about that temple only when one of the Boys' College students, was drowned in the pond during rainy season.

---

[11] Brown Sugar liquid

[12] War of the devil

Chapter 3

The community

There were two all island schools, one for girls, one for boys, therefore, students from all over the island came to these schools to get a better education. There were big hostels in both the schools and the discipline was excellent. Children learnt not only subjects but were also educated in behaviour, and in all the other things that were necessary for life. The reason why I am telling this is, although it was a small town, the people who lived there were of higher standard, because the teachers, who came to teach in the school, took this town to reside, therefore the community was of a higher level. They were not the only people. We had a district court, a magistrate's court, and with a lot of eminent lawyers residing in and around them. Mostly they were old boys of Hartley College. There were Sinhalese officers serving in the customs department, police department and excise department. There were doctors and civil servants. We had Singapore pensioners living in big houses. Land surveyors and rich business people hailed from the town. On the whole it was a town of elite people and therefore we had high society effect on the town. This part was in the north therefore it was referred as *"Vadamarachi*[13]*"*. Throughout the country people who hailed from this area were considered to be intelligent, clever and arrogant. They were proud of their origin.

After my parents were married my father was posted to the Boy's College in Point Pedro where he stayed till his retirement. It was a trend the students and the teachers referred to each other by their initials. My father was known as SVG but there were other teachers and principals called as STS, KP, RMG, SP, and WNS and so on. They also used nick names, when the students were angry with the teachers or simply for fun. Internal clashes between the teachers were there when ever jealousy cropped up between the children of the teachers. All three brothers of mine and my second sister were old students of the college. The staff room politics was always there. The school had strict discipline for the students after it was taken over by the native principal.

Independence of the county made the British leave the country, and automatically a native Christian principal was appointed for the boys 'college. With his arrival a new era began. Late comers had detention and names were

---

[13] Northern area

written in the detention book. In worse cases public canning was given to the students like in Britain. Canning by the principal was the worst punishment for the students. Students were not to be seen on the streets with their *Lungies*[14] especially when the principal had his rounds in the town either visiting the families of the teachers or simply going for a walk to the beach. News reached the students well ahead in the streets that they would be alerted. My third brother Chelva had many log book entries for various things he did in the class.

I was quite small when I learned the song in the Sunday school. It started as "There is a joy, joy, joy, joy down in my heart, glory to his name". It went on like that only with one word differing. But the last stanza was "There is a peace that past that understanding down in my heart". The boys 'college principal's wife's name was Peace. And my sister called her as Peace acca (acca means elder sister). Therefore I heard the alliteration of rhyming words that started with the letter "P". So my version of the song was "Peace acca *um*[15] principal um down in my heart". My mother noted that and when the principal and his wife visited us, the wife would call me and ask me to sing that verse. After my proud performance a prolonged gust of booming laughter was all I heard. I of course did not understand till I was old enough to know the meaning.

The girls 'school was situated on the main coastal road. It faced directly the sea with reeves, and they had steps running down to the beach. The beach was quite small and during the rainy season the waves touched the wall built. The entrance had a main gate and a side gate. Students went through the wicket gate. There was another entrance leading to the garage of the principal's bungalow. The bungalow was a huge building surrounded with big verandas in front. There were many rooms in the side wings. The main sitting room and dining room was set in a British style with settees and cushions with a grand piano in one corner. Many times I surveyed the bungalow in amazement. It was always tidied up, floors washed and not a speck of dust on the tables. This part of the bungalow was opened during the day time. Behind this building was the teacher's hostel followed by the immense girls' hostel dormitories. In front, next to the bungalow was the principal's office during my school time and then came the assembly hall. When the hall was newly built after the cyclone, there was a chapel.

---

[14] House attire for men

[15] meaning and

THOSE WERE THE GOLDEN DAYS

Only a half wall in front which extended to a high wall on the sides. Along the wall on one side not hiding the view of the bungalow were tall old casuarina trees which never lost its green in any season and whistled during strong winds. There was a science lab behind the principal's office followed by the kitchen for home science students. Our library was adjacent to the main hall. Then you had class rooms all over. The back yard had a net ball court. Near that there was a small gate for the hostellers to go to the church for the Sunday service and for the combined worship of Christian students together with the Boys 'College on Fridays. Well the excitement seen on the girls' faces on meeting the boys was surely seen. We were not supposed to talk with any of them but exchanging glances and smiles were not barred. Occasionally our principal came and then we observed absolute code of conduct. It was only conducted in English. The open air stage and the play ground ended the school premises. We used the open air stage when we had our sports meet or other public functions like Prize giving. One set of toilets were near the stage with the access to water either by pipes or well.

During my mother's time the girls' 'school was called as Girl's Bilingual School. GBS for short. Later it was upgraded and became Methodist Girl's High School. The girls' high school also had a native Christian principal Miss. Chinniah after the last British principal Miss. Dore left. Miss. Chinniah was well known for her strict discipline in the school but not that strict as the Boy's College. I attended this school, my eldest sister an old girl and later on started her teaching carrier there, and my second sister finished her General certificate in the 10th grade in the same school, before she joined the Boys' College, to continue her advanced level. My mother was also an old girl of that school but under the British principals. My brothers studied till the third grade before they went to the Boys' College.

There was one elementary school, one boys' high school and one girls' high school founded by the Hindu community. Traditional Hindu families sent their children to those schools. Typical rivalry was seen between our schools, when they had district competitions in speech, sports and music. We always wore uniforms at school. Ours was the western style short pleated dress, with the school colour tie where as the Hindu Ladies College had the traditional dress of long skirt and blouse, for the grownup girls they had the half sari but lower grade students wore the western dress as uniform. Their principal

Miss. Saravanamuthu during my time was a strong lady with a dominant voice and one of the few ladies, who drove a car in our town. The Hindu primary school was at the beginning of VM Road, about a mile long. The chairman of the town council lived in this road along with some Hindu educated families. The lane that crossed this road was Odakari. That lane continued and met the college road. Further down was a house for the deaconess from the Methodist Church: a nice dull ordinary place to live. Soon after my sister married she lived in that house for some time. There was a rice mill owned by a rich man and that road met the road leading to the Vade Hindu Girls' School. That was almost the boundary for Point Pedro town.

Chapter 4

My Father

Samuel Veluppilai Gunanayagam B.A.(Lond)

My father's background

My father was the role model for all of us. He was quintessential and a unique person. Seldom, you could find persons like him. He was a teetotaller: never involved with other women except my mother and never addicted to healthy opulence. He was prudish and handled matters with great measure of tact. He was tall, dark and hefty but his features were strong. My mother was his first cousin and at that period it was the tradition to get married to cousins. He was self disciplined. I do not personally know all about his childhood. All what I relate are the occasional information given by him, my mother, my aunt or my grandmother. Some of them were given by my second sister. My paternal grandmother was the daughter of the village headman, who received a medal from Queen Victoria, for his services. Therefore my grandmother was a proud woman. I knew her when she was about ninety years old, when she came to stay with us. Sometimes she talked about her past. My maternal grandfather said "Ponnu acca (my grandmother) always went to their own temple by a closed horse cart. She would be wearing all the jewellery, especially her ruby nose ring, would become of her, because of her golden complexion". Her husband, that is my maternal grandfather Veeravagu was dark but handsome, and was feared by people. My father was the eldest son and he had a younger sister and a younger brother. Suddenly my paternal grandfather died at a very young age, and my father as the eldest son, had to shoulder the responsibility of his family.

When my father finished his senior Matriculation, he joined as a teacher in the Methodist Boys' College in the east. Only for the holidays he travelled back to the north to his parents. His parents were orthodox Hindus owning temples. But my father was influenced by Christianity through a missionary and became a Christian. Once, when I asked him about the conversion, he replied, "No other religion has the word "Saviour" and it gives the hope for everyone to get a chance of salvation. This is the biggest hope we have in this religion". His convictions about life never failed him and he was one of the luckiest men who could see the grand children of all his six children before he passed away.

His siblings did not call my father in the usual manner "*Annan*" (big brother) It is difficult to explain it in English because she, he or you cannot be used normally in a polite sense, even the prime minister, we refer as he, she or you but in our language we can distinguish between polite and impolite forms for she, he, and you. My uncle and aunt called my father as "*Annar*" and not the usual "*Annan*" because words ending with 'n' are impolite. My uncle was working in the government service before he was called to become a pastor. As a pastor he was a very powerful speaker. He was fluent in his Tamil therefore he always gave the sermons in Tamil, even for the Sinhalese audience during big conventions. There would be simultaneous translators to translate it in Sinhalese and English because the congregation consisted of English-speaking, Tamil-speaking and Sinhalese speaking people. Sometimes he was so carried away that he went under the table, around the table and jumped while delivering his sermons. And he was appreciated for this by the congregation because he kept them alert.

At the beginning, my father's family was orthodox Hindus owning Hindu temples in the village and outside. Therefore they believed strongly in horoscope. Once a man told that my father would have an accident in water, so he was forbidden to learn swimming and never allowed to go near any kind of water. But he used to swim in the ponds of the temples. Despite the warning and punishment he continued to swim and became a good swimmer. Later when he was a young man, he was distained to travel by a big ship, which wrecked in the middle of the ocean and he swam for more than eight hours. If not for his skill in swimming he would have drowned like many others in that wreck. I would like to narrate it in his own words because we heard it several times during our Sunday sittings with him. I would try my best to give his version about the wreck. All the readers should know the experience of my father not in the third person narration but in the first person narration. Only then the correct emotion would be conveyed. I had forgotten the exact year and I have no way of finding out because all of them who could give the information are no more. But I knew it was shortly before my father got married, and my parents married in 1927. Therefore it must have happened in1926. But the date I knew because my parents always stayed at home when we went to the watch night service on the New Year's eve on December 31st in order to remember the wreck

Chapter 5

The ship wreck.

The following account was my father's words if not exactly but almost.

"It was in the late twenties. I was teaching at the Batticaloa Central College after I finished my senior Matriculation. I was a bachelor still but it was an understanding between my family and my uncle's, that I would get married to my beautiful cousin Mani shortly. She was the eldest daughter of my uncle, who was a Methodist pastor. For me it was a childhood romance. I could not get a post in the Northern Province, where I hail from. Most of the big and popular schools were Christian institutes. After the death of my father as the eldest son the urgency of getting a job was inevitable. Therefore I accepted the post and went to the Eastern Province. I had to do my London examination in the Northern Province. It was not an easy journey from East to the North. If we were to go by bus we needed more than ten to twelve hours. We had the most dangerous road ways. The biggest and dangerous jungles we came across were inhabited by dangerous animals like elephants, leopards and poisonous snakes. Usually people preferred day journeys but it was not always possible. But there was an alternative and that was to travel by big ship liners.

I was strictly instructed not to use the latter. There is a story behind that. I belonged to a predominantly Hindu orthodox family believing in superstitions, horoscopes, palm reading and predictions. When I was a child there was an astrologer, who predicted that I would have a horrible accident in water and I should avoid any situation to travel or have an adventure in water. Almost all the family and relatives knew about it. That was the ethics of a village. The general belief was different people had different ways to face their worst destiny. For some it was water for some it was fire and for the others accident and so on. The astrologers warn people not to take any risks with them. My parents were no exception. So from my very early age, I was given strict orders not to go near the water and nothing to do with water what so ever. We had the Bay of Bengal near our village and I was not allowed to go to the beach. If by chance I went, there would be an escort to keep an eye that I never played with the waves. The more pressure they gave me, the more desire I developed for swimming. I was left with the only alternative to learn swimming, and that was to go to the temple pond in the village on my way back from school, as there was no fixed time for my return. At first I was careful to see that nobody watched my secret visits to the pond. When the habit became frequent I became careless. One day while I was having a blissful time in the pool I saw one of my uncles watching me. He came near to make sure and I had no way of escaping from his hawk eyes. Pulling me by my ears he took me home and reported the event in a colourful provocative manner, asking questions like if, what and when with appropriate emotional outcomes. He knew I was precious to my family. His attempts did not disappoint him. My father called me and gave me severe beatings making me to promise not to try that again. It was more the fear they had for my life than anything else, I received the punishment. Despite the warning my affinity to water became a passion, and my secret visits never stopped, and I became an expert in swimming. What I thought was such superstitions should not be encouraged. More than that to fight against such things and to protect your self was important. To the contrary, what happened years after, proved that my parents' fears came true.

Well coming back to the incident, the temptation to take a sea voyage was so intense in my mind, I decided to take the risk of travelling by the ship. In those days we had liners from British and Irish companies. The liner I decided to take was Lady McMellem. With high spirits and courage in heart I boarded the ship. The ship sailed promptly moving out majestically to the open sea on the first leg of journey. Varieties of people were on board. There were rich and high society Tamil and Sinhalese people in the porthole cabins and young people like me happily enjoying the sea breeze on the deck of the ship. The air was cooler and fresher than in the land. The speciality was the full moon which had risen well above the horizon, casting an avenue of gold across the still water. Words could not describe the beauty of that. Being young and romantic, and having read all those literatures both in Tamil and English, my heart got carried away with that magnificent view. Closing my eyes I simply felt the beauty. I was standing on the deck feeling the tender breeze all over my body, and admiring and wondering god's creation of the ocean. The full moon appeared and lit the mists of early evening incredibly. Water! Water! Everywhere! I was lost in that world of magic.

It was about 7.30 in the evening when I felt a big jerk as though the ship had touched some big object. It took some time for us to realise, what had happened. The truth was the ship had banged against a rock and was sinking. There was a pandemonium all over the ship. Running, screaming, jumping, searching, calling and so many other things were happening. After the initial shock I started to act sensibly. I went and helped the helpless. I got them their life jackets and put them in life boats. There was real confusion, and screams and people running aimlessly trying to save their material things or simply jumping into the sea without any protection. The crew tried their best but I could see that such a crisis was unexpected. While help was distance away, and most probably even if it came it would be too late, I was helping the needy forgetting that I should also leave the ship soon. The damage was in the middle of the ship and there was a danger that we would be caught in a whirl pool while the speed of the water entering the ship was rapid. The captain shouted, "All of you get out of the ship. The ship would be sinking in minutes." I was at the edge of the ship neither with a life jacket nor a life boat to save me. I had two options either I would continue to stay and be caught in the whirlpool of the sinking ship or jump into the ocean and face the consequences. It was like the devil and the deep sea. I chose the latter. I plunged into the water of the ocean and started to swim away from the ship. I saw a life boat full of people where I had no chance to get a place. Then I heard a woman screaming "My son, my son" and a child crying" Mummy, mummy" and the third mummy was only a wobbling sound from the child. The fretful cry of a child was hushed only by the sound of the waves. Yes the child got drowned.

That was not the time for me to think of anything else other than my own survival. I was in the middle of the ocean without a life jacket or any other protection to safe guard me. I had to think of the orientation to reach the shore, but all I could see was water, water and waves from all directions. I swam for some time and at a distance I saw a dark figure floating. I quickened my speed, and nearing the figure I saw a man floating with the help of a broken piece of wood. When I touched the wood he started to protest. Then I told him" I only want to rest for sometime" and he became quiet but I could feel he was restless. He confessed he was not a good swimmer and the piece of wood was his only refuge. I felt the fear in his trembling voice. I left him alone and started to swim. I did not witness when the ship capsized totally. Sometimes I floated and allowed the waves to carry me especially when I was tired. It was the moonlight that fascinated me. The waves had shimmering silver wavy lines. The sky was void of clouds that the moon shone and smiled. I thought about the poems and descriptions about moonlight from the Tamil poet Bharathy and the Moon light sonnets of Shakespeare. Those beautiful images and emotions filled my thoughts than the danger I was in.

At a distance I saw sharks jumping above the sea level and I was all alone in that wide ocean. It seemed I was swimming endlessly closing my eyes and yet when my eyes flew open again the moon had moved. I must have swum more than six to seven hours. Suddenly I felt my feet bumping something and it took some time for me to realise that I had really touched the sand under me. Yes I had reached the shore but it was still early dawn and it was dark. From then onwards direct ahead I swam free to the thin mist of the shore. Although I reached the shore, my whole body was rigid and I could not get up and walk. So I rolled to the shore and stayed out of water. It was during the first stroke of dawn, that I heard a voice shouting "There is a corpse". A group of people approached me. I realised they were the "*Vedhas*"[16], the old inhabitants living in the forest. I kept quiet till they were very close to me. Then I said "I am not dead. Please make some fire, to warm me". Those Vedhas were very helpful and made the fire and two of them swung me over the fire. It was the Kalkuda shore in the East of the island. I was at their mercy. I had heard they were savages but for me they were my guardian angels. Later they took me to the Rest House where I was bathed in brandy. As soon as I was fit I sent a telegram to my parents stating "When is my exam?"

Meanwhile my future father in Law and my parents were highly worried because my name was under the missing list and decided that I was drowned in the sea. They were in funeral mourning. But when they received my telegram they were confused but overwhelmed. I came to my village by bus within the next few days. It was only months after, I came to know that the child who died, was the grandson of a very influential and rich person. In fact they came and talked with me about the incident"

This vivid memory I had in mind because my father related his adventure not only once, but several times to us and for others. My sister remembered that this wreck was also in the text books in the school. During the farewell party of my father, his old student and a District Judge took all of us back to this adventure of my father in his speech.

My father was an ardent fan of the game Cricket. He would sit hours and hours, listening to the cricket commentary. Those days there were no television in our country. There was an English magazine from England called "Tit Bits". There

---

[16] The early inhabitants

my father saw the black and white TVs on windows and said, he would like to watch the cricket test matches on TV. I developed an obsession for the TV, and thought I should work on a TV, which was not possible in our country at that time. This childhood dream I was able to fulfil in Germany, by working with TV companies like FAB, satellite TV the WTT, and the firm Kaiser TV and Film production.

To become a TV presenter was my childhood dream No. 1 in reality.

My team in the German Television FAB

Television Interview in the German Television with Violin Mastro Kunnakudy Vythiyanathan and his son Dr.Balasubramaniam a Tabla player

My father practiced a righteous life. He executed the New Testament saying from the Bible' Love thy neighbour as thy self'. He was a brave man, who fought for the rights, when he believed so. He was never frightened of any threats in life both by nature and by the people. He never hesitated to help people, who were in trouble regardless their status or consequences he had to face, and loyal to his family and friends. He had the highest sense of humour, understood people with compassion, especially his students and his friends. I have never heard anybody speaking evil of him even now. Challenges were like child play for him and he ventured every type of it including life threatening.

Chapter 6

Remarkable incidents in my father's life

Some of the following incidents were told by my father during our Sunday sittings. When he started his carrier as a teacher in the east he used to come home to the North by bus for the vacation. It took about eight to ten hours. To avoid the heat during the day time, they travelled in the night. It had two reasons. One the heat and the other was a good night sleep. Once on such trip a prisoner with hand cuffs was travelling with the guards. They had to go through big forests, the dwelling places of elephants. But occasionally they would stop for the passengers to answer the call of the nature and often there were boutiques, where they sold snacks for distant travellers. During one of these breaks my father noticed that all had gone to have something to eat except that prisoner. Feeling sorry for him my father shared his food with him and was acknowledged with a smile as his thank you, because obviously he did not speak Tamil. Half way through, in the middle of the forest the bus broke down, and the passengers were asked to get down from the bus, to an open place and sit around a bonfire specially made to scare off the elephants. Time was running and one by one went to sleep. The fire was diminished with the covering of the ashes and occasional red blink of the remaining charcoal and it became semi dark. Suddenly my father felt he was woken by someone. When he opened his eyes he saw the prisoner. When all the passengers were called back my father was asleep. Bu this man noticed that my father was not among the passengers in the bus. He took a risk of coming back and waking my father as though anxious to show friendship. Not every cloud brings rain. My father told us that incident taught him a lesson not to judge people superficially." Not every unpleasant appearance is deceptive" he said.

Another two incidents in his life were remembered by my eldest sister and my second sister to prove how brave he was. About 200 meters away from our house, one of the richest man in my town started to build a cinema hall for which, my father protested, saying it would disturb the quietness of the neighbourhood. The fight escalated and ended up in courts. My father had a lot of strong reasons for the protest. But the opponents were strong financially and had man power to threaten people, who opposed. Sounds we don't hear can sometimes wake us. That happened to my sister. One day, in the middle of the night my eldest sister woke up for no reason and observed a dark figure standing near the window with a shining weapon. Without making a noise she rolled from the bed and went to my father's bed and alerted him. Behind the grimy windows there were more movements. He became vaguely conscious of the noise. My father first shouted " Who is that?" and after sometime took the bar that was used to bolt the doors at that time and went outside the house to the road and stood at the junction, with the bar as a support. "There are parts in life which are impossible to play with dignity" he said. It was suspected that it was someone hired to threaten my father. But father was fearless. This was accounted by my elder sister.

There was another incident related by my second sister Rathy connected to the same affair. One evening a famous IRC[17] came by car and threatened my father about the same case warning him to face the consequence. That man was feared by all. My father was seated in an easy chair. He did not even bother to get up but said ".....You go and tell these things for people who are frightened to die not to me" and continued to read the book he had in his hand. He despised individuals of low character. That was watched by his driver, who was a thug himself, and after some time they heard that the driver attacked the IRC, when he tried to bully him. Indirectly my father gave him courage to face the IRC. There was a time to speak and a time to be silent. My father felt it was the former he should do. Of course my father was able to stop the project of the theatre. Later it became a store room for the owner who had big boats to carry cargo from various ports.

By nature my father was compassionate to people who were under privileged and did, what he thought as correct and did not heed to old traditions, which had no sense. He never capitalized on other people's weaknesses. When my father came early from school, and did not have any tuition, he used to go out of the gate, stand on the street and watch the people. Usually he met a lot of them, because they went to the public beach passing our house. One day I was with my father, I had a pink dress and was holding his hands. I was jumping up and down, while my father watched the people. Suddenly from the town centre a very tall man with a turban on his head, came carrying a cloth bag on his shoulders. It was obvious he was a snake charmer. They bring snakes especially cobras and with their kind of special flute (*moudi*)[18] they played a tune and the

---

[17]imprisoned Rigorous criminal

[18] Flute used to make the cobra show its full form of its head

snake would come up and show its full face, if you could imagine what a cobra was. He was looking up and down my father and then he asked "Do you know the family, which lived in this house about twenty years ago? There was a beautiful woman and her husband with a daughter who was about five or six years." Then my father replied "I built this house and live in this house for the past twenty years. And my wife is a beautiful woman. And I think you are looking for me." Then he took both his hands and showed the traditional respect to my father. My father was confused, so he asked him who he was. Then he related the story and I was listening. "Twenty years ago, I came with my father, who was also a snake charmer. Then I was twelve years old. One day after our rounds the whole day, we looked for a place to stay for the night. All of them refused to have us because we had the snake. They were frightened that we might let loose the snake in the house. When we came to this house and asked for a place, you allowed us to stay and sleep on your veranda and gave us some food. I could not forget this incident. So now I come to see you, just to say Thank you! My father asked him, "What did you do all these years that you remembered only now". Hefting a frustrated sigh he tunnelled the fingers through the mane of brown dusty hair that needed a proper hair cut. Then he said, "That is a long story. I stabbed my father-in-law and went to prison for twelve years and only recently came out of it." My father looked at him in shock and surprise. Again my father asked "And why now?" Then he took out a small tin and said, "I have brought a present, Sir. Here you have a black stone which you can use whenever there is a snake bite or insect bite. If you keep it on that place, it will stick there and it will fall down only when the whole venom has been absorbed. Afterwards you have to wash this stone in milk before you use it again". My father whispered 'Truth is stranger than fiction'. Believe it or not we tried this stone and found it correct. Because once our principal was bitten by some poisonous insect (or snake) and we took this stone and kept it and we found it worked. Even now my brother-in-law has that stone. A scientific explanation was given by him although he did not know it was scientific. They go to the deep jungles to get this stone. They watch the snakes spitting venom on a particular stone continuously that this stone gets the quality to absorb venom. My father said "A good deed done without expectation will be appreciated with gratefulness"

Chapter 7

My Mother

Sophia Gnanamani Gunanayagam (nee Eliathamby)

My mother was a unique person. I know her only when she was 45 years old, when I was two years old. Even after eight child births she was very beautiful. She was fair, with long hair and stylishly dressed. If she got ready for weddings she looked gorges with her silk sari. She always took a last look at herself in the mirror before she left. But I saw some old photos of her family taken just before her marriage and just after her marriage. They were group photos, where she was dressed in traditional sari with a long gold chain, tucked at her waist. When asked she replied, that was the fashion at the time. My father was dressed in western clothes with suit and tie when he got married. My mother continued the same, but my father did not like the artificial look and after some time refused to wear western dress and wore the nationals the traditional dress. My mother's personality was so utterly different. As I was born rather late in her life, I know my mother was almost middle age and that stage I remember her the best. She was strong and bounteous but with a gravity of breeding that was visible beneath her smile. There was no antagonism in her eyes no contempt only amusement and affection. She was a woman of peculiar grace with a touch of impulsiveness. She never frazzled. Though she tortured our patience, exhausted our nerves, she was all the time building up around us by the unconscious revelations of her bones, an interpretation of truths of life so unpretentious and easy, that we never recognized it then, yet so true that we never forget it.

My mother's family

My mother's family was also Hindus by origin. Her grandfather was a hard task master. He had two sons my grandfather and his brother, who was in the police force. They got severe punishments even for the smallest offence. Sometimes they got lashes from their father for the smallest mistakes my grandfather said. My grandfather became a Christian and later he was a pastor in the Methodist Church. I could say only a little about my grandmother because she died before I was born. My father and my mother were first cousins. At that time it was the tradition they fixed the marriages at a very early age and so it was for my parents. They grew up together having the idea of marrying each other. My mother had two sisters and three brothers younger to her. I do not know her second sister who died two years after she married. But her other sister married the widower husband of her sister and lived in the same town. The eldest of the brothers Gunaratnam, became a Methodist pastor like his father. The second brother Sam well groomed was attached to various companies and once even with the German Embassy but never stayed at one place. Her third brother James became an accountant and settled in the capital city. Since my grandfather had to go to different areas serving the parish, sometimes to remote villages, my uncles were sent to my father to live in our house and have a good education in a good school. The youngest was 20 years younger and the other brothers were 17 and nine years younger than my father. They were more like my father's children. There was only nine years difference between my uncle and my eldest sister. Therefore they had a great deal of respect for my mother and father. My mother was educated in the mission schools under the British principals and teachers. She finished her ELSE which was equivalent to the 10th grade which was the maximum education at school for girls during her time. She was an old girl of Vembadi girl's high school and later my own school, which was called Girl's Bilingual School, GBS for short in Point Pedro.

My parents early married life

My mother was a beautiful woman and followed that time fashion. Due to the British influence my father wore western dress before and after the marriage. But gave up when he started his married life in Point Pedro. Once I had a chance to see those photos at my father's sister's house but could not get the access of them later. I knew my mother only when she was 45 years old. Even then she was beautiful. I remember one of my aunt's reminiscences when she related about my mother. My aunt was newly married and visited my parents in the forties. She told me, "When I saw her I was mesmerised by her beautiful appearance. She was wearing a bordered sari and her long curly hair was in cascades. One could not believe she had six children. She was so beautiful that I stared at her till my husband nudged me to bring me down to the earth. Mani Acca (my mother) was a beauty of her own".

My father was the role model for all of us. He was a great person for honest dealing. He told us he loved my mother from his childhood. My mother was his first cousin and at that period it was the tradition to get married to cousins. His love for my mother started at the age of ten he said. They were first cousins and according to the tradition of our culture they were fixed for each other. But my mother always bossed my father even when they were kids and did some mischievous things like biting the guava fruit before she gave it to him to eat. My father found pleasure in those small things.

My father affectionately called my mother as "maniam", an abbreviation of "Gnanamani" which was her real name. The tradition says not to call the husband by his name. Out of respect she called my father as "Incharum" an abbreviation for "look here". In many houses it was the same. Actually it was a standard name for husbands. Small children have their own interpretation for this. I can recollect a joke shared by my mother about it. A small girl was asked her father's name. She answered boldly "Jerum Kandiah" and the teacher was confused and checked with the others about the name. Then it was revealed that the girl noticed her mother calling the father as "Injerum" and thought that was also his name and said that strange name combining it with the original name.

Soon after my parents got married they had to start their life leaving the family house in the village. The college offered them a small wooden upstairs which was the property of the college. It was an old, ransacked building which made creepy noises while climbing the stairs to go to the rooms. Water dripped off rotting eaves, the stones were slimy, wood creaked, door hung crooked but fast closed." Each plank had something to say" my mother said "They were scolding and mourning when you put down your feet". There were no houses around them. And this building was called 'Turret'. On the one side about 500 metres away was the college building, on the opposite side was the premises of the magistrate but the bungalow was about 500 metres away. On the other side there was bare land and therefore it was quite lonely. My mother was quite young as a bride. They did not have my eldest sister at that time. And she heard a peculiar noise in the house during the nights. I know my father was a sound sleeper. The moment his head touched the pillow he slept. Therefore it was my mother who was awake and sometimes alone in the house. At first my mother did not mention this, but later there were other people who talked about ghosts existing in and around the house that she got frightened. So one fine day she could not bear it any longer and told my father she would like to leave the house and not live there anymore. It was difficult to find houses to rent, especially for low rent at that time. When my father asked for the reason she told what happened. So my father said to tell him, when it happened. Since it did not happen continuously they had to wait till one day both my father and mother heard this noise. My father went in search of this noise, looked at each and every door and window. And at the end he found out the noise was made by an old window that could not be shut. It was knocking against a nail when the wind blew hard. So he took my mother and showed it to put her at ease.

But they did not stay there long because my father decided to build his own house, the first of its kind along the beach road and at the junction of the first cross street. It was the year when my eldest brother was born. Somewhere round 1935. I could not pin point the exact day because the people, who could confirm are my parents, my eldest brother and my eldest sister, who are no more. It was not easy to have everything at the same time for the house due to my father's independent spirit to stand on his own legs himself. In 1937 when my second sister Rathy was born the house got its electricity supply. That was the best thing they could have at that time because of the tuitions my father gave were possible only in the evenings. It was really a luxury at that time. The house was built in the middle but did not have a road frontage. My father was clever enough to build the house like that, to avoid the wind and the rain during monsoon weather.

The problems of ghosts did not end with that old house. When they moved to the new house surrounded by Hindu families my mother was influenced by superstitions. It was a tradition among the Hindus to offer food for the dead in the middle of the night at the junction. Usually they cut a white variety of pumpkin and smudged it with *Kum Kum* a holy red powder. They kept a torch made of cloth dipped in oil. People were frightened to trample that except the vehicles. They also believed if you touched them with the foot or hand slowly you would lose them like a leper. Even though my mother was the daughter of a Methodist pastor and a sister of the same she still believed in traditional superstitions, whereas my father was just the opposite. So whenever they did that ceremony at the junction my mother closed the doors and stayed inside. Slowly my father felt it was high time to take away that fear from my mother. So on one such occasion, when there was that offer at the junction he decided to do something sensational. After my mother went to sleep he went to the street and brought the whole thing including the torch inside the bedroom and arranged it neatly around the bed and went to sleep. Early morning, when my mother got up she saw that and screamed with fear. My father calmly said, "Was your sleep disturbed by the presence of these things? No. At least now believe me when I say that there is nothing to be frightened of these stupid superstitions. They are only for the unbelievers".

My mother had three younger brothers and the eldest of them did his Bachelor in Theology degree in Bangalore, India. He married his own cousin and settled down in life. He was a soft spoken person. If he had a choice he would always talk with a man rather than a woman, ask a man the way of somewhere, go up to a male assistant in a shop, and take a seat next to a man. He was very attached with us. He did most of the travelling for my family. Especially when my second sister entered the university he took her to the capital and visited her and informed my mother about his visits and the situation. When my father attended the Synod, the annual Methodist Conference, he looked after my father well. Because my uncle was a Methodist pastor he served in different parishes in the island but definitely once a year he visited us with my aunt and cousin. The other two brothers Sam and James lived in our house for education and left when they became adults. Her second brother was a confirmed bachelor, roaming around the island, making occasional visits to us. Her third brother was an accountant in a big firm and settled in the capital with his family. We rarely saw him except at weddings and funerals. My mother had two sisters and one of them died before I was born and the other sister lived in the town but we had little contact with her. My father had his own reasons.

My mother's second brother was an interesting character. In fact the second and the third brother of my mother, that is my maternal uncles, grew up in our house long before I was born. They lived under my father's guidance, and he was almost like their second father. They had the greatest respect for my father.

When they started their independent life in the capital city they used to visit us occasionally. Especially my mother's second brother Sam. He never married. There must be a story to that. It could have been financial or emotional. A woman who had refused or had died young and he had not loved again. He would appear and disappear in the most unexpected way. Sometimes he had money and sometimes not. When he had money he would spend it lavishly. He would visit us with presents for every member of the family. Once he brought new bank notes and gave us. That was quite a sensation for us but not to my father. My father was not overwhelmed when he had money or rejected him when he was broke. He remembered all our neighbours including the servants and the poor folks, who lived around us. He even remembered their names. He had a half a million dollar smile. Ear to ear. Regardless whether it was a woman or a man he gave a big hug to them. The local women were shy and they giggled. With his friendly voice he showed interest in them. He was tall and handsome and spoke perfect English and had a stylish walk. But he was never in the same job. While working at the German embassy and in American companies he lived in expensive hotels otherwise stayed at the YMCA. He was always on the move and never settled in life being a confirmed bachelor. As far as he was concerned 'life is what you make it'.

One day, he arrived home, showing signs of money. Then he requested my father to recommend a driver to hire a car for him to go on an island tour. Although my father was sceptic he arranged the car and my uncle took my third brother Chelva with him. He was used to unbridle extravagance. They spent more than three weeks visiting friends and relatives all over the island and at last when he came, he left in a hurry the same evening to the capital. The next day the driver came and asked for the money and my father footed the bill. My third brother Chelva copied my uncle's style of walking and followed his footsteps like a lamp for sometime but realised it was only a false appearance and he slowly came out of it. But my mother loved her brother with all his faults.

For every season my mother bought eggs and allowed them to hatch. It took about 21 days. A hen sat on the eggs and after 21 days we could see the cracking of the egg shells and the chicken coming out of them. Before that in the nights my mother took those eggs and warmed them near a lantern. And when the chickens hatched each of us was given the task of looking after them because they were the prey for the cats, dogs and sometimes the local snakes and also the hawks. But in spite of that at the end of the day, there would be at least a few chickens remaining. The hens all day pecked for the sweet bits in the ground but they were good layers. If they were cocks they will turn into our dinner, if they were hens they were allowed to live and produce our eggs.

My mother was an excellent cook specially in preparing the specialities. One of them was 'Kool' a speciality of Jaffna because you needed grinded Palmyra tuber. This is like porridge made of all kinds of seafood and greens with medical value, together with jackfruit seeds, strong chilli powder with tamarind and salt, mixed at the end with this tuber powder. This food was prepared during the season, where people were having cold. It was a semi-liquid preparation. Once you drank this the infectious cold became better. You are not supposed to drink water after eating this. In a particular season friends of ours, who visited the beach have a "Kool" party. Sometimes it was prepared in the beach itself and sometimes they prepared it at home and brought it. My grandfather's brother was one of the chief men, who took part in the preparations. We also had the *Aadi Kool*, which was prepared from the sweet toddy, which was not alcoholic and rice flower during the season in July. This was sweet.

According to the tradition neighbours and friends sent food and coffee when there was a funeral in the house. My mother never failed to send food for the funeral houses. She would personally accompany the servant carrying the food. She never missed weddings, child births and puberty ceremonies to do her duty of giving the presents or cash.

As I told you before my father was one of the first to build his house in that coastal area, especially the beach road. Later on one of his colleagues came as our neighbour, then slowly there were other Christian communities living in and around our house, but there were areas where there were local people, who were Hindus or Catholics but there was no discrimination between the ethnic groups, the races and the religions. But they had a harmonious life. Racism was unheard. Both my parents were dedicated to family values.

My mother was a friend for all but she had selected friends from the school time and they always visited her at different times but it continued till they were alive. One of them was a doctor at the Methodist hospital in Puthur about fifteen miles from our town. Once a year I went with my mother for a week to stay with her. She had two boys of my age and I played with them. Sometimes I visited the Maternity ward, where there were babies. My mother's cousin was the

GLORIANA SELVANATHAN

matron for the nurses' quarters and one of my cousins was a nurse there. It was
a beautiful place with beautiful gardens, which I enjoyed very much and I had
my meals with the nurses. The servants in the kitchen came from remote villages
and the wonders of the town were new to them. Once we were buying ice cream
from the van and each of us had the cone topped with ice cream. One of the
innocent servants from the village slowly asked my cousin "Sister should I wash
the cone and return to the man?" Words could not describe the shock we had.

The other friend was Pathma aunty from Jaffna. I had no idea what she was but
she had a big house with jack fruit trees and mango trees. During the season she
brought those fruits. Another lady was elder than my mother because she called
her as Grace Acca (acca means big sister) who was the principal of the Girls'
School in the east. My mother did everything perfect, when she stayed with us.
Once she went to Singapore she brought me a sari for my eldest brother's
wedding. Locally most of the parish members were her friends specially the boys
college principal's wife Peace was very close to my mother.

My mother was a local preacher in the church and was a senior teacher for the
Sunday school. Our school had needle work exhibition once a year and she was
one of the judges to give the best garment prize for each class. She was the vice
president for the Vembadi Girls high school past pupils association and took an
active part in MWF apart from doing social help. She was a good host, a good
cook, a good mother and a good wife.

One special friend was Sampanthar Aunty. I do not know her first name. This
was her husband's name. Her husband and my father were very close friends.
During the forties her husband owned a car, which was quite a luxury at that
time. He was also a teacher from a wealthy family. According to the tradition he
married this lady, when she was quite young: may be sixteen or seventeen. She
was not sent to school, when she was quite young. Education for women in the
conservative Hindu families in the forties was not recommended. But one day
while he was driving in the night he knocked down someone and later this
person died. My father was turning over in his mind, his conversation with his
friend Sambanthar. Mr. Sambanthar was a righteous man and he felt guilty about
this incident and day by day he underwent mental torture which he shared with
my father. He could not accept that the past is past and that's where it should
stay. In his worst moments he had asked my father "Have you ever faced the
burden of blame?" When relating this incident years after, my father said "There

54

are certain moments in your life you wished you had an answer but to your shock you hadn't". The incident made Mr. Sambanthar sick and one day he collapsed and died. Well death keeps no calendar. His wife was a young widow without any education. She took over the traditional widow appearance by only wearing white sari and blouse without any jewellery. With the help of my parent's friends she was taken as a caretaker for a school. Not because of wanting an income to survive but to keep the loneliness, her loss and sense of emptiness away. My father told her story, when I was a child asking who she was. She was fabulously rich but could not enjoy life. It was an eternal doom for women, when they were widowed especially in the Hindu community. Very often she visited us with fruits from her garden. She helped many of her nieces and nephews in education and in marriage. But she never forgot my parents, who helped her when she really needed help. Later they had a trust in her husband's name and a library, classes for music, needle work and education conducted for women. Every year they had cultural celebration and she always invited my father as the chief guest, to speak on those occasions.

Chapter 8

Second World War

The Second World War had an impact on people all over the world. So my country was not an exception. At that time my country was under the colonial regime. There were foreign soldiers in the country. We had African soldiers patrolling in big trucks my siblings said. My brother remembered the shouting *Jumbo Raffica* they said in their own language. I was not born at that time. The day my second brother Bala was born the King of England declared war. It was the 3rd of September 1939. There was no television, and radio was the only source to get any information. Any instruction to the citizens was only informed through the radio. Food was scarce and luxuries were rare. Wheat porridge and *sambol* (a quick preparation of scraped coconut with chilly salt and onions) was the common food. Sometimes rice was smuggled from India. Then they had rice. Our family was big, when compared to the other neighbours. So the struggle was more. There were times there was tea without milk, and then no sugar and at times no tea at all my sister said. Aeroplanes flew over the country. Panic was everywhere like a spreading plague. If they suspected they were the enemies there would be sirens warning the citizens to go to the hiding places. My mother had a whistle around her neck and whenever she heard the siren she blew the whistle and all the children should run and hide under the big beds and stayed there till the siren sounded that the danger was over. In the nights windows were closed so that no lights were seen. Markets opened only for a short time and they had little to offer.

Only one incident my brother recalled. We had the beach behind our house and one day suddenly it was filled with these soldiers. They were tall and hefty compared to the locals. Fortunately they talked English and requested to have some drinking water. So my mother gave the biggest pot which two people carried and gave a brass pot to withdraw the water and drink. Then to their astonishment one of the soldiers came and lifted the big pot effortlessly and drank the water. They had such strength. The army base was about fourteen miles from our town and in the nights they flashed the search light in the sky and land, that one could see the objects clearly as in the day light. The schools functioned for shorter hours. There were open bunkers round the class rooms. All the children had a thread round the neck with a piece of wood attached to it. Whenever they heard the siren they bit the piece of wood and jumped into the

THOSE WERE THE GOLDEN DAYS

bunkers. My second sister was in the kinder garden and the schools had a lot of British teachers. To divert the children from the tension, they were asked to draw pictures and they were taken and magnified by the bioscope, a wonder those days, and shown to the children. As a child my sister had often wondered how her small chick she drew became so big on the wall. The huge war ships were anchored in Kudathanai, about ten miles away from our town and my siblings went to see them. Years later they had a festival called ship festival, and people dressed as white people came down the ship and performed street operas.

My mother was pregnant and when the time came they prepared to go to the hospital. Things were loaded in the car but it was too late. My mother delivered her seventh child at home. During the World War II in 1941 my third brother Chelva was born at home and my second sister was playing outside. They brought the baby and showed him to my sister. Since he was wearing a girl's baby shirt my sister thought it was a baby sister. Only later she understood it was a brother. She went to school in 1944 just before the war ended. The British principal had different activities and in December they had the nativity and my sister's first name was Mary and she acted Mary's part. She recalled my elder sister relating the following incident. The hostel girls from the Girl's School were taken to the beach occasionally and they sang the song.

Soldier, soldier, soldier how big is your fortune

Farmer, farmer, farmer three boots old and useless

Solider, soldier, soldier then you may not court her

Farmer, farmer, farmer at home we have much fairer

The soldiers who passed that way halted and laughed at the song.

It was the Easter Sunday my parents and my siblings watched a fleet of planes flying over the sea and disappearing. Shortly after that, the capital city Colombo was bombed. They heard the news on the radio. The report appeared in its fullest version on the news papers. When peace was declared the students wore blue and white and attended the ceremony at the judicial courts building. My siblings were too young to remember the details.

Chapter 9

My infancy

Gloriana Gunarubini Selvanathan (nee Gunanayagam)

I was born rather late for my parents. My father was 46 and my mother was 43. Not only that after 4 years interval. They lost one daughter between my last brother and me. Whenever people asked my father about my birth he always answered with a laugh "Well that was an accident". I brought illness to my mother even before I was born. When she was six months pregnant she had to be operated for appendicitis. It was quite a dangerous situation, especially with limited medical facilities. But we survived. One should not wonder about that because apart from my father all my brothers and sisters were operated for appendicitis including me.

As a baby I used to have fits attacks my sister said. Very often it was a matter of life and death. As I said our town had all ethnic groups and my parents got friendly with the Sinhalese community who worked in the government sector. One day I had a severe attack and the customs officer, who was present at the time, quickly went and cut the bark of the *Moringa* tree squeezed the juice into my mouth to bring down the intensity before I was taken to the hospital. My sister vividly remembered that incident when we talked about my illnesses. This continued and someone told that piercing the ears would stop that, so my parents did that when I was four year old. I remember the gold smith coming and piercing my ears with a needle and putting *kum kum*, a magenta powder used as disinfectant.

I was in the fourth grade, when they started the preparation for the annual price giving day at the school. I was taking the main role in one of the plays and of course in singing. My mother occasionally visited her friends in the capital city, where her brother was an accountant. She was away from home when I developed fever. My father always gave us the home medicine, failing which the native medicine was given. It was detected that I had enteric, pneumonia and whooping cough at the same time. The local medical practitioner visited me and identified these illnesses. I was allowed to sleep in a separate room and my father was with me. Friends of my mother visited because that was the custom even if we had severe illnesses, just for courtesy sake. They did not come inside my room but sat in the veranda. One of my mother's friend noticed that the apothecary was putting his leg with the shoes on the mattress. My mother was informed and she came immediately. When she came the whole scene was different. She put me in a separate bed with a beautiful sheet that they got from the boys college with the college colour blue with yellow stripes. I felt great. I was still ill. My mother would sit in one of the easy chairs and read while I slept on the bed.

When she returned from Colombo she brought a packet of rosins, which was left at the side of the cupboard. With my illness I was forbidden to eat many of the food items specially solids. I think my taste buds were craving for something. When I saw the packet of rosins, I took and ate some of them. In fear I did not munch them: I swallowed them. Suddenly my father found the temperature rising, he could feel the pulse and felt that something was wrong. When they pressed me hard to find out the truth, I told them what I had eaten. It was a matter of life and death which I did not understand at that time. I could have died. My father went to the family native physician, who gave him a tablet that should be taken in the middle of the night, so that the things I ate came out without damaging my health. My father used to tell this story many times.

Due to the illness, especially typhoid, I lost my hair therefore they cut my hair short. I could not go to school and I could not take part in the play I prepared. My friend did it but I was allowed to see the prize giving because I had several prizes. For some reason I felt sad for not doing that part in the play. I was twice attacked by malaria. And the third time when I was in the hostel. Luckily I was taken home and my father knew how to handle. Usually at that time they gave Quinine pills but my father had a special herbal preparation and the extract of this was so bitter that one could not simply swallow it because the taste stayed for a long time in the tongue. Always my father brought this preparation together with a spoon of sugar and waited till I drank fully. If it were one or two spoons you could take it, but usually it was a cup full. And every time this treatment cured me.

Chapter 10

Our house and our habitual

Our house was well protected where as the houses built with the road frontage were totally wet during the monsoon season. The building was built solid with varnished wood windows and doors. We had fairly a big compound surrounding the house with a lot of coconut trees and *Moringa* trees. Each coconut tree belonged to someone in the family. I was the only one, who did not have one. May be I was born rather late. We had two big verandas in front and behind which could accommodate a lot of people specially my father's students. They were enclosed on both sides and opened on one side. When there were big dinners hosted by my parents, which were quite often, long tables were set in the back veranda. The living room we referred as Hall was set for the visitors with settees and arm chairs with cushions. And during the Christmas season we had something new added and the colour changed. Every year our house was white washed and the furniture polished: all hand done by the workers. The pillows had real cotton and my mother would periodically take them out of the covers and dry them in the sun. Water was supplied from the well, built slightly away from the house. Open tubs were there for the younger ones to fill and bathe. Every year the well was cleaned by men, who drew out the water from the well, cleaned the walls inside and disinfected it with *Sambrani* (incense) smoke. When my brothers were a bit older they helped our servant Somu with the cleaning.

On the front veranda high up in the wall we had a framed picture of Jesus praying in the mount. Strange enough we never had any photographs hanging till my sister got married. Her wedding group photographs were hung in the living room. There were three framed pictures hanging in our living-room ever since I remember. Those pictures were brought by my pastor uncle, my mother's brother, and had a good lead for us to remember things about God. First one carried "Fear God and keep his commandments" with big red roses as motives, the second one I remember said "God will supply all your needs", the third one was quite vague, because during one of the cyclones, it was destroyed but these two I read every day.

All the valuables were kept in the main room, which had access only through the living room. The children's room had a door to the back veranda. Most amazing thing was, during the day time all the doors were open and anyone could enter the house. That was the time thieves were not heard of, and anything was asked and given. But later, after some incidents that happened, the doors had bars across in the nights. On the front veranda there was a big table for us to sit and learn and some armchairs for people who made short visits. We were not supposed to come and sit with the visitors unless or otherwise called for. But being the youngest and small I would go and sit with the visitors sometimes. I was always dressed for the occasion. My siblings would be in their room but would look through the key hole and listen to all the conversations. Especially if any of the teachers or the principals came to visit us. For emergency I had done the spy work of reporting who was there. Usually visitors came without informing and I was asked to go and serve the drinks. Visitors came from distant places and stayed for a meal or stayed for weeks and months depending for which purpose they came for. Visits of school friends were allowed and we were also given permission to visit our friends. There was no hard fast rule that we had to inform where we were going, if it was a visit in the neighbourhood. Only my elder sister or my second sister, who were young girls, should inform where they were going. Usually they were accompanied by my father or if it was my second sister, I was asked to go. Overnight stays with friends were not allowed. All should be back by six O'clock at the table to learn till we were called for dinner. We had to respect my eldest sister in all aspects otherwise we were dealt accordingly. My sister saw to that. We called her "Acca" (elder sister) and not by name. All the others called each other by the pet names because they were only two years difference between them. We called father *"Ayah"* and mother *"amma"* the traditional Tamil names for father and mother. No western influence of using Mummy and Daddy.

We were not brought up in a tasteless home or disagreeable parents. Kind or cruel, loving or cold, brave or cowardly my parents stayed together. A good husband makes a good wife they say and it fitted for my parents. I do agree that anxiety, stubbornness, provocation, anger and contempt and quicker tongue did exist but above them all a peaceful harmony shone in our family. My father's voice was moderate and consoling and powerful. He kept his best card to his chest. There were situations, which were satisfying, depressing, horrifying, humiliating, discontented, intrigued and indignant. Many times the smile on my father's face lost none of its exuberance but the voice was hard as a whip crack. Mid night in bed was my parent's conference time. They talked matters of business, matters of money, perplexity to fantasy problems and solutions, worries and anxieties. Being the youngest I was often in their bed room and heard bits of that and bits of this, which did not make any sense to my small brain, while I was in that cloudy space between waking and sleeping, before I really fell asleep.

Once in a fortnight the *dobby*[19] collected the clothes for washing whereas emergency washings were done by us. Coconuts were plucked regularly by special people for that job, and there was a woman to sweep the compound regularly. Fences were renewed and the coconut leaves were woven for that purpose. The leaves were tied together soaked in the sea and woven. There were women, who could do that very quickly and we tried that for fun.

Our living room was big enough to accommodate the whole family for the morning prayers. That was how we were woken from sleep. Once people had got over their early morning moods it could be a bit fun in getting ready for school. Morning Prayer was a regular practice in the house. Whether we were sleepy or not, we had to attend. And every day somebody was named to pray and another person should read the bible. Sometimes my brothers were too sleepy, they would come to the room, and when the prayer started, they would go to sleep. They had to be woken after the prayer was over. If we were late we would be stepping in tiptoes and taking a place. My father was the only person, who could pray quite short, without fancy long phrases, and without any reference to bible texts in the prayers. My mother prayed sincere wishes. And we of course made the shortest prayers but the interesting things happened, when my grandfather came. He was a very pleasant person talking to God in a very pleasant way without shouting, but by the time he ends we would have heard a small sermon in the prayers. But the worst thing was when the father-in-law of my uncle prayed, when he came for holidays. That was unbearable. He would talk from A-Z about the bible, quoting verses as though he was reminding God about the bible. Sometimes it took about fifteen to twenty minutes. We had our schools starting at eight thirty. That meant only after the family prayers, we could get ready for the school. We would have enough time to get ready and go, but if these prayers were too long, we all open our eyes and point to the clock and do everything possible without listening to the prayer. Once it happened even my father opened his eyes and asked us to go, because grandfather was talking about the whole bible in his prayer. So when he finished, we all left, only

---

[19] Local name for the man washing the dirty clothes

my mother and father were there. I really appreciated my father's practical way of thinking.

Chapter 11

Food we had

My mother or my sisters prepared the morning coffee for all and served it. Breakfast was a hasty affair, lunch was self served because of the different times we arrived from the school, evening snacks and tea would be on the table for us to take and dinner was together. Sometimes there was mixed rice prepared by my mother made into balls and served by her. Actually we waited for that because it was really a treat. We used our hands to eat our meal, which was practical for our type of meals. Whenever special dishes were made by my mother she sent to the neighbours or friends. The task of taking them was given to one of us and not to the servants.

We had variety of food in the house, usually in the mornings we had string hoppers with curry or *dhosai* with *sambol* or *idly* or *puttu*. Rice and curry is a must for lunch. In the evenings at about four we had some snacks made out of different types of lentils and grams ranging from the smallest to the biggest Bengal grams. In the evenings it was either rice and curry or other food prepared in the mornings. For special occasions we had oil cakes, both hot and sweet, and dried rice soaked and crushed with coconut and *jaggery*. We never had strict instructions as to how we should eat, like' you should chew the food properly and never swallow in lumps', because often I did do that.

My mother was a very good housewife. She did everything connected to food preservation. During the chilly season, when it was very cheap, maybe a pound for 10 cents, she would get that and we were supposed to take a safety pin, prick the chilly and split it. Then it was boiled with salt and tamarind, allowed for one day to soak in it and then dried in the sun. This was very tasty and my mother took them when she visited her friends in the capital because it was a delicacy for them. Similarly during the citron season the similar process was done and lime pickles were made. We had a big *Magosa* tree. During a fixed season it blossomed, small white flowers. We used to spread mats and cloth under the tree to collect the dried flowers which was mixed with some other ingredients and made into round flat preparations and dried which was called as *"vadagam"*. During the Palmyra tuber season she had prepared various things. Some of the tubers are boiled and dried, cut into small rounds. Later it was treated with sugar which was another delicacy for the people who lived in the capital, where there were no Palmyra trees. All Palmyra products went from our province.

Sometimes the tubers are dried without being boiled and made into flour, which was the healthiest food my father ever liked. The fruit of the Palmira was also used for a longer period if the juice is extracted and dried.

There were different seasons for the fruits in my country. North was famous for the Palmyra tree products. That was one and the only tree, where every part of the tree was useful. The tuber when it is young was eaten either boiled or roasted in the fire. The young fruit (*Nungoo*) was eaten during the beginning of summer, which was tasty and had a cooling effect on your body. During the season servants were sent to cut the bunch of fruits from our property in the village. When they were fully ripe they become soft and juicy: one could eat as they were. When we had in excess my mother made various types of food from oil cakes to dried form to keep it for the winter. The trees were used as rafters for the house and the big fan like leaves were used for the thatched roof for the cottages and huts. We always enjoyed the whole season of this tree. Making the oil cakes was a big process. We collected a few fruits that had fallen from the tree, the outer hard skin was peeled off to expose juicy inner fruit. Then with the help of water, the juice was extracted into a paste which was mixed with flour and the thick paste was dropped like little balls into the boiling oil. The result of it was the tasty oil cake. We waited for the rest of the seed and the remaining juice which my mother would give mixed with Tamarind water. They said when you ate the fruit to extract the juice the husk in the seed would clean your teeth.

Chapter 12

My family

Apart from my parents I had three brothers and two sisters. But we had a big age gap between us. My eldest sister Gunamani was 18 years elder to me and my last brother Chelva was 7 years elder to me. Actually my parents had eight children but they lost one son and a daughter when they were quite young. We all had pet names in the house. I could never remember any of them calling me my real name. I was called *Kunchu*. All my neighbours, family friends knew only our pet names. They did not know my real name. It is a name given for baby birds. Only at school I was referred with my name. I was really a baby in the house and they never allowed me to walk when I went to the church. My eldest brother Baba or my sister Rathy carried me. Except my eldest sister all my brothers and my second sister were called by their pet names. My eldest brother was Baba, My second brother was Bala, my third brother was Chelva and my second sister was Rathy. They were all, the last part of their full name which started with Guna...Only my eldest sister we called "Acca", which means "big sister" an honour given due to seniority. If ever we had loggerhead towards any of the siblings then we used the nick names to annoy one another. The fight would go on for a long time just by repeating the nick name and it was really a serious issue for all of us. It made you so sensitive that you would be really annoyed and for hours we did not talk to each other. Sometimes it was a team effort. For all these it never went to our parent's level. We ourselves would sort them out and the anger was only short lived with the attitude of let sleeping dog lie. My father expounding with relish on the complexities of his intricate family was rarely shaken by surprises and shocks. During his long life my father made many friends who were attracted by his never failing wit, knowledge, good humour and maddening self assurance leave alone his compassion. My mother was my father's driving force for his physical activities and my father was her moral support for my mother's challenges. They were an ideal pair. My mother proved that behind every successful man there is a woman.

My family in 1956 Christmas, just before my sister got married

*Standing: myself, second brother Bala, eldest brother Baba,third brother Chelva,
second sister Rathy.
Seated: my father Gunanayagam, my mothe rGnanamani, my grandfather Rev. Eliathamby,
my eldest sister Gunamani*

My own family now in Berlin

*Back row: Eldest son in law Philipp, second son in law Timo and my son Thilak.
Front row: My eldest daughter Sofia, My second daughter Irene,
I, and my daughter in law Daniela*

Servants

I could remember most of our servants. Somu who came from the east and stayed with us till my mother arranged a marriage for him and built a small house for his family behind our house, where he lived till he died recently. When he became a man he worked in a restaurant then his brother Murugupillai came. We had another one Sunthari, who was my nanny for some time. Then we had Annaluxumi and Easwary from our village followed by Kili and her sister, who became a drag queen, Panchu and Vethalingam. When we grew up local women like Annapillai and her daughters came to do the chores during the day time and returned to their houses in the evenings. I remember one funny incident with our servant Somu. My eldest brother was very fair but younger than Somu. So he called my brother *'Baba thamby'* (thamby means younger brother). Somu was pitch dark and he was always obsessed with my brother's complexion. One day my brother was playfully making some tiny balls like tablets out of the dust and Somu happened to come that way. He saw those tiny balls and asked my brother what they were. For fun my brother told him they were tablets to get a fair skin. Suddenly Somu grabbed them and ran and before my brother could warn him he swallowed them. We were all shocked and did not utter a word. Till he died he did not know about it.

There was an interesting adventure we had during the new moon. I remember Somu since I was a baby. He came from the east and talked funny Tamil but improved as time went by. He had great affinity to the sea, skilled in angling, good in his cooking and unsympathetic with animals. We had stray cats and dogs, which were punished severely by him. He attacked them with fire wood and chased them specially while cutting fish for the meals. But he caught fish even in a stormy weather only with the line and hook. One could say angling was a passion for him. He collected used tyres of the bikes and cars for a special purpose. That was for the night hunting in the sea. It was locally called as "Chule", where they burned the tyres and used as a guide to walk in the sea to catch fish and crabs. They said the fish got blind by this light and some species hid themselves in the sand making a cloudy effect with the disturbed sand. You would not move your eyes even a fraction then the fish would swim back out of reach and stay there to laugh at you. But he would spot the place and put his hand and catch the fish hidden in the sand. My eldest brother, during his University vacation, or even otherwise gladly accompanied Somu in those adventures. During the holiday season even the neighbours' children joined the group. Then at the end of the hunt we made a bon- fire at the beach and put the catch and enjoyed the taste of the fish and the crabs. But there were some sudden developments during this venture. That was when they spot the sea snake. Then they would shout "*Anjalai* (that is the name of the snake).The next moment each one would run in different directions. And the worst was, when the fire ball dropped down and in the dark they scattered and ran towards the shore blindly. We heard stories that if that snake bit, you would permanently tremble like the Parkinson diseased patient. Not that we saw anyone suffering from that, but the fear was there. I was not allowed to go with them far only when they were near the shore. Even that was a thrill. I never saw any other girl doing that. Fear within was one thing but showing a brave front was another. Usually I and my second sister waited at the shore and collected firewood for that local Barbeque. My parents never took part in this adventure although mother was there sometimes only to watch.

Chapter 13

Pets in the house

Our house was built almost in the middle of the property, but we had plenty of land behind the house to have pets and other household animals. Only the cow's milk was delivered by somebody else. But my mother had a goat and it was said that goat's milk was good for the heart. And we had to pluck leaves for the goat and I used to watch my mother milking the goat. We had lots of hens, chickens and one of the hens was the favourite for my brothers. They trained it to echo their voice. So when they made a voice, the hen returned it. And they were very attached to this hen. In the nights it slept in one of the trees, they had their freedom. This particular hen, looked barren for my mother, and she thought that it was high time we had her for our dinner. My brothers opposed but my mother would not listen to it. My mother kept hens with the expectation of getting eggs but this hen did not produce any eggs and one day my mother said "It is high time to have her for our dinner." So on that particular day my brother took the hen and put it in a basket and covered it with dirty clothes and when my mother searched for the hen, she could not find it. My brothers were happy but it did not continue for a long time, our servant was clever enough to make the same sound as my brother and found the hidden place. And when they cut open the hen, our servant said "Madam, there is egg inside." It was such a sad day for my brothers that they did not eat the dinner. The first preference for dinner would be the cocks but occasionally a hen was not over ruled. If it was a formal dinner for the visitors then tender chicken was bought from the neighbours. Somu and my eldest brother Baba killed and peeled the skin of the bird. Especially our servant Somu got vengeful pleasure in cutting, bending, breaking open the body of the chicken. My eldest brother was a favourite eater of chicken. When my mother cooked the chicken curry while it was in the fire my brother would come and take a piece of it and run away. He was also an expert in peeling the skin of the bird whenever we had one for dinner, especially when visitors came in the absence of Somu.

We always had dogs in the house. Once my pastor uncle brought an Alsatian crossed pair, a male and a female. My father named them as Cesar and Lizzy. I think they lived for a long time in our house, maybe 5 or 6 years. My father was an ardent friend of those dogs. He would never eat without keeping a portion of his food reserved on his plate for the dogs. After he finished his meal he would take this food, call the dogs and give them. Cesar was the barking type, and Lizzy was the biting type. Sometimes people went to the beach through our house. From the time those dogs came they got frightened to come, they either barked or tried to attack and chase them. And one day a young man threw a big iron nail used for the ships to Lizzy and her eyes were affected and then she died. We could see Cesar was sad. But he continued to live. He was very much attached to my father because he fed him regularly every day. He also became ill and one day when my father came home, he left his usual place, the veranda, and got down from the veranda, wining, backed towards the coconut tree and fell down and died. My father said "He did not want to die inside the house." So they buried Cesar behind our lavatory. And we had to pass that to go to the beach. And sometimes I was sent to do some errands while the others were at the beach in the nights. But every time I passed the place Cesar was buried, I saw some shadow, which I thought the ghost of Cesar whereas the dangerous shadow was no more than a faint dappling of darkness: but for my child's mind it was a ghost, an idea instilled by my servant girl, so I closed my eyes and ran to the beach. A fear is a fear in any other form I suppose.

Admittedly my father would get friendly with any stray dog, from time to time and bring them home and feed them. There is a special word to call a dog "*Unchu*". And you could hear every night my father calling the dog, because the dogs did not have a name, only the general name "*Unchu*". And he would feed them. Once, our servant caught a parrot. And it was kept in a cage and fed and was looked after well. I was not that tall to reach the cage but I used to go and look at it. One day it opened the cage and flew. My servant followed it but it flew directly to the ocean. There was no place to rest and it got tired and it flew closer to the sea surface. And the servant came back and told "*Amma* (amma means mother but it also means "lady" when people paid respect), you know what happened? A shark jumped and swallowed the parrot." Who could change the destiny? Only after a short lived freedom the parrot died in a most unexpected manner.

Chapter 14

Parents the best hosts

Our house was a standard place both for the Boy's College and the girl's school boarders to visit: both the teachers and the students. During moonlight days the girl's school's hostellers and teachers came to our house and went for a sea bath. They enjoyed the contacts with fishes and the screams that followed. It was quite an entertainment watching them from the shores. My mother was a good host. She loved entertaining people by giving dinners in the western style. New teachers, new government officers from the customs department, and people leaving the town for good and newly married couple were given dinners at our house together with our family friends. From the morning itself preparations would be going on. As the evening approached my mother would be busy setting the table and checking the food. My eldest sister would be gliding about the room preparing the dinner and my second sister did the errands. I would be dressed tip top on those occasions. Since the two schools were all island schools, teachers of all ethnic groups were in the schools and most of them were not from Point Pedro. So every time someone joined the staff my mother invited them for dinner. Not only the staff but also new Sinhalese friends who came to the government jobs were invited. There were a lot of *Malayalies*[20] from India who were in the schools. They were also there sometimes. When someone left the school or got a transfer they were given farewell dinners. Usually the dinner was held at the back veranda, which was quite huge and convenient. A long table was placed covered with white sheets. The servants were not allowed to serve the meals because according to our custom the host must serve the food for the visitors and the hosts did not sit together with the guests and have the meal. When asked, my grandfather gave me the reason for this custom. The host was responsible to see there was no shortage of food and must be ready to prepare more in case of emergency. The host must have what was left after the dinner. Those dinners were more of a western style. The kitchen swirled with the clutter of crockery and cutlery. Gradually the kitchen was filled with the aromatic fragrance of the spices. Three courses would be given and sometimes four. First the soup with baked beans, the second course would be fried fish, boiled potatoes, beetroot with onions and chillies cut in small pieces, fish cutlets and another vegetable. Then the main meal was served with fried rice or string

---

[20] People from Kerala India

hoppers, *mixed rice*[21] with meat curry or prawn curry. And the desert would be fruit salad. Those dinners were memorable because some of the teachers are my siblings' teachers and some of them were my teachers. They loudly and happily raised their voices exchanging greetings, with friendly abuse, and news, snippets of gossip and less of politics. The continuation of the conversation, the change of topic, the inclusion of each person at the table, it was magic.

Our house was an informal hostel for many people. Visitors, homeless and boarders were often in our house. Very often different people from different areas and towns came and stayed with us. They had social, financial or health problems. Once, a sister of the Girls' School's staff came from a distant place to see her elder sister. Those days women wearing trousers and riding a bike were not totally accepted in the towns, they were seen only in the cities. This lady Devi was doing her graduation at the agricultural institute where they had to drive tractors and work in the fields therefore she wore trousers when she came. As said before although we had British culture in the school, the traditions were kept. Therefore her sister would not allow her to stay with her in the hostel. So my parents were her refuge. For me she was a very interesting person and I used to accompany her, when she went to the shop where people looked at her strangely but that was not a problem for my parents. Not only her there were several of them, who stayed with us either for a problem or for the holidays. Similarly many young girls with some kind of problems were brought to our house at various times. An evangelist's daughter after her mother's death, the third daughter of a teacher for studies, the sister of a lecturer for holidays, a sister of a teacher at the girls' school as a boarder, two sisters who had hysteria, a beautiful girl with problem of love and many others were with us either for a short time or for the holidays. My parents were respected and trusted with such tasks. One should understand that it was the time young girls were not allowed to stay in other people's houses other than their own. That made our house quite special and lively and all of them loved to carry me because I was a baby.

---

[21] Fried rice mixed with vegetables

Chapter 15

My father and politics

My father had excellent knowledge in many things such as English and Tamil literature, Latin and Logic, Sports and Music and one other subject was Politics. He was an excellent speaker. A popular criminal lawyer, who became a full time politician, wanted my father to speak in public meetings, in favour of him. He had the great gift of delivering convincing statements to his voters. My father being his best friend, he consulted about the election tactics with my father. Their famous meeting place was the public beach, where they sat and discussed matters for hours. But at one point my father realised that politics did not suit to his morals of life. That in turn made him to retreat from such commitments although his friendship continued. Once I heard him talking to my brothers. He said "Politics is a dirty game and lawyers have to live with lies, therefore I don't want any of my children to become neither a politician nor a lawyer" Well it took some time for him to realize that oil and water did not mix. Fortunately none of us became a lawyer or a politician although there were several occasions my brothers were tempted to do so.

I would also like to say about the political meetings we had in the public beach. The beach could accommodate thousands and thousands and there would be mikes and loudspeakers and stages erected for the particular day. Political meetings in our country at that time were totally different from what I see in Europe. In Europe rarely they have open air meetings but for us the previous day and the same day of the meeting, there would be vehicles fitted with loud speakers announcing about the meeting, venue the time and the name of the special speakers. It was a usual practice in our country to display posters with photographs of the candidates on them. Although at that time I did not understand politics, I still recollect a song that was sung by the opposition party about the wife of another party member. They made such a fun with that. The lady concerned never shied away from such criticism. She was a strong person, who withstood such attacks. She had the great gift of being to say nothing at length, and in a flowing sequence of polysyllabic fashionable words of talking meaningless nonsense, in fine mellifluous phrases with absolute confidence.

Two or three days before the election there would be big vehicles filled with the supporters of different parties, going around the town shouting 'our votes are for....' and then their symbol. We used to rush out to the streets to see that.

Going behind the vehicle and collecting the notices thrown was fun. One thing was sure that carpet beggars can never compete in our area. Each meeting would be a big event with special speakers, who had to address two or three meetings on the same day, in different areas. Normal party members would speak at the beginning, only in the middle or at the end the important speakers appeared. There were two reasons for that. One, they waited till the whole crowd came and the other reason was to keep the crowd stay till the end of the meeting. Those powerful speakers could turn the voters from one party to another overnight.

I as a child did not understand the worth or the reason of the political meetings. For me it was a day to go to the beach without any restrictions, play with friends, run about and enjoy. Especially the vendors will be selling snacks, popcorns and nuts, and I am given some money to buy these and eat. There would be someone from the family sitting on the beach, for me to go if I am sleepy. Sometimes my whole family and friends were there away from the bright lights. At times I would go and sit just in front of the stage in the first row, just to look at the popular politicians. At that time we never had racial discriminations, therefore the Sinhalese politicians, who were usually from the communist or left parties or leaders of those parties, came and delivered their speeches. Unfortunately they spoke only in English. Therefore my father was asked to translate those speeches at the beach. In such instances I was in the front row telling the other children "Look my father is there." I was proud of him. If in case, there was rain, then there was no protection whatsoever, except the post office building opposite the beach. The main speakers were taken there till the rain ceased. Once when it started to rain I also ran to the post office building, my eldest brother saw that and carried me on his shoulders. Then I noted we were shoulder to shoulder with the guest speaker Dr. Colvin. R. de Silva. He looked at me and asked "Who is this little girl?" And I boldly told him "I am the translator's daughter." It was very rare to have such direct contact to the leaders of the parties. Then he gave me one of the garlands he had. When the rain stopped I came home and related the whole story proudly.

There was an incident that happened for a particular politician who contested in the communist party. Even though I was a little girl, I remember this candidate visiting our house. He contested the election two times and failed to be elected. But his third attempt was more of asking sympathy votes than vote for the party.

At one point he said, if he didn't win the third election he would commit suicide. As a person he was soft-spoken and kind. That was the only time, we knew for whom my father voted. The rest of his life we never knew, who was his favourite candidate in the general election. After the polls ended the results were announced either in the government administrative office in the city or for the others through the radio. The whole night we sat around the radio to hear the results. Every time the winner was announced there were crackers cracked by his supporters. And this time my father sat with us and listened to the political comments. We heard the announcement that this candidate had won with an absolute majority. There was joy on my father's face. I think the whole town celebrated his victory.

Once the elections were over, they had a thank you meeting at the public beach. I think that was the grandest public meeting we ever had. That particular candidate paraded in an open car and almost all the houses greeted him with garlands, which were up to his nose. Every time it reached this level, he removed them and the second round started. That was the only time I saw my father supporting a politician not for his political principles but as a person.

There was a politician, quite young, whose wife died leaving him with three daughters. My father was an active speaker supporting him in his political meetings. Soon he was married to a lady who was not from the same area but her family was quite influential. In fact the age difference between her eldest step daughter and her was ten or twelve years. But those girls were quite talented and were educated in the capital city, later joined the Hindu Girls' School in our town. This lady got a baby, who was of my age. Her name was Aruna. Whenever they came to my town they never forgot to visit us. But her husband died quite suddenly leaving her as a young widow. My sister told me that was the biggest funeral procession ever in Point Pedro. My father ended his political activity and never went to speak in any of the political meetings to support any candidate thereafter, except as a translator, which he did for all parties. It was not easy for a young widow to live alone, so she had her solace only with her daughter. Financially they were well-off but she had other family problems therefore she used to come to my father to get his advice. While my parents talked with her, Aruna and I played together.

As the saying goes 'misfortune never comes alone', suddenly Aruna died at the age of five. Graves are of all sizes. She could not bear the loss. So she often came home and saw me and brought presents for me just to remember her daughter. But time changed that she fought against the conservative beliefs and wanted an out let, and the only possibility was to leave the island and she forced herself in pursuit of studies. The irony was that it looked as if she had had no more chance of escape from the forcible education than a Victorian girl from its denial. I came to know about the loss of her daughter only long after Aruna died even though I repeatedly asked after Aruna. Death at that age couldn't be explained. Since Aruna visited me occasionally I always expected she might come one day. It took me long to understand that she would never ever come and visit me.

Chapter 16

My early memories

I had a vivid memory of my childhood and one could say one of the first of its kind, which still haunts me was, my adventurous walk to my sister's school. I think I was about two or three years old then. One day my mother wanted to give a bath. In those days they have to boil water and mix it with cold water to give a bath for a baby. I was wearing my baby shirt. It was an orange baby shirt with small flowers on it. My mother asked me to stay there until she prepared the water for me to have the bath. Those days we did not have pipes, so it was only the well. But sometimes they bathed the baby in the back veranda. So my mother left me and went to the back veranda. I think I must have remembered a small, white sand dune in the girls' school where my eldest sister was a teacher and my second sister was still a student. It must have clicked in my mind and I was obsessed with this white sand. And I wanted this sand to play with. So I took a green soda bottle, came out of the house and entered the street. It was a glorious day and the fresh breeze from the sea was replaced by the dry weather and the skies were clear blue with just the tiniest cotton buds of cloud drifting by. And I started to walk to the school, which was about half a kilometre away. But the dangerous part of that road was on one side there was the sea. And I walked this road looking at the sea and reached the school. I saw the white sand dune and sat on top of it and started to fill the bottle. The assembly hall was just nearby and the principal's office was also there. The teachers who came out of the office saw only a small child on the sand dune. At first they thought it was someone from the school but I was too small for a pupil. Then suddenly one of the teachers identified me and called my eldest sister. My eldest sister came near me and could not believe her eyes. I did not think I was able to speak much those days but I was happy to see my sister. There was a big commotion and the Sinhalese baker cum grosser who lived closer to our house came to the school to deliver bread. I was handed over to him to be taken back home. Nothing ventured nothing gained I suppose.

I remember mother telling that they were searching for me all over the house, including the well thinking I had fallen into it. This became a standard joke to my brothers and sisters. Well that was one of them I should say. More of them wait for you in the coming chapters. Every time they wanted to say something the soda bottle was referred. I was sure mother would have been relieved to see me, but my adventure was something they could not believe or accept, especially how I remembered the way to the school and how I avoided any accident on my way. I think this memory is still in my head may be because I was quite serious about the incident at that time.

Last year when I met my sister in India after ten years, she told me another incident of my childhood which I hardly remember. According to her they were invited for a Christmas party at our principal's bungalow and my sister, who was about 13 years old, took me with her. There were a lot of singsongs and good entertainment. And suddenly she told me, that I went to the stage and started to sing only with the alphabets and continued to sing. At the end I was able to get the attention of the crowd and got applause from my principal. I think my stage career started that day which I am still continuing. Stage and cinema cannot be separated from me even now.

Chapter 17

My early school days

My first year in the school I had a British principal, therefore we still had the British influence although the Second World War was over a few years before and independence was given to Sri Lanka, we still had the British influence. In fact Ceylon, which later became Sri Lanka, got independence in1948 a year after I was born. If you lived in a town like Point Pedro and if your parents were directly connected to the school or college then you would be known in the town because of your parents.

I have some vague recollection of my first year in the school but nothing much. I remember two of my friends in the school, Arulpuvanam and Saroja, but not all. I was fearless even in my childhood therefore I took risks, especially climbing the trees and swinging quite dangerously and jumping from the swing but they were only mild adventures compared to what I did later. This fearless tendency was due to my father. He taught me many things I knew including not to be frightened for the smallest things. Except snakes the animal I hate to see, all the other domestic crawlies I can tackle even to the extent of killing them with slippers. In that way I was better than my eldest sister who had the habit of screaming for every small thing.

Even at the beginning of my first grade they identified that I could sing. My mother was a singer, her voice was unique and my father too could sing, especially he knew about the classical music and the ragas. I remember that every New Year the special treat for us was that both of them sang two songs for us after the family prayer ended. I could vividly remember one was a classical piece set in Raga *Kathanakuthukalam*[22] and the other one was one of the first movie songs. Although they were Christians and films songs were not encouraged by their parents I do not know why they sang this song. One reason they told was that soon after the marriage they went to the capital and saw the first Tamil film, in those days referred as 'Talkies'. They saw this film and that was why they remembered that song. They really enjoyed singing these two pieces. They never had serious fights except some mild arguments. May be the saying great minds think alike was true in their lives. They solved their difference in opinion privately very often going to the beach. Mother had her own holidays

---

[22] A name of a classical raga.

visiting her friends in various parts of Jaffna or the capital. Father travelled only when the situation demanded. Otherwise he loved to stay at home. In fact, in one of his poems I read, he wrote 'Home is the haven for Sofie[23] and me'

All my brothers and sisters were very good singers, a sure inheritance from my mother and father, but I became special in the eyes of the church people. Come to think of it they called me the family soloist. It was a tradition to have a special song composed for a wedding including the names of the bride and the bridegroom. My father was a good composer and he composed a wedding song. The bride was a teacher at the Girls' School and my parents arranged the marriage for her. The bridegroom was not from the north, but from the east. My father said I should sing this song at the wedding. So my singing career started at the age of seven. And the violinist who played for me was the wife of the Boys' College principal. I think we were a good combination together till I left my town. All the Sunday services, Christmas services and watch night services were shared by me and the violinist. In fact many years later she invited me to give a special recital for her second daughter Vasanthy's wedding, which my mother could not attend due to her illness. Three years ago I met her in England, after thirty five years, and we shared all our memories. After two years she passed away.

It was a tradition that soon after the wedding the bride and the bridegroom visited the guests, who were at their wedding. So it was not something unusual when that particular couple came to my house. I did not know why but I had an impression that the bridegroom was a white man who talked English because of his complexion. Therefore when they came and sat in the living room I uttered some of the English words I knew, which was overheard by my brothers and suddenly I saw my second brother, calling me from the veranda using the word 'come, come'. I went proudly thinking it was an honour. But later on, it became a household joke that I talked English with the bridegroom.

Come to think of it, another interesting incident about an arranged marriage, in which my mother was involved, crosses my mind. There was a young man living in one of the lanes in Beach road. There was also a young girl the eldest of nine, who was beautiful and lived in the next street. There was a marriage proposal between the two of them. The marriage arrangement was in process when she

---

[23] It was my mother's second name

visited the cinema hall with our family, because she was also a friend of my eldest sister. During the interval, the boy selling snacks and drinks came to us and gave the drinks, even before asking. With a slight doubt we asked him how come he brought the drinks. He pointed at the back and said, "That gentleman asked me to give" We looked back to see that young man who had somehow or the other found out about our visit to the cinema hall had followed us. When the girl saw that man, she refused to take the drinks and sent the boy away. Later there was a disagreement between the two families that the proposal broke off, and there was an *inter marriage*[24] for the girl. When the young man heard about that he approached my mother to find a fair girl for him as quickly as possible and he wanted his registration of marriage on the same day, as the girl's registration, previously proposed. We were friends of both the families. My mother casually mentioned that to her friend, who immediately arranged a marriage for her friend's daughter, who was only eighteen, living in Jaffna. As the young man wished, it happened on the same day one in the evening, the other late in the evening or rather mid night. I went for both. My father muttered 'Man proposes and god disposes'. So were the marriages, a choice of the family, rather than a choice of the partners themselves. Many such marriages were more stable than a love marriage due to the support of the families from both sides.

---

[24] A marriage between a brother and sister from one family to another brother and sister of another family

Chapter 18

Father's punishments

To explain my childhood behaviour, I should also explain something about my parents. My father and my mother were ideal partners, my mother taking the normal house hold decisions, and my father taking the final decisions on serious matters. My father never punished us severely because my mother never allowed us to that level. We usually got the punishment from my mother, and it would be a hard pinch. And it made us to go straight. When the worst came to the worst it reached my father, who used the stalk of the coconut fruit which had some spikes and we got only one slash from that. That was the worst embarrassment we could ever have, but he never punished any one of us before the others. We were taken separately and then punished. I was his pet and many things I took it for granted.

But one fine day I found out I should not play with serious education. My father was explaining the Pythagoras theorem, and asked me to write that. Because I did not pay attention I could not write it correctly. He asked me to write it for the second time, again I made mistakes. It was close to our lunch time and I thought when my mother called us for lunch everything would be alright. I had never seen my father losing his temper as he did that day. He made me to write it correctly and then he asked me to write that ten times as a punishment. Tears in my eyes I wrote. It took about one hour. All the others had their lunch but my father waited for me to finish and then we had the lunch together. Later in the evening he told me affectionately "You know practice makes perfect". Even now I have a sharp memory as to how to prove $a^2+b^2=c^2$.

A similar thing happened for my third brother. My father was never selective as far as food was concerned. He would gladly have any meal provided to him. It was something unusual because men in my country often thought it was their right to select the food they ate and I had seen men criticizing food cooked at home. Small complaints were made into serious issues. I know in a particular house the husband was used to his home food, that when he got married to a total stranger, he expected her to cook exactly as his mother and sisters. One day when preparing the Brinjole curry she forgot to put one particular ingredient. When she returned home after work, she found that her husband had not touched that curry. When she asked for the reason, he replied that she had not used the Cumming seed and that was why he did not eat. She was furious but kept her temper down. Another day she prepared a sauce and forgot to fry something. The same thing happened. This time she really lost her temper and told him "Then you should have married your mother or your sisters ". Even a worm would turn. After that the stress was less but did not completely vanish. You could see how the tradition was.

But my father was an exception. It was not possible that all of us could always sit together and have the meal. There were times members of the family were not there on time. But somebody at home would call father when the meal was ready when my mother was not at home. My father had many things in mind during the meal time and scarcely noticed what he was eating in my mother's absence. Whatever that was given, he ate and made no comments. Once the servants had used the salt lavishly in one of the curries and he ate it without any complaint only when my sister commented on that he realised but continued to eat without leaving that aside like my sister. That was something new among the men in our country. One day it so happened that only I, my third brother Chelva and father were at home. We went together to the kitchen to have the meal. When my brother saw spinach curry he made a vomiting sound when it was served. I had never seen my father become so angry regarding meals. But that day he did. He took the whole dish and put it on my brother's plate and asked him to eat. He sat there till the ordeal was over. At the end of it he said" Never ever criticise the food that is given to you because there are millions of people who are dying of hunger or without one meal a day. But you are blessed at least you have all the meals". From that time I learned not to throw any food except when it was spoiled. There was a reason for that. My father had seen both the First World War and the Second World War at the age of thirteen and thirty eight respectfully and had seen how people suffered from not having a square meal a day. Though I was not born during the Second World War I heard enough stories about it from my parents and siblings. I would deal about it in another context.

Chapter 19

My friends and Environment

I never had the correct people of my age to play with when I was at home. They had age differences. But I don't think I noticed that. To be honest I never used to attach much significance to whom I played with as long as they played with me. My constant play mate was a girl named Rasaluxumi. She was two years elder to me. And her family was not originally from Point Pedro but from another small town called Nelliadddy. They had cows and we used to buy fresh cow milk from them. She had two elder brothers. Her mother is a very fair woman but conservative. You could never see her on the street doing shopping or visiting like the other women. She always stayed inside the gate and peeped through the hole to see what was happening on the street. They had the biggest jasmine creeper and during the season both of us would collect the flowers and make garlands and decorate our hair. Sometimes the jasmine spilled cascading down with its mesmerising fragrance with the green carpet studded with white pearls. We were strictly ordered not to pluck the flowers or the buds on the creeper. But they gave the best fragrance than the fallen ones. To be frank I took some of them from the tree. That was the first sign I had for the affinity to perfumes which I still have with a table full of perfumes in my room and most of them have flowery smell. I don't know why but perfumes and flowers are still my weakness. When we are born they write the horoscope. But my parents did not do it although I remember my father used to read the Sunday observer predictions without missing one Sunday. Ironically when my husband's friend offered to write my horoscope I noticed among my specific characters the phrase *'Vasanai piriya?'* meaning fragrance lover stated there. I don't know how far those predictions are true but in my case it was true.

Coming back to my friend, I saw that she learned Violin under a private master. She could also dance. I had no restrictions to go to her house. So whenever I went I had to notify who ever in the house, where I was going for not always my parents were at home. This was not my regular habit because sometimes I did not tell them but they knew where to find me. Both of us mainly played in the sand and in her house they had red clay, used for pottery so we tried to make small pots and pans out of that and pretended to cook food using leaves for vegetables and stones for fish. We talked with each other not like friends but like the women in the house. May be that was where I developed my language for writing plays and now the screen plays. We copied the grand- mother of our neighbour, our servants, and the local women. My passion for writing started when I was quite young. To start with I wrote short stories but I was craving to write a novel but the possibilities were limited for a small girl like me. Only accepted authors were able to print and publish not an inexperienced little girl, unknown to the world of authors. The moment I got a chance I wrote my first novel "4th Dimension of love" in 2005.My childhood dream became a reality in Germany.

Writing a novel. My childhood dream No.2 in reality

Launching my first Novel 4th Dimension of love in Berlin

I grew up with the sea, the waves, the beach and everything connected to it. I was taught to swim by my father at a very early age. In fact all of us could swim except my mother and elder sister. That was because they were grown up women and we still lived in the conservative society. But they did bathe in the sea only in the nights when the moon was shining fully dressed. Then the danger of stumbling the crabs hidden in the sand below or the brushing fishes giving a tickling feeling could not be over ruled. As far as I know none of those affected us in any way. They became natural sequences for us. As beginners we were given two coconut husks connected with a rope for us to float. My second sister always stayed near the shore practicing with that. But I went deeper and wanted to show off and refused to have this protection. Suddenly when I went down into the sea it was a blind choking panic of helplessness. The result was I automatically learned diving not with knowledge but because of the necessity for survival. The only disadvantage we had was the salty water which made the hair sticky forcing us to bathe in the well water at home after the sea bathe.

Chapter 20

My grandfather's brother and playing bridge

My grandfather's brother went to the beach not just to talk with people like my father but to play cards with a particular group of people who came there only to play cards. The main persons were a head teacher from a primary school, a teacher from the same school, a clerical servant, occasionally an engineering student and my grandfather's brother. We called him as 'sugar grandfather', literally translated. He was supposed to take care of me while I was at the beach. I was quite small, four or five years. Sometimes he made me to sit in the sand, which was clean and white, and allowed me to play. But once he got engrossed with the game, his concentration would be on the game therefore he kept me on his lap, my feet half touching the sand and played the game. The head teacher would spread a cloth on the sand and put sand on each corner, so that the cloth did not fly with the wind. And then they started playing. And I saw my grandfather's hand with the cards. The red and black, the Queens and Aces falling down from all four directions, collected only by one person, but not always the same person. While playing sometimes they had violent arguments. And the head master had a very hot temper and shouted at the top of his voice. He had a nick name 'Kulari' meant 'shouter'. Sometimes he would throw the whole cloth and go away. A mood of blitheness rarely experienced even by young men. But this was a usual occurrence. The next day he would join again to play the game. Bridge is a very complicated game, you should play carefully. Sometimes you could mislead your opponents by giving the wrong bid.

This head teacher was addicted to eating betel[25] and *ariconut*, a combination that we usually had at home, especially for festivals: that was a tradition. Usually children were not allowed to eat this, the reason I was given was that it would hinder speech. But I became an exception for that and later on I found out there was no truth in it because I had a big mouth when I was young with a flair for languages even now. While they were playing I would look at the betel and *ariconut* in the head master's hand and ask him appealingly with my innocent eyes and stretching my hand at the same time in order to have the taste of it. He would give me a very small portion enough for my small mouth. I should say the habit of eating betel continued not only by me but also by my third brother

---

[25] Leaf you chew

Chelva and my mother: either we bought and ate it or tasted it when we visited houses, where the house hold people used it. There was an old lady, who was the matron at the school during my mother's days, two houses away from ours who had no teeth: she had a small manual grinder and she made a fine mixture. This we gladly ate when we visited her.

One could buy the sweetened betel from the local shops. I think about five cents which was quite expensive at that time because a pound of salt was one cent, a pound of sugar was 23 cents. Therefore we had to wait till we got our pocket money, which was not a regular one, but when our aunts and uncles came from different cities, they gave us 5 or 10 cents when they returned. So more than the arrival of the guests we waited for the departure of them. We could buy a lot of things with 10 cents at that time, sweets, biscuits and small magazines for 15 cents. My grandfather gave the lowest and mother's brother gave us the highest but when my father went to the capital he gave me 25 cents which is a great amount for me. That small brass coin and the wide eyes with delight went hand in hand.

I was really interested in the cards game "bridge" because at home also my brothers and sisters including my father played this game, except my elder sister, who never joined us in any of those group activities, and my mother. If we were really playing the full games it was always an odd number so that the winner is declared. You should see how my father reacted when somebody made the wrong bid. His famous words of swearing were 'Damn fool'. I used to beg them to include me. Sometimes my third brother played other card games with me. When he had good cards he would have a peculiar smile. When he cut with the trump card he would put it forcibly on the table. He would be fully engrossed in the game enjoying every minute of it. I was only a spectator till I was seven. I had to wait a few years before I was included in the group. Sometimes on Saturdays after lunch we had a session. It went up to four or five in the evening. My eldest brother used to be so quick in distributing the cards. He could shuffle them faster than any one of us.

The interesting part was my mother did not play this game because she did not know how it works. So she got angry and bored if we were playing. My father and mother played a traditional games goat and tiger, with three stones as the tigers and 15 tamarind seeds as goats. The game was to trap the tiger so that he could not go out. That she gladly played only with my father taking advantage of his affection. If she made a wrong move and if father won, she did not accept. She only says "No, no you can't take that, I will do it again.' So practically always my mother was the winner. Those small pleasures for her were never denied by my father because he loved her very much. But on Sundays we were not allowed to play cards. It was just a practice in my mother's family respecting the religion.

Continuing with the games of cards I remember an incident that I never forgot. One day father was playing bridge with us and my mother came several times and called him, my father did not heed her request. She suddenly came and took his cards and tore them into pieces. So we could not continue the game: the funny thing was my father did not get angry with her. He only smiled and went to read something. Very often cheating was done in the game, especially when they did not have a good set of cards. The rules of auction bridge say if you don't have a scoring card then you can declare for a reshuffle. Very often when they had only one scoring card with the lowest value, like a Jack of something, they slowly hid the card and showed the rest of their cards making us to believe that they had no scoring card. Once or twice it was successful but later when we found out that trick, the numbers of cards were checked before the reshuffling.

During one season of the year fisher men from another village Myillity used to camp in our beach and catch fish. They went only for whole sale so if our servants went, they got it either free or for little money. They got bigger catch than the locals and we got our fresh fish early in the morning for our lunch. But there was something we all had to be careful when visiting the shore early in the morning. The local fisher folks usually did not have a lavatory so they used to squat near the shore and wash with the sea water. Especially at dawn one could notice small blinking fire seen from those people including women, who had a puff of a cigar while at the shore. Stumbling over the excreta was a possibility. Usually the sea washed away but there were times we had unpleasant experiences with that. Well that was taken as part of life. Here in Germany we have the same experience with the dog excreta. I do not see any difference between the two. Most of the fisher folks wore only a piece of cloth to hide their nakedness and their children did the same. We got used to that sight. When I was bored, I used to go and angle or take a piece of cloth and catch fish at the shore with the local girls. Strange enough, we were not allowed to have an aquarium in the house.

We also had moon light dinners together with the regular visitors of the beach and the cards playing group. Three things were branded food only from my town. They were the "Point Pedro *dhosai*, Point Pedro *vaddai*" and the white hoppers. Almost all the people in my country knew about those snacks, and they were so famous, that we were requested to bring them when we visited people living in out stations. *Vaddai* was a snack you could keep for days and the other two were eaten either for breakfast or dinner. Sometimes there would be big queues in these places. It was not a shop but a small opening with thatched piece halted with a stick. We call them as *"dhosai thatti"* During the moon light dinners these foods were brought by different families and shared by all. When we were at the beach not always the sky was clear showing the moon. Sometimes banks of running clouds made changing caverns round the moon. I would lie down flat on the sand and look up at the sky and watch the fast moving clouds and their wonders on the sky. When there was wind we got sand in the food. But that never disturbed us enjoying the meal. It was more of the fun we had than the food we ate that mattered.

Chapter 21

Native Principal and my life till the fifth grade

The Christian schools in Point Pedro were popular for good education and they had hostel accommodation for outstation students. My first principal was a British lady, Miss. Dore, who was very strict. She was at the principal's bungalow and we were thoroughly frightened to go near that. The girls' school, where I studied, had strict rules. We had our uniforms and at the beginning had a green and yellow tie, which was changed after the first new native principal took over the duties of the principal. Then it was changed as purple and yellow, which remains even now.

It was a tradition that students attending our school from other villages, towns or even within half a mile from the school came to the school by bus, private cars and in some cases by bullock carts. Parents trusted the drivers to bring their children safely home. Years long the same drivers were doing the job. They go to each house and collect the students. We had no rules as to how many should go in a car and often those cars were overloaded with eight to ten children in one trip. The cars would be sagging at the back with the load. The drivers recognised the students' presence only by their voices. Sometimes those drivers were so demanding that the students were afraid to offend them. Sangarapillai was the oldest driver I remember and we had Sambanthan, and Maniam who transported my sister and me for a short period. But above all of them, the old man Murugappa, the popular bullock cart owner, fascinated me. His cart was always full and he took pride in challenging the motor cars. The bulls had loud metal bells jingling while they rode on the streets. The bullock cart rider was old with a red stone ear stud a tradition for men of the old days. He was proud of his bulls. You had a metal step and the rest was a jump to sit in the cart. There would be a metal piece with a hook that barred the back opening guarding the passengers from falling. Some times out of fun I touched the back bar and ran with the cart and the moment he saw me running with the cart he would give a threatening shout and I simply had to retreat.

The new principal Miss. Chinniah had some kind of affinity to me. All of them were thoroughly frightened, including the teachers. She was very hard and frightening but for me, I never felt frightened of her. I heard one story that my principal light heartedly related to my parents in one of her visits. Once a small child was admitted to the school and the mother took her to meet the principal.

The child remained behind her mother and started to cry. The mother said "She is frightened" When my principal asked the child, "For who are you frightened?" the little girl pointed her finger at my principal and said "You"

She did some good things for me. The first thing I remember was when my class went to my principal to be tested in English. I was very irregular in taking books to school because of my memory, I did not need the books. Any teaching in the class I just absorbed. English was very important in the school, because of my background at home with five of my siblings learning and talking in English, English speaking friends of my parents, and having a father who was an authority in English, it was not difficult for me to learn English.

In the second grade we were all called to come with our books to be tested by the principal. This happened occasionally. So the second grade went to her bungalow to answer the questions, and to read the book. I went without the book. So I was immediately asked to go out, that meant, I would not have marks for English in the report for my term examination. When she asked where my book was, I said I have lost it. She told me, "You find the book and come to be tested". The next day during the lunch break I went to her bungalow, where she was resting. I knocked at the door and asked 'May I come in, please?" She looked at me, and she was quite pleasant and she tested me. When I came back to the class, my teacher was surprised. They all thought I would get a punishment. To my astonishment, when my term report came, I got an honours mark by the principal to say I was the best. Of course I was good in the class and always came first but this was a feather in my cap.

There were two barriers for us, one in the third grade and the other was the fifth grade. Usually children are warned about those two classes. The girl's school that I studied was quite famous for producing good results in the public examinations because of the teachers, who were in charge of those two classes. Till the fourth grade boys and girls studied in the girls' school, only after that they went to the boys' college, the Christian college or a normal, vernacular Hindu primary school. Coming back to the third grade in the Girls' School, from the second grade itself, we were warned about the third grade teacher. Unlike these days the teacher had every right to punish the children within their limits. Canning, pinching and late detention were allowed by the teachers.

Not all of them practiced those punishments, but the third grade and the fifth grade teachers, who were conservative, practiced to the maximum, therefore going to the third grade, became a big fear for the children but the parents liked that discipline by those teachers. They were very much respected. They were regular in their teaching, correcting the mistakes, underlining with red lines, and writing the comments patiently. Both of them dressed according to the old tradition of wearing the sari. Even my mother wore like that, when she got dressed. Actually they were class mates. They wore sari, pleated it over the shoulder, bring that round the hip and pin it behind. They looked so neat and tidy. Both of them had a standard chain with a pendent but the fifth grade teacher Miss. Joseph had a necklace like a lasso. They were punctual to the school, sometimes even early and had the greatest respect from other teachers because they were the seniors in the school.

The third grade teacher Mrs. Backers had rather a supercilious face with a singing voice. In order to stop the boys talking to each other in the third grade, the teacher always saw that a girl and a boy shared the desk. It was well known that I was very talkative in the class, so I shared a desk with the naughtiest boy Gunam in the class. I don't know whether the phrase 'birds of a feather flock together' is true or not, but in my case it was true, that I and that boy were quite chummy. He was adopted by my principal because he was an orphan and lived in her quarters. Soon he did all what I asked him to do. I would tell him to go and threaten the other boys and he did. So I became a bit of a tomboy at that time. Studies-wise I was very good therefore the teachers could not complain about me. I can never remember doing any homework because I finished everything in the class itself, that's why even now I do not give homework for my students. I hated homework so I do not give it. In my opinion home work was a lazy way of punishing the children. This third grade was the first hurdle in the school. Then we went to the fourth grade, where we had very nice and soft teachers. Maybe to give us a break, before we had to face the second hurdle in the fifth grade.

I remember in the fourth grade, I was again a tomboy and I was the monitor of the class and the boys were thoroughly frightened of me. One day, we the girls, were practicing some dance behind the cupboard. I pretended to be a good dancer and showed the other girls some of the steps I had seen in the cinema. Because we did it secretly, the boys were inquisitive to see what we were doing behind the cupboard. The classrooms had only half walls; therefore the classrooms were quite ventilated. One boy, who was quite short, came round the wall, climbed up and peeped. I chased him with a stone, and threw the stone at him. He also had a brother in the same class. The stone really attacked him on the forehead. It started to bleed. I was really frightened, but I never showed it. I took him to the water tap, washed the wound and warned him, that he should never utter a word to the teacher. I did not know, why he never did, but the period after the lunch break was the English lesson. Usually I was very chatty in the English class, on that day I was very quiet. My mind was too numbed to concentrate. Of course the teacher noted that, and when she asked me, I said "I have a headache." I still remember the English lesson with the title "The good boy". It was strange how you took more care to protect yourself, when the fault was yours. The burden of guilt could be hard.

After this break in the fourth grade, we had the next hurdle in the fifth grade. Again we were prepared by our parents, with warnings about the fifth grade teacher. I recollect when my mother said "Well, next year, you will be in good hands." The fifth grade teacher was very short, my mother told me because she had an accident, and she never married. And her mother was the matron in the hostel, later she retired. She lived only two houses away from ours. Till the fourth grade I used to visit their house, in fact, my brothers and sisters, especially my eldest brother visited them regularly. Therefore when I came to the fifth grade, and she became my teacher, I did not have fear for her, but I had respect for her. If we made any mistakes in the class, in her subjects Arithmetic, Tamil and Social Science we got punishments. Either we had to go to the back of the class to correct them, or if it was a repeated mistake, then she took the ruler and hit us in the hand. We must stretch the hand and we got the punishment. Sometimes a pinch on the cheek or on the arm was not new to us. Most of the subjects were taken by the class teacher, except English and sports. Therefore during the English lessons she sat at the back of the class and corrected our papers that meant, she watched us what we were doing in the English class and then she would comment about it in her class. We had all the myriad possibilities of being corrected. One could detect watchfulness and a sense of purpose in her.

My English teacher Miss Spencer was an English trained teacher, very fair with long hair and she would wear two plaits. Sometimes when she sat on the chair, the hair touched the ground. And she was a wonderful person, and she spoke very softly. Once we had an English play directed by her. We performed it before the whole school and the principal during the Christmas celebration. It was a Christmas play, and I took the role of the mother of three children and how they realized the message of Christmas. Because I was a good singer, in between I sang English carols. The funniest part was that I asked my sister to give a sari to wear, but I was too short so it became a little bit complicated for me. But I managed and got dressed. After the play was over, the next day, my principal visited our house. She was smiling when she told my parents, how she enjoyed the play with a comment that "your daughter was wearing the sari on the wrong side."

I was a bit naughty in the class because I knew English better than the others and sometimes I annoyed my teacher. She would have the ruler in the hand but she would never hit us. She would only role her eyes and threaten "I will hit you". It is an irony that after 55 years I met her in Canada. I visited her, paid my respect and referred to my naughty behaviour but she was so good to say "Oh no, you were talented and you never annoyed me." It was very nice of her, but I knew the truth. There was a new girl in the class, whose mother was also a teacher. And we usually had a public exam for the fifth grade. When the results came, they put up the list and I found that my name was the second, and not the first. This girl got the highest total and not me.

Another incident was quite a shock for my class mates. During the small break I climbed the guava tree that was opposite my class, to pluck some guava fruits quite at the top. I was partly a tomboy at that time, not frightened to climb trees. I reached the top when the bell rang. All the students ran to the class rooms and I was about to climb down when I saw our principal doing her surprise rounds. That meant total silence in the whole school, both, the students and the teachers kept quiet. She walked and came and stood under the tree. Believe it or not, the students in my class were looking at me at the top of the tree. I stood still. I think she was there for about 5 minutes to look whether there was any disorder, and then she walked towards her office. When she went out of my sight, I came down and walked to my class. Of course there was panic in my heart but I put up a brave front. And the other students could not believe their eyes.

Most of the prominent people in the town sent their children either to our school, or to the boys school, therefore I had the magistrate's son, the district judge's daughter, the chief justice' daughter, doctors' daughters as classmates. The privilege was, I was invited for their birthdays in their official residences.

They had big houses and big gardens and sometimes the parents became friends of my parents. In fact the district judge's daughters became my friend. Usually she came to school like any other girl in uniform but her mother was a typical Muslim following the culture and whenever their relatives came, she used to cover her head. But my friend could talk hours and hours and it was interesting to hear all what she said.

I could repeat all the names of my classmates, but it is a pity I do not know their married names by which they are known now.

Chapter 22

Some more reminiscences in the school

When we were in the sixth or seventh grade we had a school tradition, I should say more or less, unwritten tradition that if you do not like one person or if she had done something to annoy you, you say "I am angry with you" and then for months and sometimes years we do not talk to each other. It so happened that I was in such a situation. I and this girl did not talk for months. She was the daughter of our family friend, a land survivor. It was a funny tradition of not touching the things she touched, not sitting on the seat she sat and not touching each other. This went on for more than a year. Ironically our family and her family were close friends. There were nine children, almost each one of them was a classmate of my siblings. One day I went to their house with my mother, her other younger sisters and her fourth brother played with me but she sat in a corner without joining us. This was noted by her father. He came and asked why was that we were not playing together. Then one of her sisters told the story. He was a lively man, always joking and having interesting conversations with people. He could not accept the situation. So he gave us an offer. And that was both of us alone would be taken by him to a film, at a cinema hall and then we had to talk there with each other. Because her father was there, she made the first attempt by giving me a chocolate and then our friendship was renewed. We watched the film which is still in my memory. The title was "Rani Lalithangi" and the special thing was, it was the first time we saw the hero doing a traditional dance. Now she lives in Australia.

I was a leader by nature. With two of my sisters as members of the staff in the school, people thought I would be frightened to do things. But it was the other way round. My second sister was teaching me Chemistry and Botany. She would be grinning when she came into the class and calling my name to say "Stand up." All the teachers knew if they stopped me from talking, all the others would follow suit. Not that I was a saint and I knew she had her reasons. Sometimes I had to stand the whole hour whereas my eldest sister, who also taught me, used to ignore me in the class. She never looked in my direction; she never gave me the highest marks even if I worked hard. She gave the reason to my parents that people should not think that she was favouring me. But my second sister occasionally gave me the highest marks to see the reaction of the students. No complaint, so I got good marks when I really did well.

During the lunch break, we used to sit in circles and have our lunch in the open ground, then go to the well, draw the water and drank the water with our hands, it is a special technique; we put both the hands together, and somebody poured the water and we drank that. Although there were taps, we preferred this because it tasted good. It was the time when we did not have bottle water or warnings about bacteria and infections. Surprisingly we did not have any rare diseases that we witness now. But vaccination was compulsory especially for Tuberculosis. There was a period the whole school was fed with milk by the CARE organization. Usually the students did not drink but threw it into the drainage. Therefore during the break we saw milk than water in the drainage. The rich children did not drink because of prestige, anything given free was meant only for the poor but I tasted it.

After lunch, we came to the classroom and then occasionally they listened to the stories I had read. This was quite an interesting event for my friends. My voice was always a bit high. You could call it "dominating", therefore one could hear my voice even outside the classroom that means I was branded for my loud voice. As soon as the teachers entered, they called my name and said "Please stand up and don't talk." It was true that often I was the cause but one fine day I had a stomach ache and was lying on the desk keeping my head down. The bell rang to commence the classes. Our teacher for that period, who was also my class teacher, entered the classroom and called my name and said "Please don't talk and stand up." Actually I did not hear, the other students heard it and settled down, and suddenly someone nudged me to wake me up. And the teacher was continuing with her talk, "I heard your voice at the entrance of the hall." It was then that I woke up and I was blinking, and the teacher asked, "Why is that you are still sitting?" I was clueless. I was incredulous and baffled like someone listening to words in foreign language. Then she understood she was barking up at the wrong tree. All my friends said "Today she was sleeping." It was an irony that I met her a few years ago, old, but fit, when I was asked to be one of the guests for the old girls' association and told this episode to the crowd while she was sitting. But it was a healthy joke, therefore they all enjoyed.

I was a born imitator, it was in my blood. I could imitate people exactly. We had a teacher for chemistry, who was a very good friend of my second sister but had a very funny way of talking. She articulated her jaws more than it was necessary, when she talked. As a person she was quite innocent and friendly. So one day she was late for the class and I was in front of the class and acting like her writing something on the board, usually my classmates laughed. I did not see her coming into the class. Because the class was so quiet, I had a strange feeling and turned to see her standing at the bottom of the class. She had entered the class by the rear entrance. Well, one could imagine the embarrassment I had. I walked meekly to my place and sat down. Strange enough, she did not comment on that, so I did not take it seriously. Sometimes there is a funny feeling you have in you, when you know trouble is being made and waiting for you. When I came home, my second sister sitting in the front veranda asked me "Did you do that?" She just questioned me but was never hard on me. Later on they all enjoyed the joke.

Another interesting class was the clay work class. All the teachers in the school were lady teachers. But in grade 8 we could offer a special subject, the clay work or pottery. For this subject a master came in his scooter. He used to wear the nationals. There was a lady assistant, who came and stayed there, a kind of nanny, for us girls. But she was so funny and she felt shy to talk with the master. When she did, she squirmed her body and rolled her eyes. Sometimes she came with a rose on her hair. We, the girls, bullied her left and right. I was good in clay work and sometimes the master gave the theory and I wrote it down in my note book and he used to refer to my notes for the other students. When the examination was close at hand, he called me one day and asked me to give the notebook for him to set the questions. He forgot to return it. On the examination day we received the question paper and for some of the theory questions I did not know the answers because I did not have my notes. So I wrote it in the answer paper "Master, you have my notebook therefore I could not study." After correcting the papers he came to the class and asked me to stand up and grinned before he said "I read your message. I am sorry I had your notes" and gave me a very good mark.

Frequently I was elected as the monitor of the class, because they all knew me. So once our new class teacher came and asked the students whom they had selected as the monitor. Unanimously my name was proposed, her only comment was "To catch a thief, you set a thief."

Chapter 23

Cinema in my life

The first theatre in Point Pedro was built in the early 50s. The first film was "*Niraparadi*[26]" and I was five or six years old. I was adamant to go and watch the film. So my grandfather's brother, who was staying at our house for the holidays, took me to the show. My parents paid the ticket for the first class. Actually he carried me into the theatre because there was no ticket for me. But even now I could remember a scene from that film where the hero Mukamala came down the steps in a very stylish way. How he walked down the steps impressed me a lot. When there was no one around I used to practice this walk at the back veranda, where we had three steps quite deep, but the last one was a cement block, which became shiny due to constant use. I used to go up and down the stairs and enjoy the walk, until one day I slipped and fell down. Having banged on the stone, blood oozed from my head. Hearing my cry my mother came running and attended to the wound, thinking it was an accident. Only I knew, what really happened. And that was a lesson to stop doing it. I think my first impression of the film continued, which became an obsession in my head. Now, after 66 years, I am still connected to films and film festivals and my activities revolve round the film industry and film people. It never ended and would never end.

Attending film festivals as jury and coordinator. My childhood dream No.3 in reality.

Interview with Berlinale film festival director Mr.M. Hyden

---

[26] Not guilty

Kamal Haasens 100th day film award with actor Sarathkumar,
Director Gautham Menen IGP Chennai and Kamal Haassan

Jury

Roman Gonther	Timo Hübsch	Johannes Selle	Dr. Gloriana Guna-rubini Selvanathan	Christine Wagner

Film Director Actor MP for film funding Int. Festival coordinator Camerawoman
Jury panel at the Jena film festival 2010

Laudatum at the award ceremony at the Jena International Film Festival 2010

Kalt erwischt

Das Studentenfilmfestival Sehsüchte gibt sich in diesem Jahr in kühles Weiß gehüllt

Jury at the Potsdam Film Festival 2009

Five years as Coordinator with Manicam Narayanan festival Director,Film directors Saran, S.V.Seher and Gautham Menen

Rasa film festival 2013: Myself, Editor in chief The Hindu, Chairman Petroleum Cooperation,Dr.Ambika, Festival Director

10 years award as festival coordinator for the International Film Festival of Tamilnadu 2013

ITFA and Seventh Channel communication's 7th International film festival 2008

Norway film festival award ceremony 2013

We used to get small magazines from India, where there were cartoons and short stories mostly stories suitable for children. My brother was a collector of those magazines. But one special feature in the magazine was, interviews with film stars and at the end, they gave the contact address. I was an ardent reader therefore I read those books without the knowledge of my brother. There was a very popular actor Gemini Ganeshan whose films I had watched. So one fine day I wrote a letter to the address of the film star Elumalai, requesting him to send me the address of that popular star. I put that in an envelope and posted it with my address at the back, but without a stamp. So obviously the letter was returned. I was not there but it was received by my brother, who opened it and called every Tom, Dick and Harry in the house and read the letter loudly and made fun of me. Every time I did something, they would always refer this sarcastically. But that was something that stayed in my mind, which developed a determination that sometime or the other I must meet all the film stars.

This was a subconscious wish I suppose. Later, when I came to Europe and started as a journalist, and did interviews with many Hollywood stars, and few years later met most of the South Indian stars, when I went for the film festivals, I thought my dream had come true. Recently, the same brother who bullied me wrote an email to say, "Who would have thought a little girl in a small town in

Sri Lanka would be rubbing shoulders with the Hollywood stars". I do not know why, but sometimes incidents that happened in our lives are reflected later in our lives. Anyway acceptance means success

Meeting international film stars. My childhood dream no.4 in reality

With actor Nick Nolte.

With German actress Juliane Köhler

With actor Mahendren

With the producer of the Hollywood film Five Days of War

With the Slovakian actress from the film Marsha

With German and Hollywood actress Maria Schrader

*With Lithuanian film director, actor Vivek, Mala Manian
and festival director Manikam Narayanan*

With actress Shobana

With Hollywood producer director Florian Steins

With the producer Mr.Swartzkopf of the German/Chinese film, I Phone You.
Best film award ITFA film festival 2012.

Film Festival of Tamilnadu 2012 with film Director Amir, actresses Luxmi and Oviya

An honorary award of the film Vetaiyadu Vilaiyadu by the producer Mr. Manicam Narayanan and Dr. Wolf Siegert CEO, Iris Media at the screening of the film in Berlin film festival

With Canadian and German film stars from the film Operation Sunrise at the award ceremony

With Actor Mathavan and film producers at the film Festival

With actor Tamer Yiğit receiving the award for the film Karaman

Going to the cinema was a real procedure in our house. First we had to ask the permission of my mother and then mother appealed to father. There were special situations when my cousin and her family came during the holidays, then of course the restrictions were less. My maternal grandfather was a conservative person and was very strict with the rules of women in the house. I was never allowed to cross my legs before him or whistle which was later allowed by my father. When we went to the cinema my grandfather was the leader. The servant went in front with the lantern, in the middle all the ladies and behind was my grandfather. Children could take either in front or behind the ladies. When we sat inside the theatre the girls sat in the middle, grandfather on one side and another male member or my aunt or my mother sat on the other end so that no man could sit or play around with the girls. Break the cover and intuit that the guard was as strong as a portcullis slamming down to keep out the enemy, if he should veer into that particular territory. So secured it was.

I remember having a servant girl at the house. I, my cousin who was three years elder to me and this servant girl, who came with us to the cinema, came back from the cinema and tried to act some of the scenes in the film, sometimes even wearing the costumes, singing tips and ends of tune that sprang in my mind like mushrooms. This servant girl was quite a vivid narrator of factoid. Moreover her imagination was well used by us in our activities. At that time I had short hair

115

but in the film the ladies had long hair and flowers, so what I did was, I took a piece of cloth, tore it into three parts and plait them like a long plait and tied it on my head. It would be hanging at the back of my head, and standing in front of the mirror, I would be dancing, pretending to be the film stars in the film. We would be singing songs interspaced with inconsequential chat. It was once seen by my brothers and they made fun of it.

Visiting the cinema hall with my elder sister and brother in law was an interesting experience. Normally the Villain in the film would run and the hero would be chasing. My sister would shout and say *"Athan*[27] tell him to go and search behind the trees ,,or "Ay you stupid, run faster, then you can catch him". If there were big fights she would close her eyes with her hands and repeatedly ask," Is it over?" She would be directing the actors in quite a loud voice. After some time we stopped going with her and gave the honour to our brother in law to face the embarrassment.

Occasionally my parents watched a film. The most interesting part was we had to sit and listen to the story related by both of them. Sometimes when there is a contradiction you could see one of them interrupting the other "No, no that is not..." Both of them enjoyed watching films and talking about it. I was quite a rebel in the house. That one fine day I cut a fringe to my hair which my mother did not like. So a deal came from my mother. If I comb back my hair and keep it like before, then I would get a film as a reward. So in order to see the film I applied water to my hair and plastered it. I enjoyed the film I got as a reward.

My eldest brother and my second sister were at the university, and of course they were not restricted from watching films, but my two brothers were still at the high school. The cinema hall was only about five minutes walk from our house and my brothers were interested to watch the new English films, which they were not allowed to watch. But the advantage was that unlike the Tamil films, which were three hours long, the English films were only one and half hours long. The show started at 6.30 and ended at 8. The boys were allowed to stay out till 8 o'clock, not the girls. So what they did was, they wore their *sarams*[28] and told they were going for a walk and went to the cinema. Because of the restrictions and lack of funds they went to the gallery which was at that time 55

---

[27] Formal name for brother in law

[28] A house attaire for men

cents and sat with the smoking crowd and watched the film, returning home on time for dinner. My parents never noticed that, they were at the cinema. My brothers used to go and remove their shirts at the well-side, and come into the house because they knew the shirts would smell of cigarettes.

Chapter 24

The games we played

Initially I played Hop scotch with the servants and Rasaluxumi. Occasionally my third brother played with us usually in the front yard, while my father rested in his favourite easy chair. There were different versions of this game. In the absence of our parents, the front yard was robbed from us by my brothers, our servant boy and their friends for their favourite game *"Killi Thattu"*[29]. Two teams played in this game, one of them must prevent the other team, from crossing the partitions drawn. Only the leader had the right to run along the whole boundary. That was also the traditional game played at the beach by professional men. Then it was interesting to watch. The leader must have hawk eyes to catch the opponents by hitting them when they touch the lines.

The colonial influence of playing cricket was quite popular among the boys and we, the girls played only when they wanted to even the team. Otherwise we were allowed only to watch. I was sent to pick up the ball when the ball fell into the neighbour's house. If they did not have proper bat for the game then the bottom part of the coconut leaf was shaped and used. When it was dry carrying and running was easy but sometimes for a quick make shift they used the green one which was rather heavy. Boys who came for tuition arrived a bit early and played with my brothers. The bottom of the coconut tree, with three vertical chalk marks served as wickets and one horizontal line, served as the stump. Soft ball was used instead of hard ball. I don't remember them breaking any window glasses with the ball not because they were careful but because we had only wooden windows.

Hide and seek was also a favourite game. My brothers found unusual places to hide themselves. Once, my brother hid himself inside the dirty clothes basket putting the clothes over him. We had various rhymes to select the person who would catch the others first. One of them was

> "Inky pinky pen and ink,
>
> You go out because you stink"

---

[29] A local group game

Another one was a mixture of English and Tamil though it had a beautiful rhyme.

My father went to Kandy

Brought a bottle of Brandy

Drank it with a *Karandy*[30]

He was a *peethal Parangy*[31]

All those outdoor games were possible only when the weather was fine. Being a tropical country we had eight months of warm weather and four months of monsoon rainy season. Rain could be in the form of showers or drizzle. When we had the rain water stagnating in the front yard we made paper boats and watched them floating. Sometimes my father made them for me. The problem came only when it was dry. The front yard would be filled with wet papers removed by the sweeping woman mumbling and cursing. We also had a very popular traditional indoor game participated by all the family members at different times. It was a very old game called *thayam* [32]which resembled the Ludo, but instead of numbers we had four special shells from the seashore the *"chohies"*[33] which could fall open or close when thrown. The coins for each player were local selection like stones, tamarind seeds, and small pieces of wood as they wished. We sat on the floor and played. There was really a thrill in those games which ended sometimes in peace and sometimes in fights depending whether the game was fair or not. Yes cheating could be done in this game discreetly. Surprisingly this was the only group game my eldest sister took part grudgingly.

My third brother Chelva and I played together more than the others. Especially he was an expert in making small dolls out of cloth. A head stuffed with cloth and tied with rolled cloth as hands. There were no legs but he would cover that with a long piece of cloth as Sari or *Dhoti*[34] the national dress. Then we used to have a wedding for those dolls. Sometimes both of us played and at times we called our friends in the neighbourhood and celebrated with all the rules of a

[30] spoon

[31] Decedents from mixed marriages between natives and foreigners

[32] Traditional indoor game

[33] Shell of sea snails

[34] Traditional dress for men

wedding ceremony like procession, sweets and betel the traditional thing they give in the weddings. Once I knew my mother took an active part with us. She herself dressed the dolls with silk and made the jewels in golden thread and dressed the bridegroom in traditional dress. We were very happy and were allowed to invite our friends and the servants were also free to attend the celebration. At the end it turned out to be a very big function in the eyes of the children. My father who never knew about this children's activity took part and I served him the orange sweets that he very much liked.

The first imported doll with moving eyes I got it from my cousin Thevi. One of the missionary, who came from England gave it to her while visiting them at the parsonage where my uncle was a pastor. Visiting us during the holidays she brought it and presented to me. I walked with the doll talked with the doll, ate with the doll and slept with the doll. My mother made dresses for my doll because it had moving arms and legs. The arms and the legs were connected with elastic. One day the elastic gave way and the doll was in pieces. I cried the whole day but no one knew how to repair it. I wept in soft faint gasps and clutching the doll waddled off breathless with outrage into the cold veranda of the house. Still sobbing I went to sleep holding the pieces. When my eldest brother came home he saw me with the broken doll. He used some nails and rubber pieces repaired the doll and the next day when he gave that I was so happy I planned to have a birthday party for the doll.

Chapter 25

My interest in languages

My father was an expert in English and Tamil literature and his analysis of the characters were new and interesting. He got carried away with the characters in the story. He was very romantic and laughed, when the characters laughed and cried when the characters cried. His love for my mother started at the age of ten he said. But my mother always bossed my father and did some mischievous things like biting the guava fruit before she gave it to him to eat. My father found pleasure in those small things. My mother was a beautiful woman. He compared their romance to those characters in the literature and with the characters in the stories. So it was not a surprise all my siblings took over that quality of reading, and appreciating literature. The verse was too difficult for me so I read the abridged prose versions. I think I had inherited his passion for literature and the characters involved in them.

In this place I should tell my interest to English, why and when it started. Although we had studied in the English medium, a greater interest in English developed because of my father. During the fifties, even the for 10th grade public exam English literature was taught, especially books written by authors like Shakespeare, Scott, Milton and so on. I still remember how the students came to learn under my father. In the outer veranda there was a big long table, where the boys sat. There would be more than ten at a time, and the girls sat inside the room, only through the window they would listen to my father's lessons. The boys came in *dhoti* and shirt and the girls came with long skirt and blouse. Modern dresses were not welcomed by the community. If they came early, the boys sat in the beach and the girls sat in the back veranda. Only one girl, Emily *acca*[35] came in western dress because she was educated at the Holy Family Convent and was a catholic. I used to sit hunched under the table closer to my father's feet and heed words and phrases from the literature while he was explaining. Of course I did not understand the complexity of the language, but I was quite interested. I saw him teaching with a combination of stormy intensity and concentrated patience. I used to admire my father's wit and satire. I felt he could accomplish even the impossible. Explanations my father gave, especially

---

[35] Big sister

about the characters in the book, were simply out of this world. This was the main reason I developed the interest to reading at the age of seven or eight.

When we were very young and I was still five or six years old occasionally on Sundays my father would sit on his usual easy chair, my mother homed the arm chair and my eldest sister due to her seniority also got a chair to sit. All the others sat around father on a mat. And there he would relate the stories from the classics giving beautiful descriptions of the story. I was too small therefore sometimes my eyes drooped but still I listened earnestly to what he said. I was sure my brothers were not that interested therefore they always sat there impatiently but not me. He had talked about all manner of things. Mostly ideals, values, old stories of love and adventure, courage, sacrifice and reward. I liked listening to fathers stories. His acting ability gave each story its own special emphasis. One of his famous Tamil semi historical story was "The Murder at the hill of Karungkuil" literally translated in English. He got himself carried away with the characters 'Alumelu' and 'Varenthiran'. He often had a brilliant eidetic memory, faces and townscapes recorded in full colour. For instance he could describe the girl Alumelu alias Marahatham without forgetting the smallest detail given by the author. Incidentally that book was made into a film years after with the title Marahatham. Watching the film my father said the book gave a better feeling than the film, especially the villain of the story was not as he expected as the evil character, described in the story, but played by a comedian which was disappointing, although the main actors in the film did their part brilliantly. When the leading actress of this film Padmini visited me in Berlin, she said that was one of her best films in her career.

Actress Padmini and my daughter's teacher Chamundeeswary at the dance debut

In between my personal childhood experience, I should also include certain episodes of my parents and my siblings to maintain continuity.

I developed the habit of reading classics both in Tamil and in English at a very early stage. My father encouraged me. At the beginning my third brother regularly bought a Tamil magazine titled *"Kalkandu"* which means Candy. This was suitable for young people. He used his pocket money to buy that. There was a series called" The Mysterious Man "and my brother loved that. The editor had the pen name *"Tamil Vanan"*. I read this magazine regularly and that was my first Tamil Magazine. Those days we got all the prints only from India except the news papers. Slowly we became a team and pooled out our pocket money to buy small comics in Tamil and later novels suitable for children. Most of them were crime stories. They were one fourth of a normal book, handy to hide inside the text books and could be read when we were supposed to learn for the school.

It was the time, when the Western films from America were gaining momentum and naturally my third brother was interested in them. They were comics in English of the same. I still watch the films Roy Rogers and Lone Ranger just to remember the old times. My brother had a wooden box where he kept his treasures and sometimes it had a lock. In his absence I used to peep into his treasures without touching. But to look at the comics was a real temptation. I was too small to understand the text written there. Sometimes when my brother was in a good mood to show brotherly affection he would read and explain to me. I started to gain knowledge and continued to develop. My vivid memory of his reading was a short story in Tamil. I think the impact of the story stayed with me for a long time and every time I thought about that story there were tears in my eyes. The story was about two parrots living in a tree. One day a hunter killed the male parrot and ate. The next day he sat and made fire under that tree and talked loudly "Today I don't have anything to eat." When the sad female parrot heard that, she jumped into the fire to be the food for the hunter because it could not live without its partner. For days I cried when ever I thought of the story.

Our interest in Western comics and films was fuelled by films shown at the Boys' College. We were able to watch the classics at the boys' college where almost every Friday they had film shows. In fact when I come to think about it, I was the only small girl in the crowd. I hanged on to my father's hand or brother's hand, when we went to watch the films in colour. Although it was meant for the students of the college, families of the staff were also invited. I saw all the films in black and white and sometimes in Eastman colour, which were rather artificial. That was how I got interested in all the classics like Shakespeare, Scott, Dumas and various other authors. At that time I had a great urge to read those books in detail. It was the beginning of my passion for reading. We also saw some of the classics like Romeo and Juliet, Hamlet, Midsummer's Night Dream, Merchant of Venice and all the other Shakespeare's dramas because they were text books in the school. Dumas's Three Musketeers and Count of Montecresto together with Captain Sir Horace Horn Blower, They Died with Their Boots On, Captain Blood, Mutiny on the Bounty and various other popular films of that time were also shown, and I had the privilege to watch all of them, when I was still a little girl

At the beginning I started to read Tamil classics. There were famous authors who wrote historical, social and love stories. I was able to read those books, the original versions, when I was about nine years old. I became engrossed with the characters. Sometimes I lived with them; especially there was a long, mega series.

It was the historical novel *'Ponniyin Chelvan*[36], written by the famous author *'Kalki'*. At the beginning I got interested in this particular book because I heard the story being related by a friend of my sister, Ariyamalar acca to my eldest sister. Before they published as a book of five volumes, it came as a series in one of the Indian magazine, and she read it every week, and related it to us on Sundays. It was not a matter of sitting and listening but overhearing because sometimes my sister did not allow me to sit with the big people when they shared their own secrets. This Ariya *malar acca'*, (we had to call all girls elder to us as acca, big sister, whether they were born with us or not) lived a few houses away from ours. She was a very good narrator. Those were the days young girls were not allowed to go out alone: they must have somebody with them, usually a little girl or the little brother. I could not understand how we could protect them but it was the tradition. Usually on Sundays I was sent to her house to bring her with. Although the story was told only for my eldest sister at the beginning, slowly all of us got interested. I watched her closely as she spoke in that husky voice that sometimes sounded weary and often sounded sensuous. I still can remember that I could not sleep on Saturdays and waited for the Sundays to come so that I could hear the next episode. The characters in the story were not only characters in a fiction but role models; they were set examples for morals and behaviour.

The moment I had the passion for reading I read anything and everything. Sometimes classics, sometimes trash, nothing escaped my eyes. When the school holidays started, I used to go with my father to the boys' college library and select the books for me to read. Because of my father I was allowed to have the books longer than the others. My father encouraged me a lot. I went to such an extent that I read the books in the nights even when all of them had gone to sleep switching off the electricity. I used candles to read the books. One day I slept with the candle burning which was noticed at the correct time to avoid an accident. Once I was having the mid-term examinations and inside my physics text book I kept the story book and read instead of learning for the exam. My father who came that way casually saw me doing this, he slowly came behind me removed the book and told "Do this after the examination." That was my father. I really appreciated the way he handled us in different situations, even when we were in the wrong

---

[36] A Tamil historical novel

I found my father liked when we the children went and asked our doubts in our subjects. My father was referred as the walking dictionary because he could answer almost all the meanings for English words. I wanted to impress my father and my siblings so when I was in the living room and my father was in the Veranda I would tell a word in English quite loudly and say "Father what is........." and then a word. My father would promptly answer me. When I did quite often my brothers got irritated. After sometime they started to bully me by saying "father what is' *gee*[37] or what is' *ree*'. They were words that never existed but used just to bully me, especially my second brother who enjoyed bullying me. I felt a sudden wrench in my heart and my action of asking father loudly slowly stopped. But I was not kept chained to his bullying demands. My father was the all in all for us as far as education was concerned. He solved our problems in Tamil, Mathematics and English.

Slowly I developed reading English books. At that time my second sister was at the university and she brought English books but I was forbidden to read because it had a little bit of adult material like love stories. One day I saw my sister reading the book "The dark Gentleman" by Ruby M. Ayres. When I peeped to have a look at it, she told me "This is not for you" and went on reading. This made me curious. After reading the book she kept it in a wooden box where she kept all her books and I was not supposed to open that box but I broke the rule and took out the book and read the story. I leafed through the pages of the book with great enthusiasm. I became soppy over dashing heroes of romantic books. Even now I remember my imagination about that dark gentleman in the book. Afterwards I tried my best to get and read all the books possible. My sister also read books published by Mills and Boones which I never hesitated to read. My hiding places were inside the toilet or a corner in the back yard. Very often I had to hide the book when somebody passed by. This reading habit developed my writing capability. I could write good descriptive essays both in English and Tamil. During the break in the school I used to relate stories to my class mates telling them they were from the books but many times they were my own creations. Apparently I said if sufficiently naturally the suspicious shadows left their faces. I think I had a flair for narration. Later I started to write drama scripts for the class and staged them in school.

---

[37] Meaningless sounds

Chapter 26

My first train journey

Not only my grandfather but his eldest son, that is my mother's brother, was also a Methodist Mission pastor. Usually every three years they went on a transfer to different parts of the island. Once he was in the town "Murungan" in the North West of the island. He had one daughter Thevi *machaP*[38] that is my cousin, who was three years elder to me. In our tradition we use the relationship of a person together with the name. Whenever she came to our place during holidays we played together. Sometimes I had to use her used dresses which I could not refuse out of politeness and I accepted. My first train trip was my visit to my cousin in this town. I went with my father. It was not a direct journey, we had to break journey at the "Mathavaatchi" station and then take the connecting train. The train arrived at the Kodigamam station where we started our journey. It was the slow mail train. When the train pulled up and for a moment a welcome breeze touched the passengers standing on the platform. As the doors opened manually by the passengers a good number of them exited the train. It was a temporary rest site. As many people boarded as had left and the carriage was full and in seconds the smell of perspiration, smelly feet and garlic breath intermingling with the stale smell of upholstery of the seat filled the compartment. I stood the journey well hugging my father and we reached Murungan station. My uncle came to receive us at the station. To my shock there were no people or houses to the nearest vicinity except the church and the parsonage. I was partly disappointed and partly bored. My father and uncle had a lot of things to discuss because my father wanted to buy a paddy land there. The first day I was tired and slept in a big bed room suddenly to be woken for no plausible reason. I saw the moonlight pouring over the window sills in blue pools at my feet: an imagery that still comes to my memory, whenever I think about that trip.

The whole day we had to sit indoors and play with each other. But after two days I met some of the parish children. One of them was Miriam, the other one was Malar. My first impression when I saw Miriam was that she had a blue stone ear ring which was unusual. Then they told me they would be coming to my town Point Pedro to our school to continue their studies. The visit to this place

---

[38] First cousin

made me to realize there could be boring places in the island and I could not imagine how my cousin lived there. Of course later she was sent to the city boarding school in the city near our town. Thinking of my cousin I think of the days both in her place and in our place how we spent our time. Especially my strict aunt used harsh words both with me and her daughter. Her temper was just under the surface and sometimes it bubbled up. She was a teacher in the primary school and she treated us like her students. Especially on Sundays both of us could not do anything. In the bible it is said it is the day of rest, but in her house it was the forbidden day for both of us. We could only read the bible. We could not play and we could not go to the cinema and we could not read story books, we could do nothing except read the bible. It was simply a prison for me. The same thing was repeated, when they visited us: not that my parents were like that but because my cousin could not do it, I could not do it.

Chapter 27

Things we did in the house when we had free time

I was the youngest in the family and sometimes considered as too small to play with my siblings. I had to sit and wait watching the others playing. The playmates from the neighbourhood used to come to play with my brothers. And I craved to take part in the games. Usually I was ignored. I felt hopeless and inadequate. My third brother Chelva had an influence on me. I used to do everything he told me, if not I won't have anyone to play with in the absence of my parents. They used to play 'robbers and police'. It looked very interesting for me, because the robbers had to steal something and go and the police had to catch them. They had sticks as pistols. And with the mouth they made the noise. After so many begging my brother agreed to take me into the game. He seriously explained me the importance of my role in the game. I must be the police station holding the jewellery till they finished their game. I became the champion of being the Police Station, sitting and waiting. Some thing was better than nothing.

It was the time, when there was smuggling going on between India and Sri Lanka especially a village near our town where most of the smugglers lived. And the customs people chased their boats in a launch. And my brother was quite fascinated by that, often they had seen that chase. So the game changed its directions in the house where we used the big wooden coconut scraper as the launch and the coconut husk as the smuggler's small boat. We have to push both the coconut scraper and the coconut husks in the sand pretending the chase of the smugglers. Very often I ended up being caught as a smuggler.

Usually my parents visited the houses in the community, the neighbours and friends who lived close by. Such visits lasted about an hour. That means we did not have much time to do any mischief. Especially at 6 o'clock, my brothers and sometimes the children in the neighbourhood sat in the front veranda and learnt for the school. Obviously I was a freelance and had nothing to learn, so I wandered in the house. Occasionally my parents went to visit the principal or teachers who lived a little away from our house. This was usually after dinner. They would always say where they were going, therefore we knew the duration of their visit. The children were supposed to sit and learn for the school. The moment their figures disappeared, the whole group got active. Not with studies but with all other activities including games. This was limited when our eldest sister was at home. Strange enough she was never part of our adventures and we also had a distance from her. She would either be reading stitching or correcting the school work

On one such occasion my brothers and my second sister started to play. As usual I was not included, I had to sit on a chair and watch them playing. But I was fascinated by one of the games which had a lot of fun. People fell down but still they laughed. It was a game with the chair. You stand in front of the chair, and somebody gave the command 'sit, stand'. They did it a few times, and you became confident. But at some point they took the chair away and the person fell down. For my brothers and sisters, and the boys from the neighbourhood, it was fun. I went and cried to my eldest brother that I wanted to do this. They warned me several times, but I was adamant. So the game started. Two three times I was successful in landing correctly on the chair, but the third time I had a hard fall, knocked my head on the cement floor. I started to scream and scream and my brother noticed that it was time for my parents to return, and they were sure whether the fault was mine or not, they would be punished. He carried me to the street and very slowly told me "If you cry and tell this to the parents, you can never ever play with us." With a whimper I said yes and when my parents came I did not open my mouth. I slowly went to sleep. The next day my mother found the bump on my head, but because I was small they did not ask for an explanation and I on my part kept quiet keeping my promise.

It was in the year 1952 the coronation of Queen Elizabeth II was held. There was the film called "Queen is crowned", shown in the theatres. And my brothers and sisters acted the same in the house, decorating the chair with mother's sari, pretending to be the throne giving a stick in the hand and a paper cap as the crown, for the person who played the role of the queen. Once I took the role of the queen. So there was a particular music for the marching of the soldiers. This was done by my brothers with sticks carried as riffles held in the upright position, then they allowed me to walk slowly like the queen, and sit on the throne. I was proud as ever. The second step was that distinguished people came and kissed the hand of the queen. One by one came and kissed my hand. Very solemnly they kneeled down and kissed my hand. My second brother out of mischief, when I was not looking, was licking my hand almost with reverence. I did not know at that time why the others laughed till my brother told the truth after the incident. And this was a big joke for them. I cried out of shame, and they had to pacify me. Complaints to the parents about such activities in the absence of our parents were not tolerated by my siblings, and in that aspect our solidarity was remarkable.

My third brother and I were better pals. We did some very funny things together. Behind our house was the great Indian Ocean. Therefore we often went to the beach and played. Every trip to the beach was an adventure. Sometimes we angled and I still remember the excitement of the tug on my line when I had hooked my fish. In the afternoons, when my mother was taking a rest, we were supposed to stay at home and read something, but my brother and I would stealthily go to the beach and play in the sea. Before my mother woke up, we returned, so we were never caught. But one fine afternoon we went to the beach and the sun was glinting and glittering on the water, the breeze invigorating against our faces. It was then that we saw a catamaran of the oldest fisherman called *"Mambalappa*[39]*"* whose age cannot be determined. He could be 60, 70 or even 90. We got into this catamaran and my brother started to rock with both the legs. Then we could see the small waves coming out. We enjoyed seeing that. But it was a superstition that one should not do such thing when the catamaran is empty; they thought they would not have much luck that day. So suddenly we saw the old man coming towards us shouting names. The quick escape was that mattered. My brother who was taller than me jumped and ran away leaving me to face the music. I tried to get down but fell into the sea. Even with that I started to run. Of course I escaped from the hands of the old man. Whenever we got wet, we rolled on the sand which was quite white and clean then the wetness was gone, the sand absorbed the water. Therefore normally I had no trouble in drying my clothes, but that particular day I could not dare to do the same taking my own time drying my dress, because an angry victim was chasing us the perpetrators. Simply out of panic I ran. My brother ran faster and reached the house and sat in the room as though nothing had happened. I was small so I was late. By the time I reached my mother was at the entrance looking at me hard. I stood there dripping wet. When she asked me, how it happened, my brother stood behind my mother and signalled not to tell. I looked at her with my innocent eyes filled with tears. My mother pulled me, gave me a bath at the well and told me not to go to the beach alone.

---

[39] its a nick name for an old fisher man

Chapter 28

Christmas and New Year in the family

Being a very strict Christian family, Christmas was one of the biggest celebrations we had in the house. Christmas came and went with the usual procedure. It usually started by carol singing, carol services, the Christmas trees, the Christmas presents, the Christmas events in the school, the nativity play, united carol singing and so on. Carol services during the Christmas time were a big event for us. In the church as well as in the school we had Christmas celebrations. But the highlight was the united choral service, where all the Christian schools joined at the town hall in Jaffna to have a grand music festival. Only the senior students from the school went for that, sometimes my elder sister and another Christian teacher went with the students. We all had to wear white dresses but we were asked to wear our white school uniforms. I think I was the youngest in the school choir, who went to the carol service. Because of my talent in singing together with the principal's recommendation I was given special permission. One month before the big event we had to go for the rehearsal to learn the new songs and the special items by each school would be timed. The final programme was a grand affair. The ladies from other prominent city schools would be displaying their new styles in their dresses. Typical western choirs and typical Tamil choirs would be represented in this event. In the later stages my compositions were performed by my school choir. The popular one was *Maiparhela*[40] for which Shanthini Navaratnam played the interlude on the piano. The school also had Christmas programmes and once I composed the ballet, text and music, titled "Adam and Eve". The whole piece was sung by me with the accompaniment of Thanadevi.Subiah on violin and a famous *Viduvan*[41] Theverajah on *Mirthangam*[42]. The students were trained by the dance teacher and they performed that ballet for the Christmas programme. My parents were proud of me. A few years ago, when I visited Canada, Manga the girl who played the Serpent in the ballet, came to see me and shared her memories with me.

In our family my father, my mother, my eldest sister, my eldest brother and my second sister were local preachers in the church. They had to do a written exam

---

[40] shepherds

[41] mastro

[42] Classical drums

to become a local preacher. My mother was a Sunday school teacher for the senior students. Every Sunday, soon after the service was over, we were divided into different age groups and different people conducted the Sunday schools. At the end of the year, we had an examination to write and then, before the schools closed for the Christmas holidays, they had a Christmas tree with presents for all the Sunday school children. There would be a Christmas papa, (our special name for Santa) distributing presents for all the children in the parish, even if they were babies.

We had two big events during the Christmas season. My mother was an active member in the church, the MWF, and would like to do social services to the under privileged people. There were special guest workers, who lived in Sri Lanka, who were the scavengers. Usually they were treated like outcasts. We lived in the First Cross street but in the Third cross street there was a colony for them referred as *"Kooli line"* given by the government, where they lived with their families. They had their own community and normal people never associated with them. My mother was the first woman who wanted to visit these people along with the deaconess and preach religion and hygiene for them. It was every other Fridays, I think. Slowly she developed this into having a Christmas party for them. She would collect money from the community and the church, the rest needed was given from her own pocket. She would do a big shopping, buying materials to make dresses for the children. For this she would write a list with measurements of the children and then buy the material. She was a very good seamstress, who could stitch dresses economically without wasting. She herself would cut and make the dresses, and we packed them, wrote the names and put them into a box. The community would clean the grounds, erect a branch of a Casuarina tree and decorate it as the Christmas tree with balloons and coloured papers. A Santa clause came to give the presents to the children. Some sweets were also distributed. Usually they were not that clean but on this day you could see a big difference. Sometimes I used to go with my mother to this place, but the Christmas celebration I never missed. This was something that no one dared to do because of the caste restrictions and conservative beliefs. But my mother felt happy about it.

The second major event was the 21st of December. It was the Christmas season but for my mother it was the death anniversary of her mother. Therefore she did an arms giving for the beggars and the poor. More than ten curries were cooked, all vegetables and we had to go the roads and call all the beggars and also the poor people around our house to get their food, rice and curry. The beggars sat and ate whereas the neighbours took it in their vessels. Early morning we would get some flowers and visit the graveyard, keep the flowers on the gravestone of my grandmother and my mother's sister, who died early together with my sister and brother whom we lost. The graveyard was in the next street so we walked there, then, straight from there, we went to the sea and washed our hands. It was something that we did without asking. It was more of a hygienic reason than a tradition.

22nd and 23rd are the busiest days for us. My mother formally put the *oil pan* on the fire to make the traditional oil cakes. One could never deny that my mother was an excellent cook. She prepared the tastiest dishes and my father used to say "Because she has some special thing in her hand". Those oil cakes were prepared on a large scale. They were put in big tins and kept in a secured place. The whole season those oil cakes would be used for the visitors, who came, and distributed to the neighbours and friends.

On the 22nd there would be the grand preparation for the making of the butter cake. It was the period we never knew making a butter cake was a child play. Being a western food it was a serious matter and a long process in the house. My mother did not do it but my eldest sister was the manager for that. I say manager because she instructed my brothers and sisters to do the tasks. One should hold the bowl while the others took turns to mix the butter and sugar. The third one would break the eggs separating the white from the yolk in separate dishes. One should beat the white of an egg till it was full of froth. There would be a kitchen clock so that the making of the cake was exactly one hour. By the time they reached the stage of adding baking powder and the essence the cake tray would be prepared. My sister would put the mixture in the tray. Baking was not done at home. One of us took the cake tray to the bakery, which was owned by Sinhalese people. There would be a row of cake trays at the bakers because all the Christians make the cake during this season. We put a piece of paper with our name on top of the cake mixture. There were two reasons for that. One to identify our tray and the other was to test whether the baker had stolen some of the mixture to produce his own cake, which many people suspected. We also had another bakery in the second cross street we used after the riots, when the Sinhalese baker left the town.

THOSE WERE THE GOLDEN DAYS

Usually there were two servants in the house but during the festival time two women would come extra and pound the rice and grind the different ingredients for the oil cakes. We took those oil cakes for the friends and neighbours and for particular families, together with their Christmas presents. The servants carried them when I went, because I was too small. But that was not all. This mass preparation was for two more major events. One was the Christmas tree celebration at home, when Christmas presents were given for all the children in the neighbourhood. This day was made colourful by having a Santa Clause, and a big Christmas tree at home. In our town there were no typical western Christmas trees. Only in the Hill Country and in big shopping malls in the capital, they had those original Christmas trees. But all the others used the casuarina tree. They look like pine trees with small spiky seeds. Our servant and one of my brothers would go and cut a suitable tree about four or five miles away from our house. Then they transported it in their bikes and brought that home. They erected the tree, which almost touched the ceiling, and decorated it with coloured papers balloons and other decorations. They hung the presents for our Hindu playmates on the tree. Those friends were specially invited and would be given a seat to sit on the veranda. The Santa would call their names and give the presents.

There was another crowd of children whom we refer as "beach lads and lasses". We take a rough estimate of the children, because we knew those families, and buy balloons or whistles. They were also given the oil cakes. It was a luxury for them. On that day not only the children but also the parents stand in a line carrying their new born babies to get those presents. Some children would be dressed for the occasion if not all. We have a front gate and a back gate. Once they received the presents they would be sent by the back gate. That was not easy. Even if they went by the back gate they would quickly run round the house and stand in the line again to get the presents for the second time. People, who stood for the first time, would complain but we could not find the truth because they hid the presents somewhere and came for the second time. Some of them my brother would recognize but we could not manage all of them. There would be a big confusion to give or not to give. My brothers were responsible for that. I would sit with my mother and watch the fun. In the later years my eldest brother found a trick. They blew all the balloons and kept them in the room and gave so that those children could not hide them easily. But sometimes the small children will break them while hugging them hard and would cry and we had to replace them of course. The highlight of this day was the Santa clause. Usually one of my brothers would dress like a Santa clause. We called the Santa clause as "Christmas Papa". The entry will be sensational. The Christmas Papa came in a Catamaran by sea and he would be accompanied by my other brothers and the crowd of children from the beach. My brother would play an old violin only with two strings the other brother would ring the bells and another would make a noise with the tins and it would draw the crowd. At the beginning they would never reveal to me, who the Christmas Papa was. Not only the children but also some of those women were frightened to shake hands. Some children would scream and as usual the children believed he came from the North Pole. It was the same for me. My father was my refuge. I would hold his hands tightly and tried myself not to go near the Christmas papa. The day would end in singing some carols. Although it was purely a children's affair our parents were the sponsors.

24th of December was the Christmas Eve. We do not have a midnight service at the church. Instead the choir from each parish would visit the houses singing carols. Each house prepared varieties of food to serve the members of the carol party. They spent at least 15 minutes in each house. When I was very small I was always frightened of Christmas Papa. I refused to shake hands with him. I would sit with my father and listen to the carols but hid myself behind father when the Christmas Papa shook hands with the members of the family. When I was ten I was the youngest member in the choir. But my father never allowed the girls to visit the houses to sing carols on Christmas Eve. The reason given by my mother was, I had to sing at the Christmas service the next day and my voice should be good. Sometimes I had seen my brothers, who went with the carol party, could not sing the next day. So I did not have this adventure of the nocturnal visits on the Christmas Eve.

25th was the Christmas day. All the family members would have new clothes including the servants. When I was very small my elder sister stitched my Christmas frocks, I remember two dresses she made for me. One was a green organdie dress with tucks and lace and the other one was a yellow organdie dress with yellow roses, the dress I am wearing in the photograph. Her stitching was very neat and tidy. I used to hang around near the machine till she finished the dress. It was the time we had only the manual sewing machine you should have one hand to roll the handle and only one hand was free. Sometimes I would roll the handle. Christmas was also a season to give presents for others. My mother would send presents for the principals of the Boys' College and the Girls' School and to the parish pastor. She never forgot to send a Christmas and birthday present, which fell on the same day, to the eldest daughter of the Boys' College principal in memory of her daughter, my sister, whom she lost. My elder sister would make night dresses or pillow cases with fine embroidery. I had seen her needle weaving in and out of the linen occasionally flashing silver as it caught the light. Sometimes garments made by her were given to non native teachers in the school.

Soon after the Christmas service at the church, my parents did their annual visits to the parish members. Sometimes till late in the night. But would come home for lunch and then continue. They did not finish in one day because they visited other parishes also. Occasionally my father was invited as the guest speaker to distant churches. Then we hire a car and go with our father. My father was quite known for his sermons.

New Year

During the whole week from the 26th to the 31st either my parents visited people or other parish members visited us. But on the 31st our evening meal would be bread, butter and jam. This was prepared either by my sisters or by my mother. Since 31st of December was the date that my father had the ship wreck my parents would stay at home. But we all would go to the watch night service at the church, which started at 10.30 and finished at 12.15. Each family would give a special item mostly to keep us awake. The preacher would be delivering the sermon but sharp at twelve the church bell would ring then he would stop and we all would kneel down and observe silence till the tolling of the bell ceased. After the service was over we wished 'Happy New Year' to the parish members. When we returned from the church, my mother would have prepared a special sweet food, which is called *"Chillu kalli"*, made of lentil flour, rice flour, sugar and coconut milk. I could not remember a New Year without this food.

On the first we got a special guest from one of the villages with his boys' troop to sing the carols in all the houses and they are given money for their performance. That old gentleman was called *"Kinnere Chatambiar"*[43] by all. It means "Music Teacher". From the time I remember he looked the same. He was

---

[43] Music teacher

very short with long hair and bald in the centre. His one leg was shorter than the other so he limped in a funny way. I had never seen him smiling and his symbol was a violin. I didn't know how many strings it had because when I was a little girl I was a little bit afraid of him for no reason. I used to hold my father's hand whenever he performed. One could not hear a specific melody but only the noise of the strings. But he played with an air of confidence that my parents used to say they felt they had forgotten the concept of music itself. Such a perfect agonizing enigma. The boys, who came with him, were not more than thirteen or fourteen. But they worked under strict discipline. The remarkable thing was they knew when to stop for the interlude which was again the string noise. In between he sang with them. That was still funny because he did not have any teeth and the words were not clear. His world of music was totally different. We were not supposed to laugh during the performance although, when it was unbearable, even my parents put their tongues in their cheeks. Our house was their first halt so they got their dinner. But my parents always treated them with respect and allowed him and the boys to sleep on the veranda with mats and pillows, when he finished his tour. He would leave early in the morning catching the first bus to his village. Every year they sang the same song only changing the year at the beginning combined with the birth of Christ. I could not precisely say when he stopped coming and my parents thought presumably he was dead. My eldest brother used to imitate him long after his visit and have fun with it. My brothers used an old violin to complete the act.

Easter at home

Being a conservative Christian family Easter was observed with vigil. Before the forty days fasting started my mother prepared many vegetable preservatives like pickles, *vadagam*, [44] and chillies preserved in butter milk. The Lent started on the Ash Wednesday and continued for forty days. My mother had only vegetarian diet all those forty days whereas we had our normal meals. It was different on the holy week. The whole house had vegetarian diet that week. We had to take part in the holy week services in the church. On Good Friday we had the three hours service and we wore only white. My mother and later my second sister made beautiful dresses for me for the Easter Sunday service. The whole family

---

[44] Made of Margosa flowers and other spices

attended the service except when my father was invited as a guest speaker in another parish. Sometimes we had painted Easter eggs but never Easter bunnies.

Other celebrations apart from festivals

Due to several members in the house more or less every month we had birthdays. Children and adults got their new clothes and few friends were invited for not an elaborate but a simple celebration only for children. But some special food was always there for all. A few of my mother's friends came for her birthday. In March it started with my third brother Chelva, whose birthday fell on the 15th of March. The following day the 16th of March was my parents wedding anniversary. Occasionally it came during the Lent season then the celebration was limited. In April we had Easter. 31st May was my second sister Rathy's birthday followed by my eldest sister Gunamani celebrating the same on the 17th of June. 20th July was mine and 1st of August my mother had her great day. 3rd of September my second brother Bala, and 26th of October my eldest brother Baba waited for their birthdays. My father closed the birthdays in the family by celebrating his birthday on the 3rd of November. We celebrated Christmas in December and New Year in January. Only February was empty. That was fulfilled later by my second brother in law by having his birthday on the 20th of February. Wasn't it ironic!

Chapter 29

My father's income

Success came slowly with him getting the Cambridge Degree, and later his Grade One Special Post at the college. After the war, the recession continued and my father had to provide an eight member family with food, education and shelter. Therefore he did additional teaching and sometimes went as a guest speaker and translator. For any church activity my father did not charge any money because it was an honour. There were conventions in the church every year. That meant, one weekend including the Friday, there would be revival meetings for the parish people, and the preachers would be popular people from the church, or missionaries from England. I say England because the Methodist church was founded by Charles Wesley and his brother John Wesley from England. Once in such convention, a foreign speaker came, and because of the fluency in both the languages my father translated the English sermons of the missionary. At one point he was telling a very serious point with theological terms which my father thought would be too difficult for the parish to understand if it were to be translated directly in high language. Therefore he only used one idiom in Tamil which conveyed the meaning the preacher expected. Funny enough, one of the words in the phrase was a raw word meaning "the backside of a person". The parish reacted with a grin. Actually they smiled because of the word but the preacher was confused. Immediately he turned to my father and asked what was funny about it, my father told him quietly "I told them an idiom. It is the best way for them to understand your point."

Again it was ironic that my father was asked to translate the Swedish expert on family planning. It was the time when exhortation to use a condom was not publicly advertised. Because of his seniority, my father was able to translate different delicate terms said by the expert in English into Tamil. There were women and men and it was a new culture for them to hear about family planning. But my father dealt it in such a casual way that one of the doctor's wives came and told "He is the best person to do the translation." But once one of them asked my father "Isn't it ironic that a man who has six children talking about family planning to the others?" My father replied "Exactly, because I know the problems of a big family". This was a paid job, not in cash but in other ways. And when my father was asked what he would like to have, he ordered two of the most expensive medical books for my brothers, who were medical students at that time.

Our judicial system was a copy of the British system. The criminal cases went to the Supreme Court especially the murder or attempted murder cases. Apart from the judge there would be a panel of juries at the session. And they were chosen among the citizens and not from the legal sector. That was another source of income for my father. My father was working as a jury for several years and later he was chosen as the foreman of the jury. They were paid a lot of money compared with the normal salary. The total sum would be greater than his salary sometimes. I did not know why my father thought only after I was born he got all his promotions that he took me whenever luck was needed. In other words I was the lucky charm for him. The Supreme Court sessions could be extended for every jury depending on how long the cases were prolonged. And my father thought I would bring him luck if I accompanied him to the bus stand when he left for such sessions. Early morning at 5.30 I was woken by my mother and I held my father's hand and walked to the bus terminals. Before he entered the bus both of us used to go to a café and have a short breakfast. Only one café was open so early. Inside the shop it smelt stale but the food was warm and fresh. They had only hoppers with banana which was my father's favourite food. After he entered the bus I returned home. It would be still dawn therefore there would be only few people on the street. My mother could see from our house to the junction of the terminals. I don't know why sometimes I was frightened. While returning I closed my eyes and ran as fast as I could to the house. One day I was just walking back I saw a young man following me. Perhaps it was my imagination there was something evil behind that. It was a terrifying experience for me. I ran so fast that my mother was surprised that I was panting. For some reason or the other I did not tell my mother what happened. May be I thought she might not allow me to go the next day.

Sometimes those Supreme Court Sessions went on for ten to fifteen days and then my father had to stay at the rest house especially arranged for the juries. Once the politician cum criminal lawyer, in fact he was one of the brilliant defence lawyers in the country, and a friend of my father, had appeared for his clients at the Supreme Court, where my father was a jury. Since my father knew his character, he challenged my father; therefore my father had to retreat as a jury. My father used to talk about the murder cases in general, not with those

141

which came when he was a jury, because he was under oath. It was interesting to listen to him especially about one particular case, which involved a famous man, whose wife was murdered. The defence lawyer was from *Vadamarachi*, our area. Although he had big properties in the best area in Colombo he also had a huge house closer to our area but nobody lived in that house that long and he himself went away from the country. When I asked my father why that house was always empty he said, "It must have been the curse on the family to help a murderer escape from his crime. That lawyer manipulated an alibi for the murderer but nobody could prove that"

My father had another source of income. Each year thousands of public examination answer papers were sent to him to be corrected. We had state examinations every December and August of the year. First the examination department would send pilot papers to see how they corrected and if they are satisfied then they would send the whole batch packed in big bundles by special post. When the parcels were delivered, they were taken to a special room and kept where we the children were not allowed to enter without the presence of an adult. My father was given a month or six weeks time to finish the correction and send them. My father was accustomed to last minute rush. In fact my mother was his driving force. She would keep on reminding him about that. By all those hard work he proved that money did not grow on trees.

Chapter 30

Father, sports and students

My father was a good sports man. He played soccer for his school team. Unfortunately while playing a match, one of the famous soccer player at that time, kicked him with the boots and my father was injured. Due to that he could not play in the team: later, when he joined the staff he became the couch. I remember him, when he was the master in charge for the Shered House in the college. The boys 'college was a model college not only for education, but also for sports and other activities. At the beginning the students were divided into four houses red, blue, green and yellow and each had the name of famous principals. My father's house was green.

The sports meet at the college was a big event. My father had a very good relationship with the students. I was my father's pet, which gave enough grounds for me to accompany him to the sports meet at the college. There was always sport politics, and till the end, the winner was not announced. There was a march past performed by every house team and the chief guest would take the salute, together with the principal. Each house would have a booth and they decorated it with best of their ability. There would be a panel of judges to give points for each house, which would be added to the grand total. The chief guest and the principal would pay a formal visit, and the student leader and the master in charge would be introduced. Till I was ten years old I was a regular visitor to my father's Shered House. That ordeal had its grandeur. I would hold my father's hand and go with him. The whole group would clap their hands and welcome my father. The clapping would give a rhythm for my father's walk. Then the captain would pin the biggest rosette specially made for my father. Those formalities were grand. Years later, the fifth house the purple house was introduced. Sometimes my father would leave me in the booth and attend other matters, and I would sit with the boys till my father took me and seated me with the visitors.

Father's relationship with the students

The students in the college mostly liked my father, because he never did any mean things. He had his judgement and tolerance of his own profession. The librarian of the school behaved like a director, and was very strict with the students, that the students had a nickname, and called him, when he went in the evenings, and he could not detect who they were. But he suspected one group. When the examinations neared, the boys wanted to borrow books from the library. Keeping the incidents with his nicknames in mind as a grudge, he deliberately denied books for those boys. They had no other alternative. And one day they went to my father and complained about it. My father said "Write the list of your books." It was a rule that, when the students borrow the books they must come and renew it every week and return it in two weeks. But if the teacher borrowed he could keep it for one month. My father went to the library, gave the list to the librarian and asked him to give the books. They were given to the boys to prepare for the examination. Such timely help was very much appreciated by the students. Of course they had some jokes about my father's absentminded quality taken jovially by my father. Whenever he heard about them he used to say with a smile "Well a truth is a truth"

One of those students was Kandiah the brother of my sister Rathay's friend Rasamani. He was very witty and intelligent. He entered the medical college and was doing well. But who could rule out the hand of destiny? For him it came in the shape of a motorbike. When they heard about a death of his friend he and his friend Wiky travelled by a motorbike and half way through met with an accident in a curve, the motor bike careening downhill at breakneck speed. His friend survived but Kandiah was not lucky. Alas the life of that young man of so much potentiality was robbed by fate half way through his life. My father had an amazed admiration for this student and said he had qualities which were unique and valuable.

One day they had the public exam in the school and one of the students got the answer paper but did not write anything and when the others gave the answers he gave a blank paper and went. While correcting my father found that he was marked present for the exam, but his paper was missing. My father could not mark him as absent because he was present at the exam but at the same time he could not give the marks. So what he did was, he gave him a double zero and kept quiet. He never informed the principal because there were harsh punishments for such behaviour but on the sports meets day, this particular student was the winner for the mile race. In fact, he was called 'miler' later on. So the principal and my father walked to the podium to give the certificate. On their way the principal said "He has achieved a lot." Then my father said "Last year he ran a faster race from the examination hall."

Almost every year the Boys' College had a drama day. Two plays both in English and Tamil were staged and the public was invited. Usually my father directed the Tamil plays and English plays were directed by other teachers and performed by the students. The college had not only Tamil teachers but also Sinhalese and Burgers. That was also something that influenced me and later made me a radio actor. My father took great pleasure in doing those dramas. Sometimes I saw him standing behind the curtain with the script in his hand. I was quite proud when I saw him. Later when my brother joined the staff, his colleagues were young people and one of them was a burger, Rosemary Cock and he produced and acted an English play titled "That Rascal Skapan" which we enjoyed very much.

I am proud to say that my father was an all rounder. He excelled in languages like English, Tamil and Latin. He was our teacher for Mathematics Religion and Logic. Much later he became an expert in Philosophy that he was requested by the Government Language Department to translate the most difficult English books in Philosophy into Tamil language for the university students. My father became popular in teaching Latin not only for the matriculation students but also for law students. Most of those lawyers later became politicians. Our local MP and former deputy Speaker of Parliament were some of them. There was a senator and his wife who came and studied Tamil literature just for the bliss of learning under my father. We had a shed at the back of the house where they sat and discussed literature for hours long. One of them who became the chairman of the urban council was a very rich man and my father after giving the lessons did not take any payment. But his parents did a very big financial contribution later, when my father needed. When my father told this story he also said, "Do a good deed without expectations then god will bless you in his own way". He also had students from other ethnic groups because his college was an All Island School. These so called advanced students had such affection that in needful time they showed it in three folds. For instance at my sister's wedding and when my brothers were at the university which I would be explaining in another chapter.

College politics

When you have children of the same age among the colleagues automatically competition invades in the minds of people. At least that was what my father said. My father was a teetotaller, married only once and without any scandals with any other woman. Some of his colleagues had more money but lacked in these virtues. Therefore they could not touch or damage my father in any way other than penalising his children. Not that my brothers were angels. But they were not that bad to be punished severely. It was only envy and personal malice. My eldest sister was out of their hands because she was already teaching at the Girl's School while doing her London degree privately. My eldest brother was the head prefect during the centenary celebration of the college and entered university of Peredeniya in 1955. My second sister was at the Boys' College only for two years before she had a direct admission to the University of Colombo. My eldest brother and second sister were out of reach while they entered the university well before their children. But the victims were my two brothers who were in the college. Very often they tried their back biting in the staff room. My father never stopped fighting for his rights. I do not deny that my brothers were average and not extraordinary clever. But they were not below average. My second brother tried his entrance and failing which joined Jaffna College where he could do his London degree privately. My third brother was at the college and there was every attempt to stop him from doing the university entrance. At the college before they attempted the final advanced level examination the teachers could decide to withdraw the application. One of the teachers gave him a mean 39% in one of the subjects whereas 40% was the requested points, thereby making my brother not eligible to do the examination. I am not Mark Antony to be diplomatic and say "Yet Brutus is an honourable man". I remember that particular day when he heard the news. He came home and fell under the dining table and cried. Nobody could do anything against the decision of the teacher.

My father thought it was high time that he removed my brother from the college in order to prevent the same thing happening the next year. Immediately he admitted my third brother to one of the best colleges, St.John's College Jaffna and supported him in every way possible. He lost one year but this failure gave him the motivation to study hard at the new college. At the end of the year both my second brother Bala and my third brother Chelva sat for the university entrance exam and entered the Medical Faculty. My mother challenged those teachers that both her sons would be doctors and succeeded in it. My parents who no fault of their own, faced disasters due to their children. When asked about those incidents my father said, "Jealousy is a monster that could drive you to any extent. Even in the Bible it is said 'who could face jealousy'"

My father's strange visitors

My father had some unusual visitors visiting him in unusual times. They included old people, colleagues, and criminals, old students, young and old. One of his students was a classmate of my eldest brother and when he visited my father there would be strong arguments going on for hours between him and my father. One could say he was a devil's advocate. When asked how come such combination of my father and his visitors developed nobody knew the answer. Most of them wanted monetary help and occasionally just to talk with him. My father would give them his help but he always closed his hand when he gave them and therefore we never knew how much he gave. There was one particular friend a teacher who had difficulties because he fell in love with a woman who was not his caste. His whole family had nothing to do with him. But he was faithful to that lady. My father said it was great of him. It was a breath of gossip for the dusty ears. My father said "a gentleman's liberty for his natural carnal appetite was certainly not a matter to be displayed before the vulgar and the inquisitive". He certainly gave credit where credit was due. Another one I remember who used to come and hide behind the wall and just give only a peep. There was a rumour that he was a criminal. One never knew how they show their gratitude in needy times. Once we needed some Lotus flowers for a big cultural event and it was January when all the lakes were deep and dangerous to go and get those flowers. When Father casually mentioned that to him he went out of the way taking a risk of going to those lakes to get those flowers. You could only marvel at his behaviour.

Chapter 31

My music talent

Music was my passion therefore it was not a wonder that I got attracted to film songs. At the beginning this was forbidden in the house when my grandfather was there, but then my brothers, especially my eldest brother started to sing the film songs. There was a Tamil film *'Chandralekha'* which is still in the Guinness book of records for running in the theatre for more than a year. The songs from this film were memorized and sung by my eldest brother Baba, supported by my other brothers Bala and Chelva and my second sister Rathy. There was one particular song my brother sang. As soon as I heard the song I would shake my head. From the beginning memory was my advantage. If I heard one song once it stayed in my mind. My father did not allow us to have a radio at home because he thought it would distract the studies. Therefore if there was a programme that we could hear we went to the boys 'college to hear that. It was only for special occasions like the guitar recital of the sister of my mother's friend. My playmate Rasaluxmi, who lived two houses away from ours, had a gramophone with LPs. Whenever I wanted to hear some music I went there and listened to the film music. Only when my sister got married we had a radio in the house.

I was talented in music and my principal knew that. Therefore for any music competition, I was selected with her recommendation. We had regular music classes and sometimes I was very naughty. I did not go for practices for the competition. I was given special permission to cut one of the classes to be trained for the competition. When I did not go for the class to be trained my teacher said, "This time you are not going to sing" and made one of the students in the next class to sing the same song to frighten me. But I was confident I would be the candidate because no one over ruled the principal's wishes. There was a competition for classical music and I was sent to the town during the weekends, 23 miles away from my place to get the training. Normally, if you went late to the school you would be detained and then the principal came and gave us punishments like detention class or to pluck the thorn creepers at least fifty of them, in the play ground. One fine day I went late after returning from Jaffna and the principal asked me the reason. I just told her I returned late from the town after the training. No questions, I was freed from punishments.

Chapter 32

School system and other activities

The school system those days were similar to the British system. We went to the first grade at the age of 4 years and 6 months. We never had a kindergarten at that time. We would have a public exam in the fifth grade area-wise and a public exam for the eighth grade in province wise and a public exam GCE (ordinary level) for the 10th grade in the island level. At the ordinary level we took eight subjects and if you got three Credits, you could continue the advanced level to enter the university. When I joined the school there were no advanced level classes in my school, but later on the school was upgraded, we had advanced level. First, we had only for the arts subjects, and then for the science subjects. in the advanced level you were separated into arts and science and you had to take only four subjects. Once you decide you cannot change. The first girl, who entered the university from our school, was our head girl, Thilagam Periyathamby, and later she became the education officer.

Our principal always encouraged not only education but also all the other extracurricular activities like music, sports and general knowledge. I could call myself an athlete because I always took part in the sports meet, especially javelin throws, discus throw and put shot. Although I tried some races and jumps, I was not that successful but I still have those certificates I obtained in the school and at the area competitions. Drill display was conducted by the province and area, and our school always took part in it. I was always in the team. I even played net ball in the school team and our school never failed to take part in championships. But once I got hurt in my leg and afterwards I could not walk that straight, even now I have that defect. We had annual sports meets in the school with March past and various track, field and team events. The students in the school were divided into four houses and there were teachers in charge for each house. The chief guest will give away the prizes. There would be judges from other schools and the highlight was the visitors and officials race.

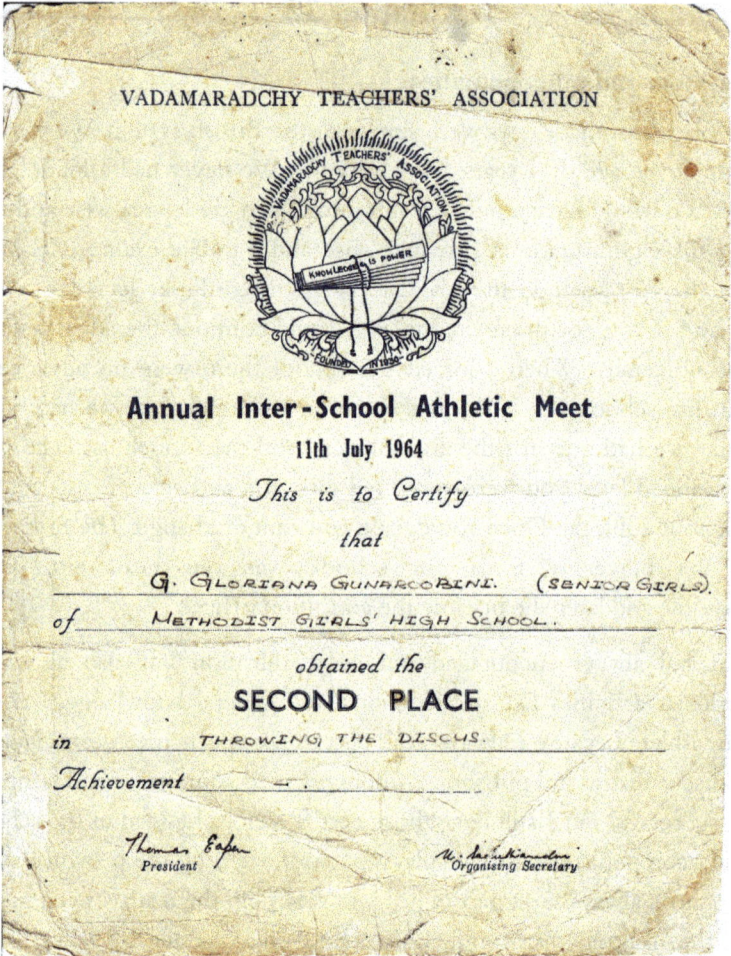

Certificate obtained for Discus Throw at the Interschool Athletic Meet in 1964

Our school was quite popular in sports; especially we had all island competitions for drill display. And once we were selected to compete in the all island competition. We were selected in the area, in the province and were the finalist for the all island competition. Twenty six of us, twenty four plus two extras and our PTI and another teacher, together with the Principal, travelled from our place to the capital in a van and in a car. Our principal sat in the front seat of the car and the children got into the van. One of the teachers also and then it was full. So there was an option that a teacher and a student must travel with the principal, everybody said no. My teacher said you are the best person, so I had to travel about 8 hours in the principal's car, of course I missed the fun but instead I had better food and small privileges like chocolates given by the principal. It was fortunate that we won the All Island Championship. We wore very short, red shorts with a white blouse and we had a pony tail. And my sister said the judges must have been attracted by those beautiful thighs. When the results were announced we cheered and disturbed the speech of Minister of Education. It was the first time that our principal did not stop us or did not stare at us. That evening we were taken to the Galle Face beach, a very popular place in the capital Colombo. And the principal served us our food. This was the greatest privilege we ever had.

Once a year Sri Lanka's biggest Navy ship named "Vijaya" came to our harbour, not directly but anchored in the deep sea. The harbour would dig out all its finery. Then the naval officers would come by boats and roam around the town area in their uniforms. The ship flood lit and dressed overall, basked like a pampered woman amid a cluster of attendant launches. The customs officers at that time were friends of ours. When the ship arrived in Point Pedro both the boys' college and the girls' school had an invitation to visit the ship. Most of the senior students above grade 6 were allowed to go to the harbour, get into the smaller motor boats and travelled in the deep sea to have a look at the big ship. One by one, climbed the shaky ladder and entered the ship. Our school was quite close to the harbour therefore you could see the big queue of the girls from the school to the harbour standing on the road waiting their turn to go. There was a limit as to how many could go at a time, so only when one batch returned the others went. Sometimes we had to wait in the sun for more than an hour before our turn came. It was interesting to note the murmuring of the students sounding like a swarm of bees. We were allowed to see all the cabins except the captain's cabin. But once one of the teachers wanted to take a rest they allowed her to sit in the captain's room. The captain was so angry he asked the cadets to put a chair outside. It was quite embarrassing. This ship was destroyed by the cyclone.

Chapter 33

My first programme on the radio and other stage programmes

Being a very good singer my mother wanted at least one of us to go and perform in the radio. Usually one particular girl went for the reading and singing competition organized by the Radio Ceylon, educational service. But suddenly my principal changed her mind and selected me to go for the programme. The Radio Ceylon people sent berth tickets for the principal to accompany the student. When I was first told the principal was coming with me I had jitters. But suddenly I didn't know what made her to change the plan she called my mother and asked her to accompany me. Well, you could imagine the happiness my mother had. New clothes were stitched for me, and I and my mother travelled to the capital. We went and stayed with one of my father's cousins, an uncle of mine, who had only one daughter, who was a musician. His wife, my aunt, was very witty and used raw language at times. Usually when any relatives went to the capital, they stayed with this uncle. It was more like a hostel, every season there would be somebody at their house. My uncle was a very interesting person and was working as the secretary at the parliament. That was my first trip to the capital. The day arrived, my uncle accompanied my mother and me to the Radio Ceylon office where we were taken into the studio, and the visitors, who accompanied the candidates, sat as audience. The announcer called one after the other. When my turn came, I went and sang the song which I did perfectly. But the reading that followed was not satisfactory. The girl who won the competition was already a radio artist who took part in children's programme. Therefore her performance in reading was better than mine. I lost the competition but for my mother it was a great adventure to go to the radio station and listen one of her daughters singing.

A few years later one of the juries, whose family was well-known to my father, came to work at the boys 'college. When he visited us he commented on my singing and said I got the highest for the singing but it was unfortunate my reading was not that good. I never thought later in my life I would be a permanent radio artist, but the sad thing was, the first song I sang was soon after my mother died. I continued to work as an artist. But my father was very proud of me.

Because we had a Christian community there was YMCA, YWCA and JICCF where I was a regular singer. The renowned colleges and schools presented their singers and choirs but I represented my school as a soloist. I had a mathematics teacher, who was also a pianist, a very soft person. For one of the united Christian gatherings, she trained me to sing a very popular song "Just a closer walk with thee" but she gave me some variations which were only composed by her. So when I started to sing on the stage there were some teachers from other colleges, who hummed the melody but were surprised to see the variations, which was quickly noted by my sister, who was sitting behind them. Later she told how they appreciated the song; even now this is one of my favourite songs.

There were concerts for tickets for fund raising in our area. I was always asked to give a performance. I had another girl, who was senior to me, who sang with me sometimes. It was in one of those programmes I was noted by a total stranger, and not from my community, who was following me when I went to school. The nape of my neck itched from the strain of resisting the impulse to look back, I forced myself. To my surprise I was only fourteen and my fan was about thirty. Afterwards he used to come to all the programmes I sang. His very presence intimidated me. We never talked but felt each other's presence. My parents knew about it, my brothers knew about it but for them it was nothing serious. I discussed this with my father, who was always my guide and he told me "You should forget the whole thing." I did not know where he went after two years and where he lived. That was a turning point in my life. It still haunts me. Even now I have a sharp memory of his face and later on, when I was in Germany, one day I dreamt about him. I told my husband and he said jokingly "Why don't you put an advertisement on the papers to look for him?"

Chapter 34

Speech contests success and down fall

I was sent to the declamation contest for English practically every year. My father would write the speech for me and I memorised and delivered. First I was trained by my father therefore the teachers did not have much work to do. They were VTA (area) and then NPTA (province) competition. My father was usually a jury for these competitions: especially for the seniors but not for my group. Once I totally forgot about the competition and went to school with the normal sandals. My English teacher was very angry and sent me to the girls' hostel to get ready with the shoes and socks. When I combed my lose hair into plaits and came she said "you are not going to win this time". After delivering the speech a gleeful feeling of anticipation invaded my heart. Yes, I won that time competing with fifteen of the other competitors from different schools. It was the same thing with the music competitions. I was always sent and I often won. But I could not deny the inner feeling during the delivery. Sometimes my throat went dry as Sahar. There was a fright you would have to stand before lines of faces that had become wet and shaky through the nervous water in your eyes. But I always remembered to detach my mind from all audience directions to dwell only on the words.

Once, my name was mistakenly given as a last minute option for the inter school Tamil essay competition. The theme given was" My favourite book." I had just finished reading a novel titled *Alai Osai*[45] written by *Kalki,* who was one of the famous authors in India. It was a gripping love story so vivid in my mind that I was able to write and review the book. When I came out of the hall the others were discussing and I heard that all of them had chosen a book from the literature or classics which were far-fetched for me. I had to compete with the advanced level students while I was still in the tenth grade. I returned home filled with bitterness thinking about the rubbish I had written. My heart sunk. I lost all my hope. I did not even tell about which book I wrote thinking that they might laugh. When the results came it was announced that I got the first prize in the competition. After that the teachers acknowledged my knowledge both in Tamil and English. Experience had taught me never to indulge in false modesty.

---

[45] Sound of the waves

Certificate obtained for Declamation Contest in 1965 VTA

Those certificates helped me a lot with interviews I had at the broadcasting service, where I became the editor for the magazine.

GLORIANA SELVANATHAN

Back to the Bible

(Incorporated in Sri Lanka by Act of Parliament, No. 17
of 1972 as 'Back to the Bible Broadcast, Ceylon')
120 A, Dharmapala Mawatha, Colombo 7, Sri Lanka. P.O. Box 1012, Colombo

RADIO BROADCASTS · LITERATURE · BOOKSHOP · CORRESPONDENCE COURSES · COUNSELLING · MUSIC · CASSETTE LIBRARY · EVANGELISM

20th August 1975

MISS G. GUNARUBINI GUNANAYAGAM

Miss Gunanayagam has been working with us since October 15, 1974. She will be
terminating her services with us as from August 31 on her own accord, to further
her studies.

We are sorry to lose her as she has been a very dedicated worker throwing the
full weight of her talents in every thing she undertook to do. As an accomplished
singer she has been of invaluable assistance to us in singing and acting for our
radio programmes and public rallies. As editor of our magazine "Sathiya Vasanam"
she has had signal success.

She was also responsible for translating a book by Theodore Epp, entitled "The
Master Secrets of Prayer," which was published and used in the work of this
ministry.

We wish her all the best for her future.

R.E. Abraham
MANAGING DIRECTOR

10th January, 1994

Miss Gunarubini Gunanayagam has since married and is now Mrs G.G. Selvanathan
(Rubini).

R.E. Abraham

Character certificate from the Broadcasting Service

I could not deny my downfalls in the speech and music competition. I and my
classmate won the VTA competition and we were selected to go to the NPTA
finals. It was a speech given by them to be memorized and to be delivered for
the competition. The text was about Florence Nightingale and we practiced
several times and were confident, perhaps I was overconfident. They say pride
came before downfall. When they called my name at the competition I went in
front because it was a room and not a stage. The VTA is different because we
see more known faces but NPTA was totally different. We see only strangers
and very strict looking judges. I started my speech and at one point I forgot the
whole thing. It was a total blackout. I was looking at the people trying to

remember but I simply could not. It was a forlorn hope. Therefore I had to return to my seat because you were given only a limited time. I sat down and felt a river of disappointment rushing through my stomach. Hot tears spurted down my cheeks. My eyes lost their sparkle and looked dull and lifeless. The next day one could see the tell-tale weepy red in the eyes. Nobody commented about it. That was the first and the last failure I had in the competition. My friend from my school won the competition. It was then that I realized, I am a person who could speak spontaneously and memorized versions were not my art. Later when I became a real stage performer both in music and speech, I never had any notes before me. I was quite comfortable only with a mental preparation and a spontaneous delivery.

Similar thing happened when I went for a music competition, I was the youngest in the group and the other girls were senior to me and quite matured. My teacher selected quite a difficult raga *Bhairavi*[46] with *Alarparanm* and *Swaras*. If you understand the classical music, sometimes we had to sing the *katpanaswara* in the middle of the beat or off beat. This was a big challenge for me and my teacher was also nervous whether I would sing that without any mistakes. I went to the stage and my teacher played the *Tampura* to take the pitch and I started to sing. There was one girl from my school seated in the front row and she was putting the *tala*[47] unconsciously. I concentrated in the singing, especially when the swaras came, I was very careful and sang without any mistake but when I finished the last swara and started the *charanam*[48] out of happiness I smiled on the stage. This was something the judges did not like and I did not get a place. I could not sleep for two days but then I learnt the lesson; in a competition you are not supposed to be light-hearted and must observe the stage rules. We all waited for my name to be announced but the secretary, who was there to announce the result, looked at me sadly and shook his head. The happiness was far removed from the flooding joy I had felt. I could not wait to get home and close the door to the world. When I came home nobody told anything but I was feeling sad. I had slept nothing all night making ghost of myself. My father said "You go for competitions not to win always but also to give chances for the others to win." They were good experiences. Then I realised stage performance

---

[46] Set classical melody

[47] beat

[48] stanza

was totally different from stage behaviour at a competition. When I was trained for the stage performances I was asked to smile which was not applicable for competitions at least then. Surprisingly I was never despond.

My mother wanted me to learn piano. I used to go to the school and use the school piano and when exams came, which was Trinity College Music exams, all the candidates were allowed to practice in the new piano at the principal's bungalow. That was a real procedure. There were huge verandas in the bungalow and each one of us would get a specific time. We had to go and stand outside till the maid came and allowed us to go to the piano. My teacher was a very strict person. She had her LTCL certificate and she was also a teacher at the boys' college. Whenever I made a mistake I used to get a knock on my fingers with the ruler. Anything disciplined was not my line. Therefore I found it difficult to concentrate and never passed the exams with honours but only with a merit. This was a disappointment for my mother. It became a strain to me because during the examination time I had to go to the town, stay with my aunt and cousins and attend regular classes at my teacher's house. I managed my third examination and then I stopped.

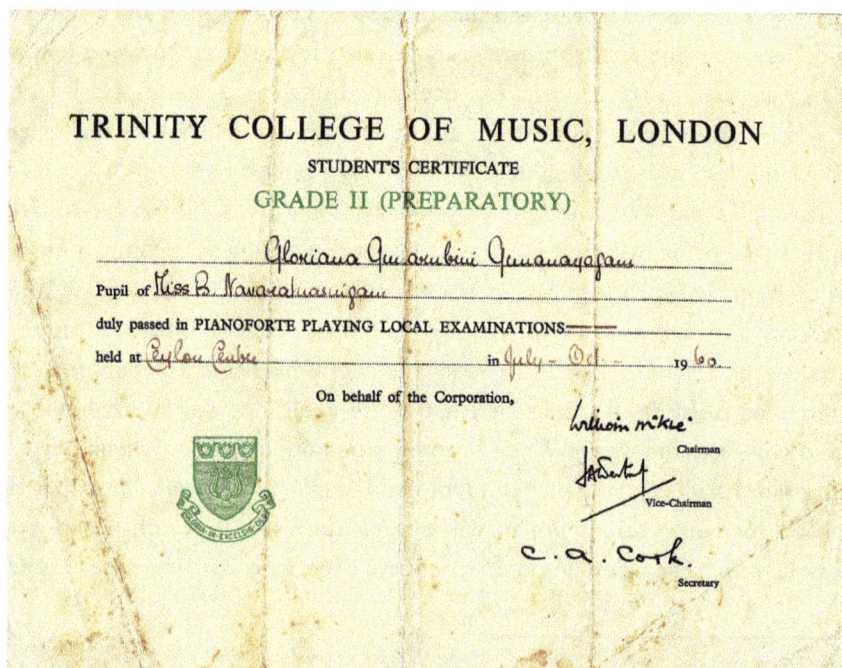

My 2nd grade piano certificate in 1960

Chapter 35

My interest in Girl Guides

Our principal was interested that our school must take part in brownies for the small children, girl guides and rangers for the senior students. I belonged to all three groups in the school. Once we finished the brownies time we joined the Girl Guide team. We had camps and annual jamborees at the old park in Jaffna. Almost all the schools had the teams, we had March past and other competitions and at the end we had a camp fire. It was there I was able to learn chorus singing. Once I became a ranger, we were asked to go for the international jamborees in the capital city where we were able to meet representatives from other countries and we were divided into groups and settled in camps.

Here I got acquainted with the Sinhalese girl Mangalika and later we were regular members to attend different camps in different parts of the island. I met some very interesting girls, who had wonderful talents. Mangalika was excellent in performing magic shows. On the first day it was a wonder for me. Ring vanishing, empty glasses getting pearls, selected cards being given, and many other tricks. At the end of the camp I was so curious that I asked her to tell me the secret of it, Well, I got it. I practiced that in different events and at different times of my life. Once there was an annual dinner for the teachers and senior students at our school. I did the magic of making the ring vanish and finding it in possession of another person. I chose a very innocent teacher as the victim. At the end of the show she was in tears telling "I never took it".

I once performed at the Indian university. There we had some very simple Indian girls, who believed in witchcraft, in magicians, and all those things, so when I performed it for the college day, the next day some of them were looking at me with a suspicious look. I could hear them talking "She has witchcraft" because of a very interesting incident that happened on the college day. The hall was filled with people and some of the lecturers were nuns. So all of them assembled there to watch my magic show, and one of them was the vanishing of the ring. You request from the guests to give a valuable ring. I put it into my palm and covered it with a cloth. Then, who ever wished, can put his or her hand under the cloth and feel the ring, to make sure that the ring was there. So I went one round and then when I came back to my place, the ring was gone. There was a big sensation; they all looked at the last person who touched the ring. Suddenly I told very solemnly "I am sorry to say, that a very special person is having the ring." Then I pointed to one of the nuns and said, "It is in your cassock pocket". Not only her but the whole crowd was shocked. She started to protest "I did not take, I did not take." But I said "I am sorry but it is in your pocket." She put her hand inside the cassock pocket and found the ring. Only I knew it was a quick movement but all the others believed it was true, that I had some magic power.

Once we had camp for the captains of the ranger companies of the schools. It was one of the tea estates belonging to the deputy commander of the Girl Guides Association. There we were trained for every situation when we hold a camp for our company. One was how to handle if somebody is kidnapped or missed. One day there was a big scream because when the members went to take food, they found the quarter master missing and the food tent was in a mess. We were all alarmed and asked to look for traces. We were running around the whole estate, and suddenly we heard a scream and we all ran there and found that one of the leaders dressed as a man had tied up the quarter master pretending to be kidnapped. Then we were called and given instructions how to behave in such situations. It was witnessed by the local people living in the estate. The next day one of the members informed that her watch and a piece of jewellery were missing. And that was a real theft. They tried their best to find but were not successful. A crime playfully done led to a real crime being committed.

Chapter 36

My parents' village

My parents' village was about three miles from the town. It proved a complete contrast to our town. Mostly sand covered lanes with lots Palmyra trees. There was one bus going through the village every one hour. If we missed the bus we used to walk the distance through by lanes. We had a very old aunt and uncle, my father's cousin, and his family, who were Hindus. My parents had a very old concrete house where they grew up. And my father's cousin lived there. There was a big mango tree and lot of Palmyra trees from which we got mangos and tubers of Palmyra respectively every year. My parents also had a land with coconut trees and occasionally our servants were sent to pluck the coconuts from the trees. The mango tree was not the usual sweet one but very sour. Therefore they plucked these mangos and my mother made them into pickles and dried them, and used them for the curries when acidity was needed. Especially for sprats, a kind of small fish, when those sour mangos were added, it gave an extra taste.

Most of the relatives, who lived in the village were strangers for me because only our parents visited them and not us. But I have a very good memory about my father's cousin Uncle Muthiah, who was a very hot tempered man. Actually he was fanfaronade. He had a walking stick and a Ghandi specs and he was a very proud man. His wife was a very soft woman and one of the best aunts I had because whenever we visited her or she visited us, she brought home made *jaggery* and other snacks. When we visited her, she never allowed me to eat by myself, but mixed the food and fed me, making me to sit on her lap. But when she died, my uncle was lonely and had problems with his children and one day he simply disappeared. There was a search all over the place. Five miles from the village were the sand dunes for a long stretch without any vegetation. In the summer time you could not walk because one could see sand, sand and sand everywhere and could easily lose the orientation in the dunes. After two days search my uncle's characteristic specs and his walking stick were seen beside a skeleton. My father went to identify that and that skeleton was brought and criminated. It was such a tragic ending for such a proud man. "Presumably he started to walk and lost his orientation and went deeper and deeper into the dunes instead of the main road and the foxes did the rest of the work" said my father.

Another cousin of my father, Uncle John, was an Ayurvedic Physician. He had three sons and two daughters. My father believed in his medicine, especially when it is connected to throat. When I had some problems with my throat I got medicines from him. But he was a funny man. He had a typical laugh, which we could recognize even at a distance and his wife, my aunt, was hard of hearing, therefore talked only with mouth movements, but a very affectionate woman. Her ideas were seldom conveyed by any other means than nods and shakes of the head. His eldest daughter was a nurse and later married the district medical officer who was a cousin and it was a fixed marriage by his mother. His third son and the daughter were proposed to another of my cousins, a brother and a sister, as intermarriage. For the wedding all the preparations were made and this doctor, the two bridegrooms and another friend went to another town Valvettithurai, which was famous for selling saris from India. They went to buy the bridal sari for both the brides. There was a place called 'Vallai', an open stretch of land with roads coming from different directions. While they were travelling on this road, they met with an accident and one of the bridegroom and the doctor died. So the wedding house became a funeral house. That was one of the biggest blows in our family but after some time the bridegroom, who survived, married the sister of the bridegroom who died. But his sister did not marry and continued to work as a nurse.

The big beach in the village was directly in front of the Bay of Bengal, which was my father's favourite swimming spot. We were never allowed to go there alone. My parents always wanted to have a Methodist church in their village. Of course they had lands, scattered all over the village given by their parents and grandparents. And one such plot was near the main road behind the village's school. Originally that school belonged to the Methodist Mission before it was taken over by the government; therefore it was a good idea for my parents to build a church in this land. But it was not an easy task. My parents had six children to look after, all going for higher education, therefore they could not afford to build a church in their own money. So they donated the land and asked the permission of the church council to build a church there. There were considerable amount of Christians living in the village. Therefore the church granted permission but could not give any funds. It was my mother, who travelled all over the island collecting funds from friends and relatives. At last they had enough funds to build the church. Nothing was impossible for a willing heart. There was a popular mason (takes contracts to build buildings), who was very dark with long hair made into a knot and golden earrings. He was called by my mother and the structure of the church was discussed and my father laid the first foundation stone with his initials SVG on it. Even now the church has my father's initials. The inauguration of the church was a big event in the village. We went as special guests and a special service was conducted by the Methodist church president, later on there was a celebration with food and drinks. Every year they celebrated the anniversary of the church and we used to go as a family and participated in it. I do not know why but I felt someone special when I went to this church.

There were different families in our village, who visited us with small presents like fruits or fish just to show their respect to my family. One of them, Ponniah, had a squeaky voice and he had four children. He was quite young when he suddenly passed away. We all loved him because he was so affectionate. My parents decided to support the children in their education, especially with books and uniforms. But then they had another idea that they would informally adopt one of the daughters. There were no strict rules when you have a child in the house in my country. Even young servants were at home and it was a custom. This little girl Satkunam, who was about four years younger to me, came and stayed with us. She was a puny little thing. Her presence had a duel role. With all my brothers away from home due to studies and jobs, I had a good playmate. She was admitted in our school and we used to go together to the school, especially when I reached my puberty. According to the tradition, girls were not allowed to go alone, even for the school at least for the first year after puberty. My parents were happy that I had someone to go with.

One night we heard a crooning noise. Then my mother woke up and found that the girl was crying. When asked she said she had ear ache. She looked so vulnerable and my mother took care of her. The most interesting thing happened a year after. My father and I went to the cinema hall to see the film "Count of Monte Cristo" on my birthday. In fact, she and I had birthdays on the same day. Although she could not understand English we decided to take her. While we were watching the film a message came from my mother that my sister was ill. In a hurry both of us left the cinema hall forgetting the girl. Those big chairs had hidden her figure and in half way through the film she had gone to sleep. When the show was over the watchers were checking and found this little girl. She woke up and started to cry and they asked where she lived. She told my father's name and they all knew my father. So a man from the theatre accompanied her to our house. Only when we saw her, we remembered her.

Chapter 37

My direct and indirect grand parents

During my parents time most members of the family married among the cousins. My mother's younger brother did the same. My aunt Thevenesam was the only daughter to her parents. She lost her mother when she was a child and grew up in a girl's hostel. She became a teacher. Her father Nalathamby, in a way a grandfather to me, was an interesting man. I knew him only when he was in his eighties. His daughter referred him as the "Pentecost old man". He had read the bible thoroughly and could quote any verse. His Tamil, that is our native language, was pure and not colloquial. It was a pleasure to hear him talking that language. He often had brilliant eidetic memory. To watch his facial expression was an experience of its own. He winced and coughed as if screwing up his face a normal preliminary to clearing his throat. In his opinion all the educated people were fools. One day, while we the children, were sitting in the beach and talking to him, he said "Ghandi is a fool". Then he made a pause and added "Gunanayagam (my father) is a B.A Fool" Because my father held a Degree from Cambridge. My father hearing that only smiled. He was an idiosyncrasy. During his last days, he lived with his daughter, my aunt, and uncle in Trincomalee in the east of the island. He became seriously ill, and wished to come to his home town. My uncle hired a car and brought him to north. Somewhere on the way he must have passed away.

They arrived home to find him dead. They rushed to get the coffin. That was the first funeral at our house. Quickly sheds were put and the dobby tied white cloth everywhere according to the tradition. It was quite a new experience for me to see the crowd, and food arriving from the neighbours. Till the funeral was over, cooking was not done in the house. Friends and neighbours in and around the town would bring food and coffee. It was more of an obligation for people, who had received the same. My mother always sent food for most of them. So food started to come. It was a lot more than needed. Usually they asked and informed when they brought the food. But that was not happening to us. Food came in abundance with or without informing. According to the tradition, after the eighth day we cooked a big meal and invited all the people, who attended the funeral and sent food. All these things were new and exciting for me more than the funeral and the meaning of death. I was too young at that time to know about death.

My maternal grandfather Rev. Eliathamby had six children, three girls and three boys. My mother was the eldest. He was a Methodist pastor and served in different stations of the island. He resembled the first Prime minister of Sri Lanka Hon. D.S. Senenayake. He was very tall and heavy built and his characteristic moustache was his best feature. He used to visit us while he was in service and stayed with us for sometime visiting his other daughter, my aunt, with whom we had little contact. When he lost my grandmother he used to invite my brothers to come and stay in the parsonage during the holidays. When he retired he spent his days sharing with his children. My uncle Gunaratnam built a house in the village and he stayed there. Whenever he stayed with us he observed what was happening but never interfered with the administration of the house. My father was the head of the house and he had the greatest respect. I had three remarkable incidents. Once I was sitting in front of him crossing my legs. He called me and said in soft words that women should not cross their legs and sit before men. It was impolite and unfeminine. Well I did obey him then. Long after that, when I asked my father about that: he said it was only an old tradition. But ironically my grandfather could not control his daughter in law, who was the principal of the Nurses Training College in the capital. She was highly educated and went to foreign countries to get further training and adapted the western style sharing the idea, women were not second class citizens. She always crossed her legs and sat and my grandfather never uttered a word. The second thing he told me was girls should not whistle. I used to whistle the songs I liked but I stopped that when he was there. Again out of curiosity I asked my father about that and he told the same answer. So I had to compromise and out of respect stopped whistling when he was in the vicinity. One day he called me and asked me to put the thread in the needle because his eyes sight was not good. When I pulled the thread quite long he smiled and said, "One could see a thrifty woman by the way she handled the thread. You should always take the thread long enough and not too long". After that piece of advice I tried, my best to follow that when I was tempted otherwise.

One should understand the background in which I grew up, morning prayers in the house, in the school the assembly prayers, then learning religion in the school and doing Christian activities in the school, then attending Sunday services, participating in the Sunday school, conventions, in a way we were saturated with Christianity. But it was a beautiful thing that my father never insisted on formalities of the religion. When my grandfather retired from his service as a pastor, he contributed little money to the central Methodist council and this was awarded to children, who participated in the Christian scholarship examinations conducted all over the island in all Methodist schools. Whatever said and done, in studies I was good in the school, therefore such scholarships I often won. And one day my grandfather called me. He had the annual magazine from the Methodist council, where the names of the prize-winners were published. Once he called me and showed, Reverend EK. Eliathamby's scholarship prize, and below that, won by Gunarubini Gunanayagam from Point Pedro Methodist Girls 'High School. He said he was proud that his granddaughter won his scholarship with an undiminished smile on his face.

My grandfather Rev. Eliyathamby was fortunate to see his great-grand-daughter and great-grand-son before he died. Suddenly he developed a chest pain which was obviously a heart attack. He was taken to the hospital and a few days later he passed away. He was 81 years when he died. It was in January 1960, a few days after my nephew was born. Till the end, even at the age of eighty one, he was never crotchety. That was our second funeral in the house that I saw. Because he was a Methodist pastor and served in different parishes, a lot of people came for the funeral. That day it heavily rained, there was thunder and rain outside, suddenly my cousin, my uncle's daughter said "Come, let us go and see grandfather in the coffin. This will be the last time for us to see him." I was a little afraid, but holding her hands we went to the coffin and looked at him. Although there was electricity they always kept an oil lamp at the top of the coffin. My cousin was commenting "Look, he is smiling". A fleeting bitter humour swallowed instantly in the reality of loss. I still have the image of that face when suddenly the electricity went off. A kind of tightness came to my throat. But my cousin said "I am not afraid to stand here." And I believed it and stood with her.

My mother's second brother Sam, sitting in a corner, was the one who cried a lot. It was strange because he was always a lively person making others to laugh. A father is a father. Being a Methodist pastor my grandfather's funeral service was in the church, a privilege given only for the pastors. It was a beautiful service with all his children and grand children circling the coffin and singing. He was buried near my grandmother and his second daughter. Soon after the funeral many of the relatives, who came from the outstations, went away. My mother planned a memorial service at the church, where I sang a song especially for him.

Being a grandparent is something special. They are the only people, who never get angry or try to control the activities of the grandchildren. They get angry with their children but not with the grandchildren. It is the special relationship they have, which I realised, when I had my granddaughter. Of course, we missed our grandfather for several years.

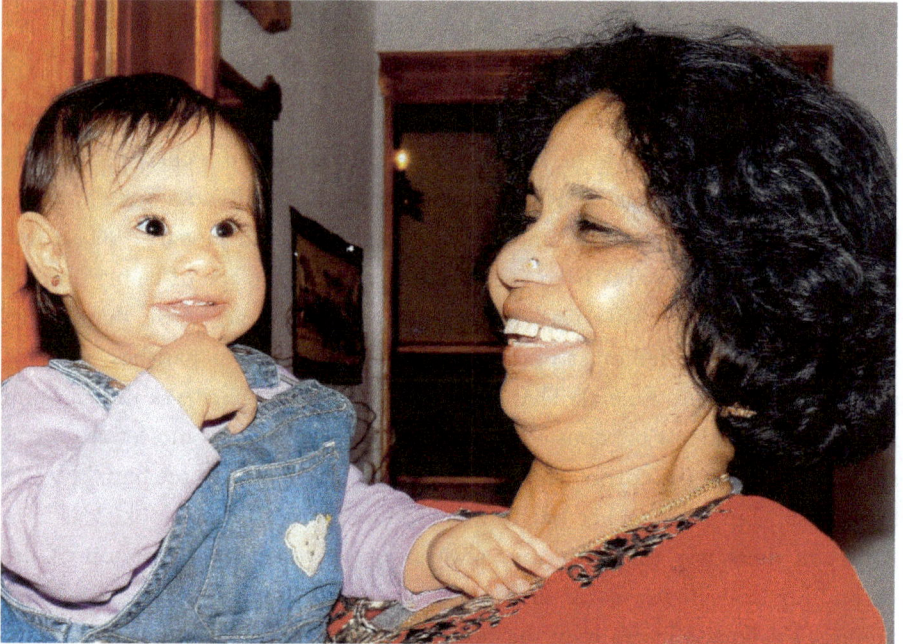

My granddaughter Mina is a turning point in my life.

My paternal grandmother Ponnu lived up to the age of 91. My father was her eldest son and my father had a younger brother and a sister. Due to the early death of his father he was the man of the house. My aunt was married to her cousin and had seven children. And my father's brother worked in the railway for some time and then became a Pentecost pastor and he was the chief pastor for the whole mission in Singapore and Sri Lanka. His mother was taken into the Faith Home, which was the church and the residence of mission workers, and was looked after. Where ever my uncle went, she also went together. She was in many hilly stations but Rakuana was her favourite.

When she was about 89 my uncle Pastor Nadarajah requested my father to keep her in our house. So she was living with us in the house, a very proud woman. Because of her bad eyesight she used to ask me to bring water and to tie a piece of cloth to the neck of the jug so that nothing fell into it. Her manner was peremptory, a little off handed, with a cool and controlled voice. Due to her age she was evanescent. She would be always praying. We got accustomed to her prayers but then my mother told "If you listen to her prayers, there are things that she does not want to happen in the house." She never called her husband by his name, but referred him as *"thambiayya[49]"*. And she used to pray that he should come and take her away. One day my eldest sister and her friends were talking about something in the room and laughing. She misunderstood and in the night prayers, she said "God, please punish the people, who laughed at me" Hearing that my mother and father only smiled.

---

[49] Means father of my son

Chapter 38

Superstitions in the house

Being a Christian and being a pastor's daughter never prevented my mother from observing the local and traditional superstitions. The prediction of the lizard was quite famous. The small reptile lived in houses, and was often seen on the walls, occasionally making an utterance, was feared by many people. When it fell on the head or on your right side then death was predicted. When the utterance came from right above, then good message would come. Usually it is cream in colour but when there was a black one it was unlucky. My father was dead against those beliefs and quoted this idiom "The lizard that predicted the future of the others fell into the pot of hot porridge".

There were particular people with negative vibrations. When these people came people avoided going out at that moment and went a little later. When you comb the hair you should spit on the fallen hair before you throw it. The usual cat crossing your way meant you would not be successful on the mission you wanted to do. We were never allowed to wear black dresses for it was the sign of death. When you went to a funeral or visited the grave yard, you must take a head bath. The most popular one was the evil eye. If you went for a wedding or a function and the people had appreciated your appearance, then when you came home they took red chillies, pepper and salt touched your whole body and put it in the fire. If it did not give a smell then evil eye was there.

You should never keep the broom stick, where you could see when you got up from the sleep or when you went out. To see a widow was a bad omen. There was a particular nocturnal bird similar to the owl. If this bird made an utterance my mother always spit three times, because it would bring some bad news. I think my eldest sister continued with these than the others. Whenever we travel and pass the grave yard she would put a cross on the fore head of her children. When there is a funeral the dead body was kept in the south north direction. Breaking a mirror or a glass framed picture was a bad omen. When somebody was sitting on the floor with stretched legs we should not walk over that. If we did we had to go back the same way. If there were quick beats on the left shoulder or eye that indicated good omen and on the right side it was the opposite. If by accident, turmeric powder spills on girls then news of marriage was expected. But they were observed only by my mother and my eldest sister whereas my father was just the opposite. He never bothered because he believed in himself. May be that was the reason the rest of us in the family were not particular about it.

My father was never ever frightened of ghosts. His theory of ghosts was "If at all ghosts exist they are in a different dimension and they cannot harm us. People get unnecessarily frightened if or when they saw a ghost" Soon after the suicide of our neighbour's servant the house was empty. Nobody wanted to live in that or rent that house. That house was in my parents' care. Occasionally my father used to go and sleep there. This suicide story was known to us but not for visitors. Some years later, there was a young boy about fifteen, who came to learn under my brother in law for his OL examinations. My third brother and this boy went to the beach in the evenings. And there they met other friends. One of them was the son of a man, who also committed suicide because he had insomnia. His wife was a teacher at the Boys' College. And the children studied at the boys' college.

One day, when they were sitting in the beach, the talk of ghosts became their topic, and whether tumbler talking was true or not, also cropped up. Then my brother Chelva had a good idea to test that. Without telling the other boys about the suicide that happened in that house, he took them, and on the veranda wrote down the ABC as the usual procedure they had for tumbler talking, switched off the lights and had only a candle. He kept a glass upside down and they decided not to touch the glass, so they held their hands above the glass, and called a ghost. Nothing happened when my brother did but then he remembered the other boy's father committed suicide so he asked him to try. And the boy called his father, suddenly the tumbler started to move. They were in such a panic, shock and fear they stopped and switched on the light. But the electricity was cut, they were in total darkness. All three of them came running out of the house. One boy went to his house and the two of them, the visitor and my brother, came home but did not utter a word. But in the night the visitor started to have fever. Nobody knew the reason but he said he wanted to go home. And the next day he packed off and went. He never came for tuition in the future. The secret of this adventure was revealed by my brother years after this happened. But it was an irony that when my father gave our house to my eldest sister we had to move to this house. Maybe because of my father's strong mind, we never had any such thing, although I was not aware of this incident at that time.

There were people who were involved in witch craft. I had a class mate Sakunthala, who was the daughter of such person. They were Malayalies. They were descendents from Kerala India. She used to tell some frightening stories about people who came to her father with evil wishes, and how she helped her father to draw some images on a copper plate. She also told that they collected personal things like the hair, the sand foot print and the spit from that person to burry with that charmed plate. She liked me because I helped her in her studies. Then we went to different classes in the eighth grade, and I lost contact with her. I had forgotten the whole story because it was not acceptable.

Some years later an unusual incident happened in my life connected to superstition. My father was a well known teacher for Latin. During that time, Latin was important for law students, and one of the languages you could take for your Cambridge Bachelor degree, as an external candidate. Therefore a lot of men and women came to my father to learn privately. They came not only from my town but also from other towns. A lady teacher Navaratnammal also came once. She learned for two to three hours at a stretch and had a break for lunch. At that time, my father had retired and we stayed temporarily in a big house just opposite the public beach. I was still a teenager. Next to our house was a man, who had ten children. But his wife would always look as young as ever. When she went to the cinema with her daughters nobody would believe she was their mother. Her husband was a proud man doing whole sale business in fish. They were doing very well until suddenly he fell ill for no reason and was almost bed ridden. They believed it was the curse of a demon, which could be done by some special curse created by those people, who dealt with such things. We never experienced but heard a lot about how they did it. When this witch craft was done that person would fall ill without a cause and left the place or slowly died.

On this particular day I and my father's student Navaratnammal went to the beach and looked for shells. It was afternoon and the sun was in its peak. Suddenly I saw something shining, which made my eyes to look at that spot. Thinking it was a piece of jewellery I went and took it. It was a thin copper plate and there were some inscriptions on it. I thought it was something valuable and ran home and showed it to my father. When he looked at that first he smiled and then took it and put it in the fire. He also warned me not to tell my mother because she might get frightened. Later he explained about this evil thing. Our neighbour became better and he was back to normal. But somehow or the other our neighbours came to know about it. May be they heard us discussing or someone else saw that. After some weeks the woman saw me and asked about it. She also said because it was removed and burned her husband became better. I could not give a plausible reason for that neither my father. The only thing he said was people with strong will power would not be affected by such things. But I still wonder

Chapter 39

A journey from Jaffna to the central province

This chapter I write for the young people displaced from my country and have no chance of returning, for the tourists who may visit, and Sri Lankans, who would visit these places after a long break. They could see the differences from my time in Sri Lanka to that of present Sri Lanka.

There was a time our school principal allowed the classes to go out on picnics to different places. We started in the morning and returned in the evening wearing our coloured dresses and not the uniforms. This was fun for us because we travelled by a van, opened all four sides; we sang songs and shouted, clapped and enjoyed the picnic. Usually two teachers were in charge for us. In one such picnic my physics teacher Miss Ayathurai brought a mouth organ. I can play the mouth organ well. On our way back I borrowed the mouth organ from her and played the music. We had good fun, and on the return trip they dropped me home, on their way to the school that I brought the mouth organ with me to my house. The next morning I took that to the school intending to return it. It was quite early and our class room was next to the principal's office. There were only two girls and I started to play the mouth organ quite loudly. Suddenly the door opened and the clerk from the office came and said, the principal ordered her to take away the mouth organ, and she took the mouth organ with her. Now the predicament was, how to answer my physics teacher. So I contemplated for some time during the lunch break. Buoyed up with the confidence of youth, I went straight to the principal and stood there. Usually we had to tell the reason to the clerk and stay with the clerk, till she allowed us to go. But I went straight to the principal's table. She was writing something and looked at me over the specks. "Yes, what do you want?" I just said "I want my mouth organ", "Take it and go" she said. The clerk was surprised; my friends were surprised that I did not get any piece of advice from her about my behaviour. In the afternoon I had my physics class. My physics teacher came to the class. Usually she was forgetful. But that day with a frown on her face she said, "A funny thing happened this morning. I saw my mouth organ on the principal's table. And I did not know what my mouth organ was doing on her table" When she heard the story she could not help herself laughing.

Those class trips became popular in the school. Especially during the weekends one class or the other went on day trips. I think our ninth grade was special. All the talented children were in one class. For music competitions, declamation competitions, essay competitions and sport competitions many girls were selected from our class and because of that our principal had a good impression about our class. One day we sat together and thought about a long tour visiting the historical places predominantly Sinhalese areas. We never feared any racial attacks or even racism those days. That was the time we all lived in peace and harmony. The plan was first put forward to our class teacher and the English teacher Mrs. Samuel, whose husband was a teacher at the Boy's College. We needed a man to accompany for emergency. In the sixties, in our country women depended on men for certain things, which they dared not do alone. One of them was a woman travelling alone for long distances, although occasionally people did that. When her husband agreed, the next step was to put the proposition to the principal. It was always a case of who is to bell the cat. Taking the courage the teachers went and discussed the matter with our principal. To our surprise she agreed to the proposal but advised that in every town we visited, we had to make sure of a safe place to stay. Plans were made with the highest intensity.

The route was to visit the Central Province, to see a lot of historical places important for our education, and then moving to the hill station to visit the famous University and tea plantations together with the most holy Buddhist temple, with the relics of Lord Buddha. It is important to name these places for the benefit of the people interested in the geography and the history of Sri Lanka. We wanted to visit Anuradhapura, Polenaruwa, Dambulla, Sigiria, Kandy, Peredenia and Newara Eliya. We needed a base in Anuradhapura to stay overnight and in Kandy to stay for a few days. Kandy was not a problem because we had the Methodist High school, which belonged to the same denomination as my school Methodist Girl's high school in Point Pedro. But the central province was predominantly Sinhalese Buddhist area and we did not have anyone whom we could approach for a stopover.

I took this problem to my father because this tour was my dream. My father thought for some time and said," I know someone who could help you". When he said who it was I was speechless. It was the deputy speaker of the parliament, whose constituency was Anuradhapura. He was an old student of my father at the Boy's College. Without any hesitance he wrote a letter to him. After a few days my principal got a call from the deputy speaker and she was highly excited.

Then he asked for Miss Gunanayagam. My second sister was teaching at the girls' school. A clerk was sent with the message to my sister and my sister hurried to the office to take the call. When she introduced herself the Deputy speaker said "I heard from your father you are coming on a trip to Anuradhapura. I have made arrangements for your group to stay at the Anuradhapura Convent". Then my sister explained that it was not for her but for her younger sister and she would convey the message gladly. To know he actually wanted to talk with me was the greatest honour. In that way our trip was fixed.

Well the plan was made; it merely remained to be executed. Words could not describe how we all felt when our principal finally showed the green flag. For one week that was the talk in the class. Simultaneously, we prepared our bags at home and the day dawned for us to start the journey. Our class teacher, another junior teacher, the English teacher and her husband accompanied us. The van was packed with the bags and people. I, being the brave one, asked our principal what she would like us to bring for her. She replied "Bring some boys" with a sense of humour. For most of us it was the first time leaving home for such a long time. We enjoyed the journey. Throughout the journey we sang, spoke, laughed and slept. It was night when we reached the first stop Anuradhapura so we directly went and slept at the hall provided for us by the nuns. They were personally there to receive us because it was the Deputy Speaker's request.

The next morning we went on a round trip of the Town. We visited the Holy Banyan tree brought and planted by Sangamitha, the daughter of the great Emperor Asoka of India, after he became a Buddhist. It was centuries old and had decorated sandalwood pillars to hold it from breaking. Pilgrims and Buddhist monks were all over chanting *"Butham saranam kachammi sangam sarnam kachami"*[50] Then we went and saw the *Dagoba Ruwanvelisiya* built by Dhuta Gemunu. We went to see the thousand pillared king's court where some of the pillars were damaged. That was in 1962. I do not know how many pillars remain now. It is twenty eight years since I left the country and fifty years since I visited those places.

---

[50] Prayer of the Buddhists

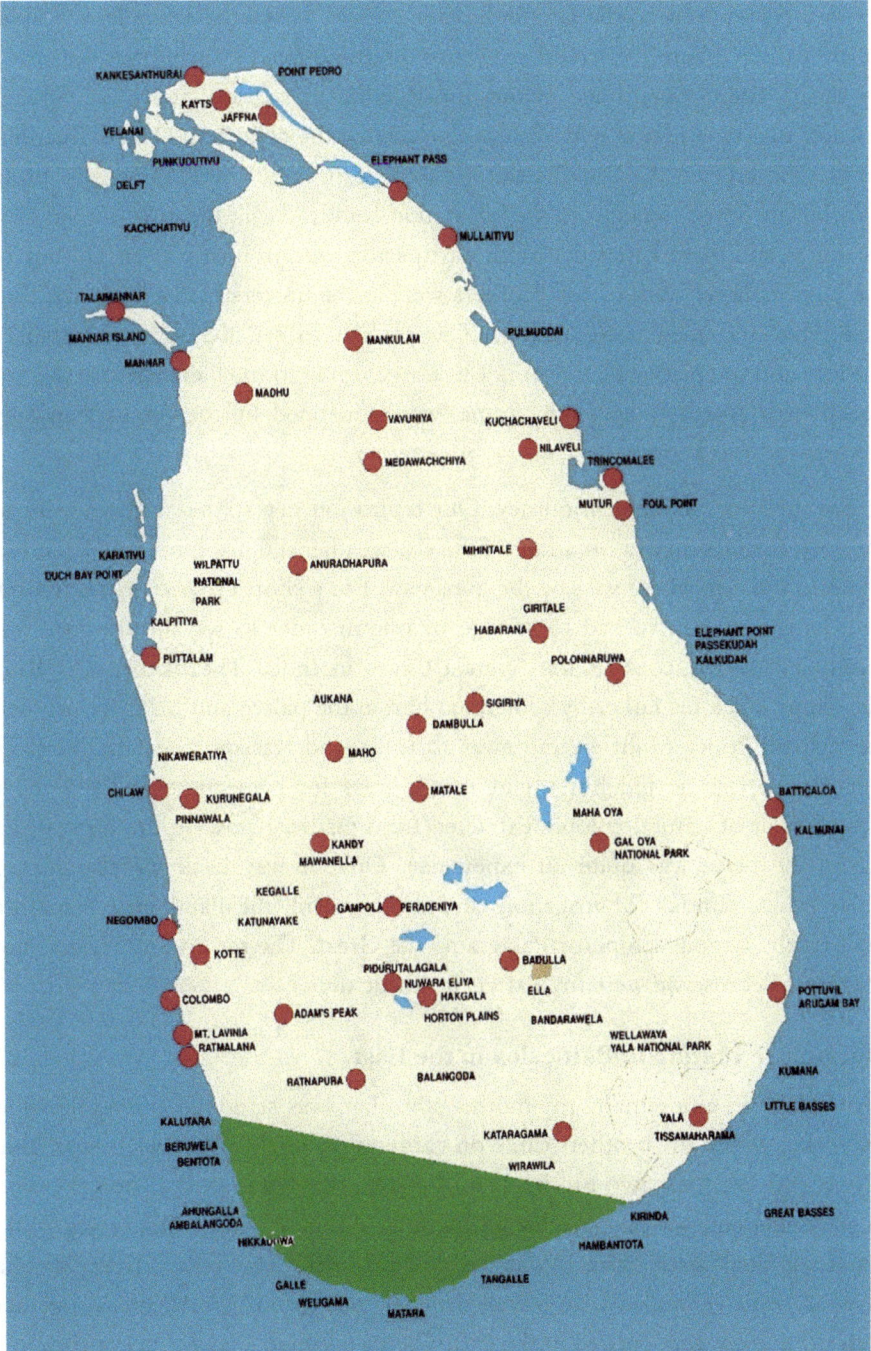

Map of Sri Lanka showing the towns I visited and the area I did not visit in dark.

From there we went to the Dambulle cave temple, a rock cave temple, a wonder of the nature, where you could see water dropping from a spring but only drop by drop. There were huge statues of Buddha in various positions. Strange enough we saw a Hindu god Vishnu also among the collection. Those Buddhist kings, who erected the Buddha statues, gave respect for the Hindu gods. From Dambulla we went straight to the hill station Kandy. Again the girls' school gave us refuge and there I met the Methodist pastor, who in turn was an old boy of the boys' college. Both of my brothers were at the university in Peredenya. So I met them and then continued to Neware Elia to see the famous botanical gardens and the place called Seetha Eliya. According to the literature, Seetha, the queen of a North Indian king Rama, was kidnapped by the Sri Lankan king Ravana and was kept there.

It was time for our return journey. Our return journey started and we went to the rock fortress Sigirya on a rainy day. The weather did not hinder us from our climb to the top, where we saw the lions paw. For a short distance it was narrow and dangerous but we had to go one by one in order to see the frescoes that resembled the frescoes of the Agenda Caves in India. The history was King Kassiappa killed his father by cementing him in the palace and his elder brother, the rightful Prince Muhalen, ran away to India, and Kasiappa became the king. But due to fear he hid himself in this fortress for some time and did those frescoes out of natural colours extracted from plants. Knowing the history and seeing the place was quite an experience. On our way back we also visited Polonaruwa, famous for irrigation, and the big dam, the Parakrama Samuthra built by the famous Emperor Paragrama the Great. The return journey was not that great because we were tired after the hectic tour.

Our private venture to Batticaloa in the East

My uncle Rev. Gunratnam, my mother's brother, was stationed at Thirukovil in Batticaloa. When my brothers came on vacation my uncle invited us to visit him. My second sister, my two brothers and I started that big journey. There were no direct trains and we had to change trains at different places before we could reach our final destination. It was fun and my uncle received us. Every day he planned some outing and we travelled in his old Austin car. All of us together with my cousin were packed in the car. When we visited a pastor in Ampara, my uncle parked the car in the town to buy something. When he started the car, the engine was making some funny noise and would not start. You could imagine the embarrassment of being in an old car in the middle of the town, packed to the brim with people, and the car refusing to start. My third brother Chelva made some funny noise combining with the song 'Young ones'. Fortunately, my uncle was wearing his pastor's collar and some parish member seeing that came to our rescue. After half an hour our journey back home started. My uncle never got discouraged with his car. In fact he was proud that it took him everywhere.

Another day we visited the animal sanctuary in Lavugale and Yale to see the elephants in their natural life. We were not allowed to go near but were given a complicated gadget to watch them. One day my uncle took me to meet my old servant Sunthary, who looked after me, when I was a baby. She was married and had children. Though I could not remember her she was delighted to see me. My uncle's neighbour Zamsudin was a Muslim and a good hunter. One day he brought wild rabbit meat as a delicacy for us to eat. That was the first time I ever tasted that. At home we never had it. Only once I tasted Venison at my neighbour's house, after he returned from one of his hunting trips to his estate. We returned home from the east bubbling with joy.

My visit to Negambo and Puttalam

Having seen one third of the island I had another opportunity to see the South on another occasion. My mother's third brother James, who was an accountant in the capital, was married to Poomalar aunty the principal of the Nurses Training College. They invited me to come and stay with them for two weeks. They had two little girls born after six years of marriage and I had a good time with them. One weekend they decided to go down the South to Puthalam, Chilaw and Negombo by car. We stayed in hotels, had nice fresh fish for our meal and saw the angry Indian Ocean.

In another place I had described my visit to Trincomalee in the East. Therefore I had seen more than eighty percent of my country at various stages of my life. I had visited the places marked in red in the map although I have not mentioned some of them because they were visited later in life at different times. What is marked in green were the towns I did not visit. I have no hope of seeing those places in the future and there is no guarantee they would be the same even if I were to visit them.

Chapter 40

My siblings

My eldest sister Gunamani Acca

Cecilia Gunamany Rajaratnam (nee Gunanayagam)

My eldest sister Acca (we called her as big sister and never use the name) was a character of her own. She was fair and beautiful, with long curly hair. At home she always kept to herself. Her bed was spotlessly clean and her trunk was neatly arranged and her drawers were tip top. In other words she never had haphazardness. She was an ardent reader and had a talent to narrate stories expressively. She was excellent in English speech, pronunciation and had a picture like hand writing in contrast to mine. Always best dressed, in that aspect my parents provided her with everything. She was a good cook but used us for the errands while cooking, moreover she was a good singer in the church but during her young days we still had to stick to the tradition of not going in the public, which I broke by becoming a singer on the stage. As soon as she passed her senior Cambridge, she was given a place in the school to teach. She was a brilliant seamstress and did the most wonderful hand embroidery. Something to marvel at. For some reason or the other we always kept a distance from her. I had never seen her joining us and having fun. She had her own set of friends at school and at home. She continued her studies as a private candidate for the Cambridge University degree. She had special students, who got tuition in Latin and other subjects. Two names I remember. One was Sunthari, who later became the first lady judge and the other one was Matilda. Sometimes she took those private classes in the school. My eldest brother and she never hit on with each other for any logical reason. The privileges she got because she was the eldest daughter for my parents, who were themselves the eldest in their own families, in addition she was the first grandchild for my grandparents.

Time never stood still. As she became a young woman my parents looked for a suitable young man. There were no such match in the close family circle and they looked outside the family circle and found a young man Rajaratnam happened to be a distant relative, who was teaching at St. John's College Jaffna. He was an English trained teacher. When everything was satisfied to both the parties my parents insisted, that he should go to India and finish his higher studies for a better future. So only with a promise he went to India to continue his higher studies. My sister had to wait for three years. In the mean time he visited her while on vacation but was not allowed to take my sister out alone. Whenever he came on vacation I requested him to bring me ribbons and bangles from India. Those days we got beautiful ribbons and bangles only from India. He wrote his finals in March and my parents thought it was high time they got engaged and married.

In May 1957 my parents decided to have a quiet engagement for my sister because of the grand wedding they planned to have three months later. We all travelled by car to Trincomalee in the east. It was my parents' friend Mr. Namasivayam, a land saviour, who took us in his car to our uncle's place. At that time we did not have any rules as to how many people should travel in the car. My parents, my sister, another friend and I travelled in his Ford Prefect car. Because I was small I had to sit on the lap of my mother. My eldest brother and my second sister could not come since they were at the university. My other two brothers were asked to stay at home as guards for the house. I was sure they enjoyed the freedom they had. My brother in law travelled separately and came to my uncle's parsonage one day before the engagement. We travelled about 250 miles sometimes through forests. The high way sped beneath the car's wheels. We had a break in the middle to have our lunch. It was the government quarters and my father's friend carried me and showed the forest. Our journey continued till we reached Kanya, where we have the seven hot springs. I was able to feel the temperature of those springs. We did not have much time to have a bath. Some of these things I am relating because before I had ended my high school I had seen almost eighty percent of the island. And this was part of it. My sister had her engagement at my uncle's house. He was a priest there. It was a quiet ceremony. I still remember that my sister wore an orange sari with gold border. Soon after the engagement my brother in law travelled back and we travelled separately. The incident was not big but for me it was my first longest travel. Of course I slept half way through but I could not forget that journey.

Usually weddings are very colourful in our town, but my eldest sister's wedding was such a colourful event that the town had never seen before or to my knowledge even after. I was in the fifth grade, and it was late summer in August. Exactly three days after the summer holidays started, to be precise19th of August. But to my knowledge the preparation started about one year ago. My parents started to collect all the addresses of their friends and relatives, who were living outside our town and in other provinces. In fact, my parents' family extended to a bigger clan, the uncles, the great-uncles, aunts, cousins, the list went on. Most of them lived in the east, where they were married and settled, but they also lived in the capital city Colombo, due to their profession and in the highlands where they worked in tea estates as supervisors. Here I have to mention there was a special reason why my parents were looking for people working in the highlands. It was from there the flowers came for the wedding. Flowers like lilies, carnations, anthuriams, chrysanthemums and a lot of ferns, which you get only in the cold areas. I remember there were baskets and baskets of flowers from different sources, which arrived by train and someone collected them at the railway station fourteen miles from our town. Even after the wedding, flowers arrived. I saw my brothers throwing the baskets, even without opening them.

Once the list was finished my parents wrote formal letters to the close relatives inviting them for the wedding. This was the procedure. You did not send only the invitation but also personal letters accompanied with those invitations. You sent invitations only to the second round of friends and people, who were more or less acquaintances. They had to decide, who would be the bride's maid, the best man, the flower girls and the page boy. My eldest brother was the best man, he was thought as a fortunate man because he received a gold ring from my brother in law, when he returned from the church after the ceremony. Bride's maids were my second sister Rathy and my first cousin Thevi *Machal*[51]. Flower girls were Thevi, another cousin of mine and Nirmala the daughter of my brother in law's friend. One might have wondered why I was not included in the

---

[51]Cousin and we use the relationship with the name

group. In fact even I was disappointed when my mother told me when I asked her whether I would be the flower girl with a very polite NO. Although I did not say anything, the disappointment was there. They must take one person from each family to bind the relationship she said. The only consolation was, I got the same dress as the flower girls.

Two days before the wedding they packed the things for the bride groom and it was a custom to give a bottle of perfume with the dress. Valuable things were inside that room and my aunt was sitting at the entrance of the room and kept an eye on things. I entered the room and saw the perfume. It was a Goya no.5 a very expensive one at that time. I opened the packet and put a drop of it on my dress and came out. My stupid brain did not realise it was an act easily detected. It was very strong and my aunt smelt it and called my sister and mother. But my father came to my defence and said he would buy a new one instead and took me secretly and told me not to do such things. In difficult times my father had been my solace. Not everybody's children came flying to the bosom of the father and mother, when misfortune struck but I always went to my father, even after I got married. I had been able to pour out my despair and distress to him, and he had comforted and consoled, making me feel that I was a good and kind human being. I never had cause to regret that trust. I knew my sister was furious. But nobody could hurt me after father spoke. So was the respect for my father.

My eldest brother Baba and second sister Rathy came from the campus only one day before the wedding. Relatives from distance places started to arrive. There were thatched sheds all round the house lined with white cloth specially done by our dobby and we had fun in sleeping in mats on the veranda. All the cousins young and old went to the beach or sang songs and played around. There was no control on anything and the fun we had was great. The house was full of people. The servants old and new had their hands full with cooking and washing almost round the clock. The house was full of laughter. Many people in the town and from our village had been helping for weeks, making oil cakes and preparing breakfast, lunch and dinner in large scales. The new dresses I was supposed to wear did not come on time so my mother hurriedly bought some readymade dresses in the town when she went on various errands. My father's brother in law was working in a missionary project and had a big van to do the transport. He was going up and down to the railway station to collect the visitors arriving from out stations.

Here I would like to mention one of my father's distant aunts who came from the east a few days before the wedding. It was the first time I saw her. When she talked with my parents I clearly heard imperious and throaty feminine voice. She brought a special preparation known as *Thothal*[52]. Usually it is a like a jelly, and very soft when prepared in the correct way but if they miss the correct melting stage of the sugar then it could become hard as a stone. Presumably this aunt brought the latter. My mother asked our servant Somu to cut that and bring it. After some time he came and stood near the door, signing my mother to come. With a grin on his face he said, he used to call my mother as Amma (mother): "Amma I am sure I need a hammer to break that." My mother hushed him saving an embarrassment for her aunt and replied in a normal voice "I will come" But it was funny; it tasted good for children like me because our teeth stuck together when we ate that and we needed a lot of time to finish it. Nobody commented on that out of respect.

The members of my family were too busy to notice what I did on the wedding day. It was a blue wedding. The bride's maids the flower girls and the page boy were attired in blue. The bride's maids' saris were painted in gold and they carried a long bunch of pink Anthriums in their hands. The flower girls had a blue basket filled with flower petals. The page boy, my brother in law's brother's son was attired in a blue suite with a cap. I could vaguely remember going to the church sitting in the choir seat because I was the youngest member in the choir but everything was like a dream in my mind. The ceremony at the church was very grand. The church was decorated with Arum lilies for the seats and the arch was with green ferns and white flowers. The church was packed with guests. It was so full there was no room to lift your arms. The bride groom arrived with the best man, my eldest brother and stood at the altar. My father brought the bride to the altar followed by the bride's maids carrying the veil, the flower girls with their baskets and the page boy completing the picture. My sister carried a bouquet of white lilies and orchids. There were five priests officiating, two regional priests, my grandfather Rev. Eliathamby my uncle Rev. Gunaratnam, and the chairman of the Methodist Church Rev. Dr. D.T. Niles who delivered the homely. My grandfather did the auspicious ceremony of giving the *"Thali"*,

---

[52] A traditional sweet

the special chain tied by the bride groom when they removed the face veil of the bride. Usually it was done by the sister of the bride groom but my brother in law had only brothers so his elder brother's wife did it. When they tie the thali they should be careful not to drop the screw of the chain.

There was a special way of asking the witnesses to sign the marriage certificate which I have never seen in Europe. Soon after the wedding ceremony, the bride and the bridegroom went and sat in the vestry. My father got up while all the others were seated and went outside requesting the two witnesses to follow him to the vestry. One of them was my father's cousin Mr. J.N Arumugam, who specially came for the wedding. We were specially honoured by his presence because he was one of the few civil servants holding the highest post in the ministry. The other witness was the principal of the college, Mr. Pooranampillai with whom my father was very close and my family, too. During that process there was a guitar recital by the principal's wife's sister. She played the famous "*English Metu* (means Melody) set in *Raga Sangaraparanam*.[53] After officially signing the necessary forms, the bride and bride groom walked from the vestry, came outside, and went directly to the studio. Unlike in Europe you need not go to the registration office separately. The priests were given permission to officiate and sign the papers at the church itself.

The rest of us had to walk a short distance and wait at the junction for them to finish the photograph session. From the studio to our house the bride and the bridegroom walked on the street in a procession with all the traditional pompous. Traffic was forced to walk on our street. Below their feet they had special white sheets put by the special people and above their heads they had garlanded, umbrella structure with four people carrying. Most of the houses on their way had a table with garlands to put them for the bride and the bridegroom. That was the honour they showed to our family and of course my brother in law and my sister looked great. So when they arrived home, my brother got his ring by washing my brother in law's feet. That was an old tradition. Throughout the church ceremony my sister wore the white Manipuri silk church going sari.

---

[53] Classical melody

The traditional Nila Pawadai (street carpet)

Traditional Poom Panthal (garland top) over the couple

At the reception, my sister with going away sari Manipuri tissue

To my parents' surprise, the seats arranged were not at all enough for the guests, who came. Three sides surrounding our house was filled with chairs but still there were more people so the chairman of the town, Mr. Nadarajah, who owned the theatre, went and sent immediately the gallery benches to accommodate the people. The normal chairs were already there. On that day two of the theatres did not run a single show. Hundreds of greeting telegrams arrived, which had to wait to be opened only after the honey moon. The wedding gifts started to accumulate in the main bed room, and it was difficult for us even to enter into it. Food was lavishly given, I remember going and trying those short eats to the best of my ability. Afterwards they served freshly cooked dinner with a big menu. One of my great aunts was the supervisor for the menu. Curd and honey from east came in abundance. Wedding cake packed in boxes, with my sister's and brother in law's name was prepared by the principal's wife, was served after the short eats. I still remember the taste of the sandwiches that were served on that day which I ate with watering mouth. When the guests left after the meal bags of oil cakes and betel with lime were given for them to take home.

It was a pity we had a black and white era in the fifties, therefore we had only photos in black and white without the possibility of videos. There were few photos that were artificially coloured. I still remember her bridal Sari, the white one, and her going-away sari, the red Manipuri Tissue sari with gold brocade, worn for the reception. If it had been a coloured photo the beauty would have been doubled. She wore traditional jewellery in gold.

My eldest sister's wedding was such a big affair and was spoken for months by the people. Then suddenly my father showed signs of bad eyesight. And it was detected as cataract. Those days we had only limited facilities for cataract unlike the modern times where it is finished in one hour and the next day you are all right. It was recommended he should be operated. Most of the family members are superstitious therefore they said it was the evil eye of people after the successful wedding. Anyway, he was admitted to the Jaffna General Hospital twenty one miles away from my town. My eldest brother and second sister had returned to the campus, the only alternative left was my two brothers to look after me. My mother could not trust them to look after me a girl of ten. Mother herself had to stay in Jaffna to attend to my father's needs after the operation. She had to take a quick decision. In the end I was sent to live with our neighbour and my fifth grade teacher Miss Joseph, who lived three houses away from ours. That was a horror. Well beggars can't be choosers. There were two reasons for my fear. First she was my class teacher, second thing was at her house as the rules says "Thou shall not make a mistake" Everything was done on time. It was a stumbling block for my freedom. Early mornings the food was packed and both of us walked together to school. Nobody could imagine the tension I had. It was like breathing in and not able to let it out.

Hearing the message my eldest brother Baba came from the university. So one day, when we were returning from the school, I saw our house open and my eldest brother was sitting outside. Nobody could describe the relief I had. I ran and hugged him and said "I will stay here." So he came to my teacher's house, took my things and I was very happy to come home. In the meantime my father was taken to the operating theatre and he was given an injection in the eye, some mishap happened and it started to bleed so the surgeon had to stop the operation in the middle and my father was sent back to the ward. The neighbour of my father's bed had visitors and one of them suggested that there was a native treatment in a place called Alavetti where this cataract could be cured. He has to put two drops of this medicine mixed with honey. So my father left the hospital and went to the native physician and continued with that medicine. Afterwards, till he died he never used glasses.

Chapter 41

My eldest brother

Edward Gunaseelan Gunanayagam

My eldest brother Baba Anna was always attached to me, I may say till he died. Mr. Navaratnasamy, who became popular by swimming the Palk Straight was honoured in Point Pedro. They had a monument erected for him at the big beach, which was closer to our house. The beach was filled with people. It was my first day outing after my illness, for more than four weeks. That was the last of my illnesses I referred earlier. I cannot remember any serious illnesses afterwards except once or twice I had an attack of Malaria. Well coming to that day, while waiting I could not see the unveiling of the plague. I remember wearing a pink dress with small black motives holding the hand of my brother trying to see that. When my brother noticed that I could not see, being a tall man he lifted me on his shoulders so that I could see that properly. My eldest brother had great affection to me. He was 12 years elder to me. He entered university when I was 8 years old. He was very tall, fair and handsome. We walked a lot especially to our grandparents' village. He used to carry me. Of course when I was naughty I got clouted by him but only occasionally. There were a lot of Hindu temples near our house and they used to have big celebrations. In one such temple the God was taken out on a Chariot along the road and in another the god was taken to a big pond with lots of lights. For all those festivals my brother took me. The crowd visiting the town was all over the town. Loudly and happily raised their voices with laughter as people moved and women gave little screams when they thought they would be crushed and men pushed out their elbows to make the way with jobs they were doing and more laughter followed. The fun of buying roasted beans and peanuts was great. We needed only five or ten cents to buy them both. We used to sit on the wall closer to the pond and watch the celebration. Sometimes I would go to sleep and he would carry me home.

When my eldest brother was in the advanced level, he was studying late in the night and early in the morning he went to the well to take a bath. He fell into the well. Hearing the big noise our servants went and shouted that my brother had fallen into the well and within minutes half the neighbourhood was there. One of them got down and the others pulled the rope and slowly lifted him and he was still dazed. My neighbour brought a cup of coffee in his expensive crockery. Our well was not that deep therefore it was not dangerous. I was pacified by my father when I started to cry.

When he passed out as a graduate he taught in the boys' school for two years before he went to the capital to continue his studies to become an accountant. During this time he was the boys' hostel warden, not living there but visited the hostel in the evenings. Sometimes he used to take me there in his bike. There were other teachers and one of them was a burger. He was teaching English and trained plays. A very funny person. My parents always invited people from other cities, working in the boys' and girls' school for dinner and lunch. Once when he came, my sister had just given birth to her daughter. When my mother showed the baby he made such a fuss making "ah" and "oh" like the characters coming in the series "Desperate House Wives"

My brother Baba became a member of the recreation club. This club organized a very big carnival with merry go round, circus, magic shows and various other amusements. Often I went to this carnival because it was only three or four blocks away from my house. Being a member of the recreation club my brother had free entrance. So I went with him. They always started the event at 6.30 in the evening by playing a popular song which carried the name of the chairman of the town council. I memorised many songs from the loud speaker I could hear from my house. Once I went with my second sister and brothers and got acquainted with the Khan family, who performed the magic shows. They performed their high light magic of disappearing in the cupboard and appearing again. That drew delighted cheers and clapping from the audience. On the final day film stars, the famous comedian Maduram and her group, came to perform dramas. I was eager to see them because the south Indian film stars came rarely to our town. My brother promised to take me. I got ready wearing my best silk skirt and blouse and waited for my brother. Time was running he never turned up. I waited at the gate looking for him. My father saw that and took me to the entrance, only two minutes from the house, hoping my brother would see me and he was sure there was no danger among known people at the same time asking the guard to keep an eye on me, in case I did not find my brother. I entered and searched for my brother at the entrance of the drama hall, there was no sign of him. Suddenly I got an idea. I went straight to the announcement booth. The announcer was Nanthagopal, an old student of my father. I went and told him that I was searching for my brother, who was a teacher at the Boy's College. He announced it two times and then I saw my brother grinning and coming with another teacher. Actually he had totally forgotten his promise. Anyway I got what I wanted and enjoyed the drama.

Another time the famous wonder girl in numbers, Sakunthala, visited the town and there was a big crowd for her show. My brother took me for that. After solving a number of questions she said she could tell the day if the date, year and month were given. My brother, just to test her, wrote 29th of February 1942 and asked for the day, knowing very well that it was not a leap year and there were no 29 days in that year. But she promptly answered "Nobody would have been born on this date because it was not a Leap Year and February 29th in this year never existed". My brother had to admit his defeat. Recently I read she passed away and I was proud I met such a great person at least one time in my life.

My eldest brother was very compassionate for poor people especially the servant boys. He used to teach them how to be clean and asked them to wear white *lungis*[54] and shirts so that they would know when it was dirty. We had a servant boy from the hill country, he was a teenager and my brother took personal care in keeping him clean and also gave him lessons in English. He had something close to sympathy for this boy. The servant boy Muthu was proud that my brother cared for him and had the greatest respect for my brother. My brother was teaching at the boys 'college and was living with my parents. Muthu always attended my brother's needs giving him tea or coffee and always answering his calls but then he had to leave within a year.

---

[54] Home dress for men

But that did not stop my brother. We had a girl helping us in the house. She had a brother. They all looked like Africans. There was no reason why they looked like Africans but he had curly hair, thick lips and very dark skin. Somehow or the other my brother was interested in this boy. So he employed him in the house paying him monthly wages and saw that he was clean. Sometimes he stayed in the house, sometimes he went home. Till then people had dismissed him as a near idiot. He was like a bodyguard for my brother. He was always with my brother talking to him giving my brother the local news and my brother used to give him tips, especially the ticket fare to go and watch films. His name was 'Panchu'. He was an ardent fan of that time South Indian film idol MGR. He would never miss a film of this hero. We had one theatre near our house and two theatres in a town called Nelliaddy, about five to six kilometres from our house. Sometimes, if he did not finish the housework on time, he could not go for the first show at 6.30 but went to the second show at 9.30 in the evening. According to my brother's instructions, in the evenings he dressed up tip top in white and went to the cinema getting the money from my brother. The funniest thing was, he was so dark that when he dressed himself in white, people could not see his face in the night. Sometimes we identified him only by his shirt and *lungi* and not by his face. We never paid attention to that except one day he came and told us a very funny story. Three miles away from our house was the government hospital. And there was a junction and on one side of it there were only paddy fields. There was a rumour that people saw ghosts in this place. We never knew but people said that it was a female ghost, called *'Mohini Pissasu'* meaning female demon. People were frightened to walk on this road in the nights. One day Panchu went for a second show, in other words, he had to return only at mid night. There was only one bus that he could catch to come home. That was the late bus returning, collecting the passengers from the last train. If you missed that, then you had to walk the five mile stretch. It so happened that day, he missed the bus. So he started to walk. Although he was used to it, due to the rumour of the ghost, when he neared the third mile he got frightened. Then he saw another person walking ahead of him about 300m away. So he called him 'Brother...' The man turned and quickened his phase. Panchu did not realize that the man was afraid: he ran to catch up with him then the man started to run too. And when Panchu neared him, he shouted "My God, it is the ghost." Panchu had to pacify that man to make him believe, that he was also in the same boat. He came home and repeated the whole story with a grin:

we joined in the fun squealing all the while with laughter. Due to my brother's profession he had to leave Point Pedro and when this was informed to Panchu his whole face began to sag suddenly, and the smile gone. His whole mask of flesh was melting quickly into a sallow leer of unveiled malevolence.

My eldest brother Baba had a proposal and there was an engagement, which was not successful after some time. I was too small to understand the implications. Anyway he started a fresh life in Hingurana sugar factory in the east as an accountant. Later he himself found his wife Rachel, who was from the Sinhalease community. Although it was the first of its kind in our family there were some resistance but then my parents were convinced because she came from a very good family and she was very beautiful. She was trained as a nurse but at the time of her marriage she was not working and she was living with her aunt and uncle, who were like her god parents. Her uncle was the chief of protocol at that time and her aunt was an exhibition cake maker. I was the only one present at his quiet engagement in Kandy. Later the wedding took place in the capital. My sister in law, Rachel, wore a light blue shaded lined white lace sari with a string of pearls. My sister in law looked like a dream as a bride and my brother as handsome as ever. The wedding ceremony was held in a big church in Galle face Green, in Colombo, which was followed by a very grand reception hosted by the Lake House owner at his Colombo residence. We all attended the wedding in the capital except my two sisters. Both were pregnant and could not travel so far.

My eldest brother Edward and his beautiful wife Rachel at the wedding

Their wedding cake was one of the most beautiful cakes I had ever seen. Her aunt Edna, an expert in cake making, made the cake taking more than two months of preparation. There were finely made swans and roses. Rachel's going away sari was a magenta Manipuri silk sari. She wore long gold ear rings and again she looked like a picture. After the reception amid a medley of laughter, old shoes and the clatter of empty tins in their car they took their departure for their honey moon. They started their married life in Kandy but continued in the capital after buying a flat there. I used to stay with them after my mother died and she taught me a lot of things about social behaviour.

I thought about the up's and down's my brother had and how he achieved a satisfied life at the end. We never knew that the possibilities gave a greater humanity to a man, whose competence and strength were no match to his temper and weakness.

Chapter 42

My second sister

Mary Gunarathy Thavaratnam (nee Gunanayagam)

My second sister Rathy was very quiet and quite small for her age when she was young. She did a lot of housework. She did not even cry loudly. And in her time girls were very conservative therefore she was under strict discipline, with close neck, long sleeves and long dresses, later on pleated sari and always with plaited hair. She was demure. She was quite intelligent, not only in the school work but also in general knowledge. They used to have "Do you know" contests for schools, which she attended together with four other classmates in the capital Colombo for a live transmission on the state radio. She remembered the deciding question they were asked and that was, who was the author of "*Kanjanajin Kanavu*",[55] a Tamil novel written by one of the first Tamil women writers in India with a pen name 'Lakshmi'. By answering this question they won the competition. The Independence Day celebration of my country was celebrated in the capital city on the 4th of February 1948 and she represented the school in the capital. She was quite good at remembering facts, dates and places. She was a recording angel to receive and remember.

She had one friend Kannagai and both of them went to the matinee shows, one of them was the Hindi film "Awara" starred by the Hindi legends Raj Kapoor and Nargis. Her friend had a niece, who was of my age. All four of us went to watch that film in our local theatre. I vaguely remember one of the scenes,

---

[55] Dream of Kanchana

where the hero brought a jewellery box and put the necklace around his girl friend's neck. This film ran for a long time in our local theatres. Although we did not understand the language Hindi, we would go and watch if they were good films.

My sister Rathy entered the university in 1956. Then I was about 9 years old. She was the only person, who obeyed and fulfilled my parent's wishes before and after her marriage. After passing her ordinary level with flying colours, she attended father's college, where girls were admitted only to the 11th and 12th grades. There would be few girls and a lot of boys in the class. One of her classmates was quite tough with the boys.

Both my sister and her friend Rasamani entered the university at the same time. That was the period admission to the university was quite different. If you had done well, then you were given direct admission. But if you were in the borderline you were called for an interview. But my sister Rathy got a direct admission. Then she was faced with the difficult task of finding a hostel in the capital. She had to go to the capital and stay in a ladies hostel, which was quite new for young girls to do. Her friend Rasamani was a real fighter when it came to her rights. Her manner was peremptory and a little off hand whereas my sister was a quiet person. My parents felt there was quite a balance between them. So they were accompanied by my uncle, who was a priest, and were taken by him to the Salvation Army ladies hostel to stay and attend the university.

Sometimes, when my eldest brother and sister were at the university, my other two teenage brothers had their own plans. I was left alone with the servants in the absence of my parents, which was not unusual. One day a medical student Kathiravetpillai came home telling that my sister needed some of her certificates and he was travelling that day, he would like to take those certificates with him. I did not know which certificates they were but I knew that they were in my mother's trunk, where she kept her jewellery. And it was in our main bedroom. He was in a hurry to go by bus to the railway station and catch the train to the capital. So I asked him to enter the bedroom and showed him the trunk and told him to take the certificates. It was fun watching him, taking my mother's things out and at the bottom the certificates which he sorted out and took. He was quite serious at that time but he had gone and told my sister about this episode and had a hearty laugh. Later not my father but my mother warned me not to allow strange people inside the bedroom.

My second sister Rathy did not break any rules after entering the university by breaking the traditions and become modern in her behaviour, especially in dressing but she did not want me to suffer the same situation. At that time wearing sleeveless dresses was a taboo. When my sister came back from the university she stitched me boat neck and sleeveless dresses according to the fashion of that time. Although my mother was shocked and protested she overruled by saying "Don't give too much pressure for her. Let her enjoy the privileges I missed". It was a curious remark and I had the fleeting impression that it was made with some deeper meaning. During the three years she was at the university either she would stitch dresses for me, while she was in the capital or did the dresses when she came on vacations. Therefore I was a well-dressed girl in my town. She was very artistic and I still remember the dresses that she painted. There was a white dress with red roses; a green dress with yellow flowers and grey dress with red and black cord work, an orange dress with black and white cord work, a yellow dress with red roses, a blue sleeveless nylon dress, they were endless. Not only that, knowing my interest in music she always brought the latest English blues and film songs when she came home for the holidays. She had ample opportunity to hear the songs in the radio and memorise them in the capital than in my town. Whenever she was on vacation she would sing those songs and I would memorise them and sing them for concerts. Songs of Doris Day "Que sera sera", "Wall flower" and other songs like "I have got a sweet heart", I'll never be married", "Catch a poling star," are some of the songs I still sing when I do book readings in Berlin.

Usually Christmas shopping was done in the town. Both my eldest brother Baba and my sister Rathy were at the university and my mother trusted their judgement in selecting Christmas presents for friends and family. They were sent to Jaffna town to buy the presents my mother wanted. Once, I went with them. We were supposed to return before 8 o'clock. After finishing the shopping we had two hours to kill. There was a Tamil film running with a sensational title "Honeymoon". I wouldn't think my parents would have allowed us to see the film seeing the name. My brother and sister decided to watch the film but soon after the interval, we realized we had to return home, otherwise we would miss the last bus. So we had to leave half way through the film. That was a disappointment for me because the hero was my favourite actor. And the film showed nothing about a honeymoon. It was only the name. Actually the honeymoon was for an elderly couple, after their second marriage. When we came home none of us told about the film adventure because we knew there would be a big lecture from our mother. A few months later the same film came to our local theatre and we all wanted to go and see the film, my mother was sceptic about the title, but my brother and sister convinced her that there was nothing bad about the film and ultimately revealed that we had seen half the film. To our surprise both our parents came to see the film. It was the time my mother became a little bit liberal with her conservative ideas. When my sister passed out from the university she was appointed as a teacher at her old school and I was still studying in the same school. She had two friends, who are now living in Canada and Australia, where as she continued to be in Point Pedro with the same job but not as a teacher but as the principal of the same school

Chapter 43

My second brother

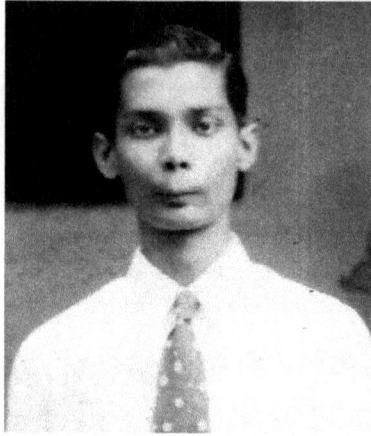

Solomon Gunapalan Gunanayagam

My second brother Bala was a little bit different from the others. We never played together but he was good in reading and good in his vocabulary content. But he was quite an interesting character as far as his behaviour was concerned. He was very conscious about his appearance, therefore getting ready for school or getting ready to go anywhere, he needed a lot of time. He would get ready, powder his face and take half an hour minimum to comb his hair, using Brill Cream and water. His hair style was Yankee style, a kind of Robert Mitchum style. They comb vertically in front and horizontally at the back to get a bump in front. Then he would pull the shirt a little bit lose to cover the waist line of the shorts or trousers. The worst thing was he left the comb with all the mess. When visitors came or for an emergency, if he was asked to go and buy a drink or sugar or milk or whatever was needed for the visitors, he would take half an hour to get ready. By the time he brought the things the visitors would have gone. He was oddly stiff and unbending. He indulged possibly a show off streak in his character. I do not know how he managed later when he became the Surgeon Commander in the Navel Force of Sri Lanka, often travelling in big ships and reporting for duty. He was a doctor by profession. Those professions needed punctuality, maybe he got up one hour early.

Even in his school days he was searching for difficult vocabularies for his essays and sometimes used them at home. For the family members it became a standard joke that our second brother always used English that needed a translation, because of the high vocabulary content in the language. In other words he used professional language jargon. Later in his life he wrote a poem, for which he got the best poetry award with a gold medal in 2012.

When my second brother Bala was 10 years he was in the cubs company at school. During the weekends they went from house to house asking for chip a job. They had their official cards and collected the money given to them by doing some errands in the house. One day he and his friend went to the District Judge's house. The judge was a class mate of my father and knew how intellectual my father was. First the wife came out and when they told her she said, only the previous week two boys came and got money. My brother argued in English that those were the scouts and he was the cub. Fathers training in the language made him to talk fluently. Hearing the noise, the Judge sitting in his office room asked his wife to send the boys to him. Entering the office room my brother continued his argument in English. At one point the judge asked whose son my brother was. When he told my father's name he just said "No wonder". Then they were given the job of watering the plants although the previous day it had rained heavily.

My second brother Bala was bold in doing certain things. Painful and pleasurable at times. He never stopped an argument till he had the last word. He would be the first to go and have his meals and chose the best. But the most amusing habit was how he got a place to sit. When he went to the church or travelled in the bus, he would go and sit where ever he wanted to sit, disregarding the fact that there was enough place to sit or not. First he sat between the people and when he was not comfortable, he would rise a bit and sit with a hard press that the people automatically moved to give room for him, to avoid another hard push. He would be sitting comfortably, while his neighbours stared at him.

There was a big wooden store box in our dining room, where prepared food was kept. Those days, having a fridge was not usual. One day my second brother Bala climbed into it and started to taste the food. For safety sake he closed the lid, so no one knew somebody was there inside. My mother's friend came together with my mother and sat inside the dining room. In fact my mother's friend was in tears. She was telling my mother the secret family melodrama. If it was to be known to the others her whole family prestige would be lost. My brother could not come out so he listened to the whole story smacking his lips over the crackling oil cakes and sugar syrup. Long after they left the room he managed to come out. He was shocked by the story but did not dare to tell anyone because he was sure he would be punished for eavesdropping. Time did not kill the rumours to the contrary it multiplied. Years later when the tragedy leaked out he told us how he knew the story years ago.

.When both my brothers were at the university my third brother had a major operation which was both a research and a necessity. Obviously being a medical student my second brother was called to watch the operation. The moment he saw blood coming out of my brother's face, he became faintish and walked out of the operating theatre. How strange that one could not see his or her own blood but could see other people's blood. No wonder people said blood is thicker than water. Both my second brother and third brother were very close, although there were only two years difference between them, my third brother always gave my second brother Bala, respect in calling and in talking with him. Fights between us cropped up occasionally, we did not use our hands but we used our verbal attack quite strongly, sometimes using nicknames, which was the greatest attack.

When he was at the medical college insurgency broke out, starting at the university within the Sinhalese community. Several undergraduates were arrested and killed and the government was forced to close all the universities. Students were asked to go home and my brothers came home with an indefinite holiday. They related several incidents. It was then my second brother told me about the well known rebel Che Guevara. My brother read the history of Che and used to wonder about such people, and their brave activities. That in turn, made me to think about doing documentaries about such people. Finding the truth about legends in different fields, by talking to them, and film them with their interviews. I very well knew they were fairy tale wishes and occasionally, when such desires cropped up I would tell myself, "Keep quite you stupid, such possibilities are only for the rich and the influential, not for you, just keep on dreaming" But years later my dream of making documentary films became a reality. With my own private production, I was able to produce three documentary films in Berlin Silent Plea, Thirst for Life and Magic Moments. They were screened at the Berlin Film Festival. And one was selected for the Amsterdam film festival and Israel film festival

Producing documentary films. My childhood dream No.5 in reality

From the top: Carol Gould's *Long Night's Journey into Day* in Israel; Rubini Selvanathan's *Silent Plea* among India's art deco palaces; Heiner Stadler's war-reporting drama *Kriegsbilder*; and Yamamura Animation's *Kipling Jr.*

Silent Plea (Germany, 1996). Documentary. *Dir*: Rubini Selvanathan.

A portrait of Polish painter and interior designer Stefan Norblin, who became famous for his work as official court painter of the Indian palaces in Jodhpur and Morvi in the early forties. From their former glory, these palaces are now in need of major restoration.

•Ein Portrait des polnischen Malers und Innenarchitekten Stefan Norblin, der Anfang der vierziger Jahre durch seine Arbeit als offizieller Hofmaler für die indischen Paläste von Jodhpur und Morvi bekannt wurde. In der Zeit seit ihrem einstigen Ruhm sind diese Paläste stark restaurierungsbedürftig geworden.

Betacam - 23 mins - English - Colour.

Contact in Berlin: Rubini Selvanathan (see Section 4).

Market screening: **Sun 16, 15.00, Studio 10**

GLORIANA SELVANATHAN

Thirst for Life (Germany, 1996). Short documentary. *Dir*: Rubini Selvanathan.
A documentary chronicling the life of the Indo-Assyrian author, poet and singer Dora Samuel, which also examines the fate of the Assyrian people, now reduced to living in small groups scattered all over the world.
•Ein Dokumentarfilm über das Leben der indo-assyrischen Autorin, Dichterin und Sängerin Dora Samuel, der außerdem vom Schicksal des assyrischen Volkes handelt, das heute nur noch in kleinen Gruppen auf der ganzen Welt verstreut existiert.
Betacam - 23 mins - English - Colour.
Contact in Berlin: Rubini Selvanathan (see Section 4).
Market screening: **Wed 19, 17.00, Studio 10**

Watching my documentary Thirst of life, at the High Commission of India, in Berlin with Dora Samuel

Magic Moments (Germany, 1996).
Documentary. *Dir.* Rubini Selvanathan.
A portrait of young Indian doctor SM Balaji, who
is becoming world-renowned for his skill at cur-
ing facial deformities, transforming both the
appearance and the lives of his patients.
•Das Porträt eines indischen Arztes, SM Balaji,
dessen Geschick beim Kurieren von
Gesichtsmißbildungen das Aussehen und Leben
seiner Patienten verändert und ihn weltberühmt
werden läßt.
Betacam - 25 mins - English - Colour.
Contact in Berlin: Rubini Selvanathan (see
Section 4).
Market screening: **Sun 16, 15.25, Studio 10**

The most surprising thing happened in one of the film festivals, at the beginning of my career as a journalist. There was a documentary film about Che, *der Reise der junge Che* (The Journey of Young Che) screened at the Berlin film festival. I went late for the screening. As a result I got a seat right in front. After the screening they had the press conference and Che's son Ernesto was the special guest. He spoke only in Spanish. After he answered the questions, many of them wanted to take a photograph with him. He refused to do it. Suddenly he pointed at me and called me with his hands to have a photo. Words could not describe my feelings. I gave the camera to my neighbour requesting her to take the photo. I did not know what she had in her mind she pretended to press the button but actually she did not take the photo. Professional jealousy I suppose. Eagerly I came out of the hall and checked for the photo. To my disappointment there was no photo. My heart sunk to the bottom. Che's son Ernesto also came out. I ran to him and said that I did not have the photo. Immediately he took the camera from me, came closer and took a photo, raising my camera in one of his hands, and left with a smile. That photo is one of the photos I treasure. He never came to Berlin again.

Che Guevara's son Ernesto with me after the press conference.

Chapter 44

My third brother

James Gunaselvam Gunanayagam

My third brother Chelva was another type. We were better pals at home and he was patient with my silly questions. When I was very small and could not read properly he used to read the stories in Tamil. We used to go to the books shop to buy story books, did small shopping at the market, go to the beach to catch fish or prepare our own snacks with bread and *jaggery*. Sometimes when I returned from school I went to his class which was closer to the short cut lane and waited till he came out of the class to return home. Once I was wearing an orange long skirt. I was sitting outside in a makeshift classroom. The skirt was a hindrance to walk on the side walls so I lifted it a bit too high. From his class he was making signs to put my skirt down. He was too busy looking at me that his teacher Shanthy noted and she was highly amused. That evening the lady teachers visited our house and his teacher showed how he frantically showed with hands and eyes when he tried to contact me. In fact I did not see him doing that.

Both of my brothers were ardent fans of the book "Tom Brown's School Days". My third brother was highly influenced by the incidents in the book. He was very mischievous. After all boys are boys. Breaking rules was nothing to him. I think he had more entries in the log book in the school, than any of my other brothers. He lived in his dreams about the western films, with guns and shooting. Once in the middle of the lesson, he started to say *"Tut tut doom doom"* sounding like a gun and the lesson was taken by a Sinhalese master. He thought actually he meant to insult him by that sound and warned my brother. Another serious thing happened. One day, he went to town, which was twenty one miles away, to watch a film without going to school. News reached my father. And he was waiting restlessly at the gate, and my mother and we were out in the veranda, wondering what would happen. Without knowing what was happening at home, my brother was coming from the bus terminals. When he saw the unusual gathering of the family and my father's look, he entered the gate of the house with a mixture of shock and incomprehension but there was markedly fear in it as well. My father caught him: with the cane in hand took him to the bed room. My mother and my sister begged my father not to punish him. My father was in a rage and entered the bed room, closed the door and the windows, and he smote the coverlet. The savage whirr and the succeeding whack sounded all over the house and the door opened, my brother came out crying. My father went out and my mother was consoling my brother because he was her pet. This news reached the principal of the college, who was a strict disciplinarian. Usually for such offence the students were publicly punished. But he escaped with a warning and an entry in the log book. It was years later I heard from my sibling's discussion, which was not meant to be heard by me, that father punished him to save him from a severe punishment by the principal. Till today, I do not know whether my father really hit my brother or not. May be it was a gentlemen's agreement. Though I was raging with curiosity, I refrained from asking. All truths are not to be told I suppose.

My third brother was crazy in eating bread and jam when he was quite young. For him that was the best food. He was the pet of my mother and once he told "When I grow up I will ask my mother to sit on a chair, and keep one sack of bread on one side, and one sack of jam on the other for her". One could see a child's dream was centred on his favourite things without knowing the reality was far away from that.

My third brother could do mischief without the knowledge of the others. One of them, which he told us years later, was quite shocking. He was in the seventh or eighth grade and he had a fight with a classmate. And in his anger he had hit him. This was during the second period, this boy threatened my brother that he would go and inform that to the principal. That means, my brother would get the canning from the principal. My brother had a quick thought, before the break he ran to the principal's office and told the principal that this boy had hit him. So the principal said "Ask him to come." During the break this boy went to complain about the fight but the principal thought he came because he was asked to, and gave him some canning and sent him back. The boy was in confusion and came to the class and my brother had a mischievous smile on his face. He could not help finding a kind of cruel and mischievous joy. Even that boy did not know, why he was punished, till today.

My third brother Chelva had a good sense of humour. Especially when he related incidents with his own comments, laughter was inevitable. When they entered the university usually they came home by the night train from Peredeniya, where the big campus was. They came home directly or took another road, the second cross street, where they had to pass the Christian cemetery. The road was quite lonely and weird, especially when you reached the entrance of the cemetery the shriek of the cicadas was deafening even drowning the dogs' barking. My brother always took the latter. My mother was not happy about it when she came to know. When asked, my brother replied "I come that way and look into the grave yard to see whether the ghosts of any of my teachers, who punished me unfairly, are there to give them a knock on their head". I remember seeing a calculating gleam on his face, when he said that. When my mother heard that she was horrified but my father only smiled at his sense of humour. During the insurgency, when university students were arrested and there were riots and curfew and the transport was stand still, he had the courage to walk through the insurgents' territory without fear. That kind of adventurous spirit he must have got it from my father I suppose.

I could not avoid remembering a very funny thing that happened in one of the weddings witnessed by my third brother. When my third brother Chelva related the story we were filled with amusement. Our neighbour's daughter's wedding was planned to be held in their house with temporary sheds serving as reception hall. Unfortunately on that day the rain started to pour without stopping. That meant, people could not go to his house and sit inside those sheds because they were leaking. In our traditional weddings in those days, even the rich people served the food according to the traditional method. All the guests sat on the floor and their lunch was served on a plantain leaf. One could not deny, that it was the easiest method of disposing the rest food, without much washing up to do, especially when they were hundreds of guests.

Wedding Lunch Served at my friend Gawry's marriage. Second from the left is me.

The rain prevented the lunch party at the house so while the service was going on, the boys' college hall was temporarily arranged for the reception. There was a temporary settee only decorated with a printed velvet sheet. The bride and bridegroom came to the hall and the guests were already there. They had to just cross the road from the church. There were so many makeshifts done because of the emergency. They brought all the drinks and kept it in one of the classrooms and arranged those tables and then the glasses were brought. Being a neighbour my third brother Chelva also went to help in serving the drinks. I do not know why at that time people thought if you were served with a drink, you should not drink the whole glass but leave a rest. So those used glasses with the rest drink were brought to the classroom to be washed and used again. One of them started to pour the rest drink into one of the glasses. They were for a moment distracted, at that time a relative of our neighbour came. He was a little funny and also a little macho, and he wanted to show his authority in supervising the serving of the drinks. Then suddenly he took this glass and before anyone could stop, drank the whole stuff. My brother and the others, who were there were speechless, and they did not dare to say a word. He left the room whistling happily without knowing what he did. When I heard this episode I laughed and I was blind with tears and my ribs ached by laughing.

Chapter 45

1958 riots

Our country faced the biggest racial riots in 1958. All the Tamils living in the out stations were attacked brutally, robbed and physically tortured and the whole capital was in chaos because they could not bring the riots under control. There was no discrimination between the rich and the poor, the educated and the uneducated except, if they were Tamils they were attacked. Tamils from all paths of life were attacked by the Sinhalese. Of course, it was due to the political situation of the protest for Tamil only and Sinhala only concept. Most of the attacks were done by the thugs, hired by the politicians. There were horrible scenes and horrible stories heard from people who returned to the north. They declared a curfew all over the country from 6 O'clock in the evening to 6 O'clock in the morning. That means, nobody could get out of the house, even for an emergency. Shops were closed at 4 o'clock. Most of them were temporary shops. And we had to stock the essentials within 6 hours every day. We could see army and police patrolling. No one dared to break the curfew although there were small incidents of riots in our town they were not as horrible as they were done to the Tamils in the Sinhalese areas.

I do not deny that there were some good Sinhalese friends, who helped the Tamils and hid them in their houses in spite of the risk they might face. One could not say the riots ceased but it reduced and Tamils, who had lived in the capital became refugees in their own country. They were sent by ships to the north and our town being a harbour, they were sent to our school. All schools were closed and our school being near the harbour was turned out as their temporary home. From the harbour they were brought to our school to be fed and cared, later on they were sent to their relatives in various parts in the north. There were a lot of families, who had to wait for a long time before they could get in contact with their families. I would get up early in the morning and go to the school not that I did much there but to quench my curiosity. Our home science department and the science lab were filled with food. I had never seen so much food collected in the rooms. Food started to come from all over the places both individuals and organizations. There were voluntary scouts, to help the refugees to disembark from the ships, and be transported by bus to various destinations. People returned, brought whatever they could bring with the main aim of saving their lives. Every half an hour people arrived at the school and it was totally busy. The stories of those people were heart-breaking but I was too small to understand all of them.

One incident that took place shocked the whole volunteers. A Hindu priest, who came as a refugee brought a very heavy suitcase, the volunteers found it very difficult to put it on top of the bus. Still painstakingly they did. When they came to the school, while trying to bring down the suitcase from the top, the handle broke midway and fell down with a big crash. To the shock of the volunteers a stone grinder was facing them. They were really angry with the man, but he said it was a holy stone used for marriages. Of course, he got all the curses from the people. Some of the refugees, who came were Tamils but not really from the north. They were the highlanders. Therefore they stayed for a longer period in the Boys hostel whereas people who had relatives, stayed in the Girls' school. One of those High Landers brought a bird locally called Myna in a cage with him. With all the rush he could not leave his pet and he was at the boys' hostel. The bird repeated many things in Tamil. All of them were fascinated by this bird because it was trained to talk. My brother being the hostel warden took me once to see that bird. After seeing the bird my brother said "No wonder he did not have the heart to leave the bird behind even in an emergency"

The whole nation was under shock. Although in our town we did not have many Sinhalese they did not harm them in any way because they were living there for more than ten to twenty years. The riots had a major effect on the schools. All the children, who came from the capital, were admitted in the local schools, so we had overcrowded classes and the teachers had to cope up with that. Many of them were from very good schools from the capital, stylish and a challenge for the local students. When the school reopened after the riots subsided, we had six hours session instead of eight, starting from eight in the morning and closing by two in the afternoon, mainly due the curfew declared at six in the evening to five in the morning. We had a few people staying in our house. There was mass cooking. For me it was fun to have people at home. Most people, who returned from out stations, stayed in the north permanently because they saw the horror of it, but some of them returned to the capital because of their jobs, after two or three months, leaving their families in the north.

In the same July 1958 my sister expected her first baby and the curfew situation made my mother to be cautious. The private maternity hospital was about eighteen miles from our town. According to the family tradition the car was loaded with things from fire wood to food and other essentials, enough for a month. At the hospital there were cottages with rooms and beds including kitchens. My mother could not allow me to stay alone in the house so she took me with them. It was like a holiday camp for me. Ever thing was perfect, except in the nights we had mosquito bites and we had to sleep under the mosquito nets. It was rather boring for me so as soon as my mother dressed me in the mornings I would go for a round in the hospital and return for the meals. I think we stayed for more than two weeks before my sister delivered the baby. That was the greatest event in the family. She was the great-granddaughter for my grandparents and the eldest granddaughter for my parents and she was my niece. I was her eleven year old aunt. We saw the fourth generation and my parents and my grandparents were very proud. According to the custom we had thirty one days quarantine, especially if any Hindu people visited us they took a head bath when they returned home. There were many other rituals in the house. On the forty-first day my niece was baptised. She wore the dress my sister wore with a pink ribbon. She was named Sophia after my mother. In fact my sister and brother-in-law lived separately in a missionary house even before my niece's birth. My sister had to return to her teaching job after six weeks of maternity leave so my little niece grew up with my parents. My sister and brother-in-law would come in the evenings to have a look at the baby and they would return. She had a small pillow that she would carry every time, sucking her thumb. That was a blissful time for my parents. She was quite active and was the pet of all.

A rare photo of four generations
Seated: My paternal grandmother Ponnu (89), my father Gunanayagam My mother
Gnanamani with her eldest granddaughter Sophia, My maternal grandfather Rev. Eliathamby
Standing: My brother in law Rajaratnam and My eldest sister Gunamani

Chapter 46

My father's retirement

My father retired in 1961.According to the rules they should retire on the sixtieth birthday. Surprisingly he was allowed to work till the end of the year because he prepared the advanced level students appearing for the examination at the end of the year. My brother in law joined Hartley College, when my father retired after forty one years in service. The school had a farewell party for my father and the old boys had a separate one. At the farewell ceremony the president of the Old Boys Association prepared the toast followed by several other speakers including Mr. Arasu Walton, the District Judge, and a student of my father who reminded my father's bravery in swimming eight hours after the Lady McMellem ship wreck in the twenties. I felt so proud of my father when such praise came from a prominent person. When my father finished his reply and came down the steps there was a bursting of applause and a deep silence which was even more eloquent than the applause. My little niece was dressed in a pink, frilly dress with roses made by my second sister and was walking about in the party catching all the people's eyes. Two days afterwards my second sister Rathy was bringing hot coffee for the others and she was behind the curtain and my little niece hearing the footsteps rushed and hugged her in the legs. The whole hot coffee fell on her, especially on the chest. It was a horror for us. My second sister was devastated; day and night she looked after my niece. Slowly it started to cure because it was only a superficial burn. Again all the people said it was the evil eye at the function. Superstitions always accompanied us.

In 1961 there were mass Satyagraha demonstrations by the politicians in different parts of Jaffna; one of them was the proposal against using Sinhalese script for the car number plates. Slowly it spread to the schools, where students also started to demonstrate. They wore a black symbol on their uniforms. One day the students of our school decided to have a Satyagraha, and a strike supporting the politicians. In my class also we all sat together and decided to take part in it. The next day as usual, when my two sisters got ready to go to school I did not get ready. Then my eldest sister complained to my father that if I did not go to school it would reflect on them as teachers, therefore I should go to school. My father called me and said "Get ready and go to school". I swivelled on my heels and went out of the room anger burning inside me. One should understand it was not my decision to go to school. Half the students in my class turned up. The next day the principal called all the students, who were absent, and they were punished, even their badges as prefects were stripped off. I was conscious of abandoning someone to the wolves. Seeing my classmates being punished somehow or the other I felt guilty. In fact, I supported them in the strike but was forced to go to school. It was an unsolicited repentance of a teenager. Even now it pains my heart that I broke the solidarity rule of the class.

Chapter 47

Social status for different people doing different jobs

As everybody knew there was caste system existing in our country, according to the job they did. My mother was quite conscious about it whereas my father never bothered. The dobby, the barber and the low cast people would only sit on the ground while speaking to my mother. Each of these people was referred only with their caste name and the names themselves would show to which group they belonged to. The people, who washed and ironed our clothes, the people, who cut our hair, the toddy tappers and so on. There were others, who were referred with their profession and one of them was Pathar the gold smiths, who were allowed to come inside the house. There were family gold smiths and ours was the *"Choku Pathar"*. It was more of identification than a tradition because he had big cheeks. Choku means cheek. He would be called for every function, where gold was used. Usually they pierce the ears on the 31st day after a baby was born and there would be a big cleansing ceremony for the mother in the house and people were invited for a meal. The other ceremony was melting gold for the *Thali* the special locket for the gold chain tied to the bride by the bride groom. But in normal days, when my mother wanted any jewellery to be made, then he came home and took the orders. But going and buying in the shops was also a custom. There was another group who did all the rituals at the weddings and funerals. A special woman came and did the chanting when a girl attained the age to become a young woman. There would be special offerings for such tasks. They got the dress the girl was wearing on the day but they demanded a sari the national dress instead. Even for an emergency a person from one cast would not perform the tasks of the other caste. They all came from our village. Whether he believed it or not my father never interfered in such things when my mother insisted.

There was a low cast woman named "Ponni", who swept the whole compound of our house. Sometimes she brought her dumb daughter with her. I was allowed to communicate with her, and during the break I gave the food that my mother gave. They were dirty and I had a poor impression about them. My eldest brother occasionally told me I was bought from Ponni and not my mother's child. They knew it was a joke but for me, it was the greatest insult because I thought it was true and ran to my father crying. My father would pacify me but my brother continued to bully me till I was old enough to know there was no truth in it.

Chapter 48

My father's concepts of religion regarding discrimination

All of us remember some of my father's sermons at the church. Although the Christian religion taught equality to all the people in the parish, due to the traditional and cultural setup of the community, the high caste people in the church refused to accept the low caste people, to sit together in the church. Therefore there was a separate seat in the church for those families. There was a heated argument in one of the synods about this, and also at the local parish meetings. My father was totally against that and said "It should be brought to an end one time or the other." So it was decided the leading parish members would visit these people's house and have a meal together, which was new of its kind and never done before, to break the tradition of separating them in the church. They lived about six miles from Point Pedro. So on a particular day, it was decided, they all go to this house to have a meal. There were various methods of transport at that time, bullock karts, buses and cars. But my father loved walking. He could walk up to ten to fifteen miles at a stretch without feeling any kind of strain, perhaps it was one of the reasons, why he lived longer without any serious illnesses. My father never waited to meet the others before going, but started on his own and reached that house, to find nobody from the parish turned up. But my father went into the house and had a hearty meal and returned. After that, the barrier was broken and they were allowed to sit anywhere in the church. This was told by my father, because it happened long before I was born. But to the surprise of those people, the children of that family became highly qualified and held bigger posts in the society that even the parish members had to go to them for favours. What an irony. After relating this incident my father said "Never judge a religion by its congregation, but by its principals." Some of the parish members took prominent places in the congregation by asking, threatening, cajoling, coercing and learning nothing. My father hated their willing blindness.

He had some favourite sections in the bible all pointing out the basic truth of 'love thy neighbour as thyself', which was the teaching of Jesus in one line. Once he dealt with 1. Timothy chapter 1, verse 9 "God loved the world so much..." and that...ended "the worst sinner is me." It was said by St. Paul in the letter to Timothy. 'Very often people point their fingers to the others in judgement without realising the four fingers pointed at them'. This was the example he gave. The main thing in Christian religion is love and judging others was not our job. Another quotation was from the 1st Corinthian, chapter 13, where St. Pauls talks about the qualities of love. And I personally feel he tried to live up to that level. He practiced what he preached. And his motto was "Never fear to do a good thing." He was a local preacher and he was allowed to take turns to conduct Sunday services instead of the pastor. When he was on the pulpit, he spoke in a voice, not so loud or too soft, as though he was speaking to the family. His sermons were never too long that the congregation never drifted into their own world. They were gripping and logical. No sign of hypocrisy what so ever. His code of conduct was based on the following bible text:

"These six things Lord hate yea, seven are an abomination unto him. Proud look, a lying tongue and hands that shed innocent blood, and heart that deviseth wicked imagination, seek that be swift in running to mischief, a false witness that seeketh lies, and that soweth discord among brotheren" *Proverbs*

Chapter 49

Interesting traditions

Puberty in a girl's life is very special in our country. We, the Christians, had a limit whereas the Hindus handled it in a different way. The girl should sleep in a special room or on the veranda with someone as a body guard. There would be a line drawn with charcoal, a protection against evil spirits. A metal piece or a knife would be given to the girl to carry, if she went to Lou. Only food consisting of lentils, Gingili oil and egg would be served to her. The dobby brought the clothes for her to wear. For thirty one days it was this agony. In some families they had a big celebration. It was the total contrast to the western system. Invitations were printed and almost all the known people and relatives were invited for the festival. The girl concerned would be taken to the well and bathed with milk and grass. The wife of the barber sang a traditional folk song. That was actually to inform the neighbourhood that the ceremony had started. The uncle from the mother's side poured the first bowl of water and the rest of the relatives and friends follow suit. The girl was dressed beautifully with silk sari and adorned with jewels and flowers. Different types of oil cakes were prepared and the girl would be seated in a decorated platform. Ceremonies would be performed and all the visitors would be served with the meal. At the end of the celebration, the visitors would stand in a queue and give their presents to the girl, mostly money. The amount depended on how much they valued that family and how much they were obliged to the family. When the time came for the visitors to return home, they were given paper bags with betel, *ariconut* and lime. If you were very close to the family, then they also gave some oil cakes to take with. Not all families did it in a large scale. Some people would limit with their close relatives. The ceremony was done by the poor families for two or three days. The whole reason was to collect some money.

The Christians did not do in such elaborate scale but to a certain limit. They also did not have those rituals and celebration. I remembered mine. We had a prayer meeting at home and friends of the parish and the pastor were invited for tea and snacks. I asked my father about the different way people celebrated the puberty ceremony. He gave me a plausible reason. He said according to the old tradition girls were not sent to school or were not sent out after they reached their puberty. The only alternative they had was, to give them in the hands of a man. The puberty ceremony and the invitation were to inform the village or the town that there was a girl ready for the marriage, and anyone interested could propose marriage formally. Collecting money in such ceremony in the middle class and poor class, is to make some jewellery or for the dowry for the bride to be. The parents of the bride gave some capital to the new couple to start their new life. But later dowry became the central point of a marriage. The bride grooms parents demanded rather than requested. The amount was fixed for different professions. Doctors, engineers and accountants got the highest. Therefore parents were obsessed to educate their sons just for that sake. There was another tradition. If there were educated boys in the family they had inter-marriages, where the brother and the sister of one family married the brother and the sister of another family. Proposed marriages were the tradition in the fifties and sixties. Love marriages were rare and conservative families were opposed to that: especially when they belonged to different castes or different religion. At the beginning if a Christian married a Hindu the Christian family was excommunicated by the church for three months. A marriage between a catholic and a protestant was also not allowed. Later these rules changed. I knew one Christian girl, who underwent such torture, but she married the man she loved and then totally changed as a Hindu. My eldest sister and my second sister had proposed marriages, while the rest of us went on our own way. I think traditions changed in our time.

Because of the big public beach, flying kites was one of the biggest past time for the local people, especially in January when the wind was high. We were no exceptions from this hobby. At the beginning my eldest brother did it, there was a special kind of kite called "Eagle"-kite and "Stork"-kite. If he was making one of those then we, the younger siblings, must do the errands, like cutting and collecting. And then once the kite was made, we all went to the beach and flew the kite. It went quite high. Since our house was in front of the beach sometimes we used to bring the kite through the coconut trees, which stood as obstacles and tied it in front of the veranda. Our servant Somu, who was of my brother's age or a little bit elder, also took an active part in it. Later my third brother made kites economically, not using coloured papers bought in the shop, but with newspapers. He made a very big kite and fixed a battery and a bulb, that in the night we could see the kite moving with the light. Quite a sensation at that time. But there were experts in our town, who made record-breaking kites and when they brought their kites to the public beach, there would be a big crowd behind them. My brothers usually went there to see the kites flying. They used to fix the

'*Vinn*', a string-like attachment which made quite a musical tone, when the wind was strong. There were different techniques in those kites. And my brothers were amazed by those kites from these experts. But one of the incidents I remember was the kite that was made for me, by my father. He was very good in making '*tail-kites*'. Not often he did but once, when my brothers refused to give their kites, he made a kite with white tissue and green heart-shaped papers. Once it was finished, I went proudly with my father to the beach to fly the kite. Both of us were very happy and suddenly the kite went and hanged in one of the tallest coconut trees. We tried our best to take it out but at the end what I got was a torn kite.

There was another art of sports during the festival times, especially in January, the 'Thanksgiving Day" and the "Tamil New Year" in April. This was called the coconut war'. The coconut with the husk was socked in the water for a long time so that the shell became very hard and the coconut becomes very narrow and small. It was very hard to break them. So during the festival seasons they sold those coconuts and we had competitions, as to whose coconut was the strongest. My third brother was crazy about it. There were two people in my town, men actually, who were experts in breaking the coconut, not only with another coconut as usual, but with their fists. One was the grocer, Rasa, and the other was Maniam, a man, who worked in the cargo-ships. There would be a crowd of people watching them doing this. Well, they did it for a bet and people got money. Sometimes there was a different kind of bet. Before they started the performance, they would bet if the opponent's coconut did not break then they would sacrifice their own coconut. You could see the loser's sad face when he lost his coconut. But it was the greatest fun we had during the festival seasons. I and my third brother used to go behind the crowd, each time there was someone breaking the coconut. My father also showed some interest at the beginning. The beach lads came to collect the broken pieces of the coconuts. There was a thrill in fighting for that and eating.

I had seen the dark moods and the pleasant moods of the sea in my childhood. I was never frightened of the rough sea and the big waves. Near the harbour there was a reef functioning as breakwater, between the deep sea and the shore. There was only one opening which led to the harbour. Those were the days, when cargo was transported by big ships, especially rice and food materials from the city. Therefore we had big wooden cargo carrying ships. There were people, specially trained to handle those ships. They had long hair, knotted and big red earrings. Once, one of those ships carrying paddy sacks sunk in the deep sea, just behind our house. The owner of the ship, who was always called as "*Thandayar*", was devastated by the wreck and many people swam and dived and recovered the paddy individually. Nobody could help. Those ships were constructed in the beach behind our house: sometimes it took months to finish. First they constructed the wooden part, and then all the intervals were stuffed with coconut husks, blocking those holes, later they were painted with tar, which was water- resistant. The day they launched the new ship would end with a big celebration. They would decorate the ship and have a *pooja*[56] according to the Hindu tradition and offer various food items to God. My mother a strong Christian never allowed us to eat the food offered to this God. And the whole crowd would be standing and they would distribute the food offered to God during the pooja, to the waiting crowd. Usually such offered food was forbidden for the Christians but we, the children, standing in the crowd, ate it. It was more of fun, than rules and regulations. But we were careful to wipe our mouths carefully before going home. The only thing that I did not like and avoided was, when they sacrificed a goat. That was their superstition but for me, it was horror. So I would run away from the place, when this ritual was performed. They had rhyming phrases chanted by the men, who pushed the ship into the sea.

---

[56] Prayer for Hindu gods

Chapter 50

Local Fruits

One of the seasonal fruits was *Naaval* the local blackberries. Usually women carried these fruits on the street and shouted the name, to attract attention from the prospective buyers. Those women swung their hips and walked very quickly. We had to run fast, to stop them to buy those fruits. They said that it was very good for diabetes. There was a village Nagarkovil, where the shrubs of these fruits were all over the place. Sometimes our servants together with my brothers went to this open place, plucked them and brought them home. The same tree was in the boys' college which was the target for me and my brother when going to church. Climbing trees was second in nature for me proving the theory of Darwin I suppose. One thing we should have in mind. You could never escape the purple shade in your tongue when you ate those fruits. There was a wood apple tree in the college, which I could not climb but when the fruit fell down the care taker Sithamparapillai collected them and gave us. Once, one of my father's students, a girl, related the following incident. My father was taking the class for the advanced level students and suddenly he heard the wood apple falling from the tree. He sent one of the student to collect it and told the rest of the class "This is for my little daughter, *baby pot* at home" With all my faults his affection for me was great till the end.

The other fruit was the guava. Some friends of ours brought those fruits from their garden about eleven miles away from our house. But there was one tree in the school, for which I was a friend. Often I climbed the tree and plucked the unripe fruits and ate them. They were not tasty but for adventure sake I ate. Another tree that we had in the school was the *Twisted Tamarind*, when ripe, it was quite sweet, but unfortunately, we, the girls, tried to get the fruits by throwing stones, whether they were ripe or not. In one of the parallel streets was the first Bank of Ceylon building. There was also another variety of Tamarind, which were long fruits, when ripe, sweet like syrup. But it cuts your tongue because the outer coat was very hard. Yet there was another tree inside the Hindu Temple premises called the *Magulam* fruit. My third brother and I used to go to this temple's back premises, for which we have to go through the temple, although my mother had forbidden us to enter any Hindu temples. The other one was the Mango fruit, this was at our neighbour's house, but at school the girls, who had mangos in their houses, sliced them and brought them and my task was to take chilli powder and salt. During the breaks we all shared it and enjoyed the fruit.

You could see bunches of fruits belonging to the *date family* but smaller in size called *Eechai*. They are seen as stray plants in places like Vallai, Kudattanai. They are also brought by women and auctioned on the street. The black fruits are the ripe ones and they were very sweet. When they were raw, they were red, but there was a danger that there were snakes near those bushes, therefore we were not allowed to go and cut those bunches. There were two other small fruits, which were seasonal, one the *Paalai* fruit, which came once a year and it had milk like secretion, which made your mouth stick. There was a special technique to eat that fruit, otherwise you would be in trouble. You had to split the fruit, take out the seeds and then put it into the mouth without touching the lips, and then you would be fine. Sometimes during our secret visits to the market we bought those fruits but then we had to be careful not to be caught. In case our lips touched that fruit, then gingili oil was applied to the lips to take away the effect of this stickiness. Therefore eating that fruit without other people's knowledge, was seldom possible.

The other one came only every three years and sometimes five years. It was called *Muthali* fruit. The reason was, people cut the trees to use them as wooden planks, so that it would take three to five years for the trees to grow and produce the fruits. One of the famous fruits, the jackfruit, was the biggest fruit in our fruit world, it has a spiky outer skin and inside you have bulbs with seeds, which were very tasty. Sometimes it was sweeter than the honey but we have the same problem of the milky secretion, which can stick all over your mouth and hands. The middle part of the fruit had the milky secretion which was very sticky, so they applied gingili oil to the knife before cutting the fruit: usually this dirty job was done by my mother and we simply enjoyed the fruit. We had various varieties in plantains, but the green bananas we see in Europe were usually seen in the southern areas.

About six miles away from our town and three miles away from my village, there were cashew nuts trees grown wild. During the season our big servant and my brothers went to this place and plucked the cashew nuts together with the fruit, and brought them home. They detached the nuts and we ate the fruits. But the fruits could damage your throat and you could lose your voice if you ate a lot. Those nuts were put into the burning fire and when they secrete an oily fluid they took them out, smashed it with hammer or stone and took the cashew nut which was inside. The process of getting the cashew nuts was more interesting than the cashew nuts themselves. My uncle, who lived in the East, used to bring another fruit which we called "*Silk Tamarind*". He also brought cashew nuts and curd in big clay pots and these things were specialities for us because we got it only once a year.

Often there were no walls between the houses only fences. There would be trees grown in regular intervals along the boundary, which served as pillars to thatch the gaps with coconut palm leaves. The trees were *glesiria, poovarasu* and sometimes *moringa*. The only disadvantage was the caterpillars. If you came in contact with their hair, you could have a terrible allergy with swollen skin but the worst was the itching sensation. I get goose pimples when I think about it even now. There were only two treatments to soften it. When it was mild you apply the juice of red onions. In worst cases Gingili oil was applied and with a knife the hair was slowly scraped off. This was a common occurrence for us, when we were children, because we went and pluck the flowers from those trees to play with. Once a year, the farmers came and bought the leaves with small branches for their fields, to cover the sown seeds the birds tried to eat: For two to three months the trees would be bare and then the new shoots would come out. Good for the trees and useful for the farmers.

Chapter 51

Home medicines

The home medicines recommended by our grandparents and parents were quite popular in the house. For Adenoids we were asked to take the roots of the traditional grass, red onions and fennel seeds, crush them together, and keep the mixture in a piece of old cloth tied with a string. Then with face facing upwards, the mixture was squeezed till drops of liquid fell into each nostril. You had to do a few times. It eased the block and your breathing became back to normal. For migraine, on a rough surface, usually the cement floor, you squeezed the lemon juice and rubbed *Ver Kombu*[57] to get a paste. This paste should be applied to your fore head and the migraine would vanish. If you had sore throat, especially just before you sing, then you chew *Athimathuram*[58] a special herb. For baby's stomach problem, they took the betel leaf, warmed it in the flame, and then kept it on the stomach. For toothache a clove was taken and bitten for some time then the pain would go. Moringa leaves with small onions were boiled and drunk for allergy. When you had heavy cold lentil flour, milk and sugar with fennel and pepper powder were boiled together and drunk while it was still hot. When my sisters were pregnant during the last stage they had pseudo pain exactly like the real labour pain. They asked me to get the *"Arakeerai"*[59] a local herb. This they boiled with water and gave my sisters to drink. If it was falls pain it would vanish. Whenever we took native medicine, it was taken care that a particular vegetable *"Pavaikai"*[60] was not included in our food because it had the tendency to break the effect of the medicines. If we had any food connected to tapioca that famous tuber in our country then Ginger should not be taken. The combination would be poisonous. If we had mild ear ache then peeled Garlic was put into the ear hole then the pain would go if it was not an infection.

Whenever anyone of us was ill then father was the first person to feel the pulse and decide what medicine should be taken. There were different products manufactured by the company M&B. Father always gave one product or the other. They were sulphur products. When we had fever and cold he would give Sulphur Diazine and when anything connected to digestion he would give

---

[57] Dried ginger

[58] A sweet tasting dried root

[59] Small herb grown wildly

[60] A vegetable with bitter taste

Sulphur Thalesol. We never knew anything else unless or otherwise we had to be admitted to the hospital, which I never remember, except for my appendicitis operation. Even during her pregnancy, my sister always consulted my father, asking to feel the pulse. Two other native medicines prepared with gold were popular in the house. One was *"Thaga Elathy*[61] for general health like weakness and *"Maha Elathy* for my mother's heart. The former was recommended for other friends, who benefited. One of them was a friend of mine, who was the neighbour to my aunt in Jaffna. Now she lives in London. I met her last year after 30 years and she referred to it. The other product was the balm from the company Vicks which still exists.

---

[61] Native medicine prepared with gold.

Chapter 52

My operation

As I told before, our family was an exception, because all of us were operated for appendicitis, except my father. One day I developed a pain in the stomach while I was in the kitchen, followed by nausea. Affirming my suspicion that my nausea and head ache and pain in the stomach had been caused by the heat inside the kitchen, I came out and sat in the living room. The sweat beaded like morning dew. Suddenly I had a spasm of pain in the abdomen that almost blacked me out. My father noted my signs and with the experience of six of his family members with the appendicitis condition, immediately took me to the General hospital in Jaffna. I was operated for appendicitis at the general hospital. That was a memorable event in my life. I was operated by a famous Surgeon Dr. Gabriel. I was taken to the operating theatre, not the first time for the family, because we had six cases of the same in the family. I was given a spinal injection instead of Morphine. I was asked to sit and bend and was given an injection in the spine closer to the 4th vertebra. The whole part of stomach became paralyzed but I was awake. I did not know till they started to make the incision. I could feel every movement except the pain. I heard the doctors talking and only then, I realized I was wake. I had closed my eyes during the process of the operation, that's all. The operation was over with only switches and not stitches. The other family members had big scars but mine was only a thin line. I was in the recovering room for some time then the doctor came and tapped my leg. I did not have any pain and I smiled thinking that was all. When they brought me out I saw my father and my eldest sister and I said "Father I am back". My sister hushed me to stay quiet, warning that every move would affect the wound. Only in the middle of the night, I felt the pain of the wound, when the effect of the injection was over. I woke up with pain numbing my senses. To keep my pain low and make me to sleep, they gave me Pethedine.

I stayed at the hospital for a week and every day someone was with me. Such a contrast to the treatment in the western countries nowadays, where the next day you are asked to get up and walk. After two weeks I returned to the school. My class was next to the principal's office. There was a door connecting both. While the lesson was in process, the door opened suddenly, and the clerk brought an arm chair with a cushion, saying "Principal wants you to sit in this chair during the lesson". Yet another privilege I had from my principal, showing her affection to me. I was the seventh to be branded with appendicitis mark in the family

Chapter 53

College, school and university jokes shared by my family

My mother had a cousin, my aunt, living in Jaffna. Quite suddenly my uncle passed away in his fifties and my aunt became a widow quite young. She had five children, they were only one or two years difference between them. One of them was of my age, therefore my mother took me for a weekend or sometimes for a few days to their house and we became playmates. Then to prepare for my advanced level I was sent there to get classes. So I stayed with them as a boarder and it was there that I learnt to be independent. Although my aunt did not visit the cinema hall she allowed her children to go. We were teenagers and we went to watch films during the daytime, especially on Saturdays. Since I was crazy about films it was a great opportunity. We had such fun. My cousin, who was one year elder to me, was so witty that on our way to the cinema and back we were only laughing in the bus hearing his jokes. One of the jokes I still remember. He was in the boys 'school, where in the Advanced Level there were some girls. There was a physics master who was very soft with the girls. One day when my cousin and his friends went to do the practical, my cousin said "Today the girls are having the darkroom test, I am sure he will put a repeat" Unfortunately the master was behind him and he replied "No, I won't."

One day during the English class one of the students had difficulty in saying the word 'persevere'. She repeatedly said 'pershevere' with an 'sh' pronunciation. Getting tired of correcting the student my teacher tried one more attempt and said "Persevere, say" The student confidently said "Pershevereshay". My teacher was speechless.

There were also college dinners, where the students could crack jokes about the teachers. My brother's botany master was a short person, so they cracked a joke saying one day a car entered the college premises without a driver, but suddenly the door opened, and the botany master emerged from the car. I had him as my botany teacher when I attended for special training at an institute. We had the lessons in a big lecture hall. I was at the lab doing some tests and suddenly the test tube burst and the chemical spilled vertically and fell on my eyes. The botany master, who was in charge, came running and helped me. Luckily nothing serious happened. He knew that I often looked down, grinning at him and talked because of his height. When he found nothing serious had happened he said "That is the advantage of being short Miss Gunanayagam, if it had happened to me the liquid would have gone above my head".

There was one boy in my class from the capital, who was extremely clever. His father thought he was distracted by other activities and neglecting his studies, and sent him to Jaffna. He always made some comments and rubbed with the botany teacher. One day both of them had a heated argument about a theory. Seeing the losing battle, the teacher wanted to put an end by saying "What would happen if two snakes try to swallow each other by their tails?" After a short hesitation the boy replied "Happy union Sir"

Similarly there was a dinner joke about my third brother; he went to see a film of the famous actress Marilyn Monroe. He saw the film three times, it seemed, and every time, he said "I am so disappointed." When asked for the reason he replied, "Marilyn Monroe was slowly removing her clothes to swim, when she removed the last piece, a train passed by." He thought if he could see before the train passed he might see her taking off her clothes, so he went early to the film. Other jokes from my father at the college dinner was about a young teacher, who did not take alcohol or eat meat and my father said "My young friend does not eat meat other than human flesh" because he was a lady's man. Those jokes at school dinners about teachers and students were not supposed to be taken seriously; students were allowed to do so. From the university my second sister Rathy brought this joke. One of her colleagues asked her "What is in front of a woman and the back of a cow?" She showed her fists and said "I will give you this" But he said "It's the letter 'W'.

But a tragic incident that happened at the university while the senior students were ragging a fresher pained my heart. At the beginning the medical faculty was only in the capital city Colombo. The senior medical students told a fresher that he should go to the mortuary and feed the bodies, in the middle of the night. He obliged and when he finished, one of the drawer opened and a student pretending to be a corpse whispered, "What about me? That unexpected voice in the mortuary frightened the boy and he collapsed and died. What started as fun, ended in a tragedy.

Chapter 54

Interesting characters in the neighbourhood

A woman lived behind our house had a name, literally translated as "Meaning child". We used the literal translation if we had our private comment. She would come and sit on our veranda with a bundle appearing to leave her husband, when her husband hit her. Occasionally she came out with surprising philosophy. Sometimes she brought her children, who were obviously not under control. They would run here and there, when bored they would turn their attention to the bundle their mother had brought with and tried to dig. Then she would be giving the child a vicious yank with one hand and administering a slap with the other. She was quite calculative but subtle. She would swear she would not go back to her husband, but the next day she would be feeding her husband openly; when anyone asked about the change of mind, she would simply answer "Mind your own business". There was one particular man, who fished only with his net along the shore. He would watch the sea intensively and throw the net. More than anything his facial expression was interesting. He had a very nice wife and two sons and one of them I remember was called "Yapan". These people were beaten by poverty, ignorance and dirt.

My mother had certain people to do the odd jobs at home like putting up sheds, renewing the fence, cleaning the well, sweeping the compound and plucking the coconuts in the compound. One of them was Arumugam. He was a barber by profession but did carpentry. Well sometimes he did some crude work but my mother was satisfied with him, because she could boss him in every way. For every repair in the house her slogan was "Call Arumugam". His wife was very proud of her husband because he had long hair like women and he always came as the goddess "Amman[62]" in the local street opera.

When we had visitors staying at our place and all of us were going to school, sometimes my mother ordered the breakfast from the local people. There was one woman called Achimuttu, who delivered the food for us. She was the type of woman, who chattered incessantly about inconsequential things and would very quickly get on your nerves. Her eyes spoke of sublime self confidence or an ability to lie effectively, someone, who could look you so boldly in the eyes and hold your gaze. She would bring the local gossips to my mother. Sometimes she

---

[62] Incarnation of Hindu goddess Kali

was allowed to go into the kitchen and keep the food while my mother was somewhere else in the house. We had a big wooden box full of brass things, old traditional lamps and pots. When the trend was out of fashion for brass, my mother kept them inside this box. But for festivals we took them out and used them. It should be polished with tamarind, to give a good shine. This woman slowly started to steal these brass things from the box hiding them in her sari. It went on for a long time, I think, because one day, when my mother opened the box it was half empty. And she never had a clue, what happened to them. She could not remember having given them to someone.

Two years later Archimuthu came and invited my mother to come to her new house warming ceremony. She had recently built the house. My mother went to the local people's houses when she was invited for weddings, puberty ceremonies and when new houses were built. Usually she gave them money. So taking the envelope with the money, my mother went and to her surprise, she saw glass cupboards on the wall decorated with our brass things. It was unfortunate that we never had a mark on those things therefore my mother could not claim. But of course, she could identify them as ours. Afterwards she was never allowed to enter our house.

When my mother passed away I was wearing a chain that looked like gold but it was not. I removed it and kept it on the table. People were coming and going. And this woman came to the funeral and her long fingers were tempted to take it. The next day when I looked the chain was not there, but I did not bother because it was not an expensive thing. After a week, she brought some food, It was a custom by neighbours and friends when there was a death in a family, and was telling us "Nowadays people do not wear gold things, and sometimes these people give them to pawn it, and we find out that it is not gold." We were confused by her talk, but after she left under the mat she was sitting, was the chain again. I think most probably she took the chain to sell and the shop man must have said that it was not gold. My father said "You can never correct the long fingers. Habit is stronger than conscience"

Chapter 55

Different denominations of Christianity visiting us

All kinds of Christian communities were accepted in our house. There was the Salvation Army sector, who visited us often. Both my parents were glad to entertain them and support them. They were given food and monetary help. There was a couple, who were in charge for the area and had many children. My parents helped them with school needs. They were very good singers and came as carol singers during the Christmas season.

There was an American couple who, belonged to the Jehovah's witnesses. They were one of the first people, who used the motorbike with the side car. It was quite new in our time. They would come home and preach bible, and my parents and who ever in the house, would sit with them and listen to their talk. That was not once but several times. My father's principle was hearing scripture any time and from any one revived your spirit. One need not be converted to that denomination, but no harm in hearing the teaching.

My father's family was predominantly orthodox Hindus and my father was the first member to become a Christian. My father had only one sister and one young brother. His brother Nadarajah, after the high school worked in the government sector. But soon became attracted to the gospel of the Ceylon Pentecostal Mission joined the mission in 1943, and later became the chief pastor of the mission. He never married, and served in India and Malaysia, before he came back to his mother land, and remained there till his last days. He was a powerful speaker and in the later stages even my father was attracted by his sermons. His name was Pastor Nadarajah a typical Hindu god's name. Usually when the Hindus are converted as Christians they change their Hindu name. But he did not want to change because he said "I want to be a witness for the others". Then his sister's family and his mother all of them became Christians. Therefore members of the Pentecostal mission also were regular visitors to our house. Preaching and prayers were in abundance in our house. Whenever my uncle came to our town, he never forgot to visit my father and had the same respect for him. I still have the last letter he wrote to me before he entered glory.

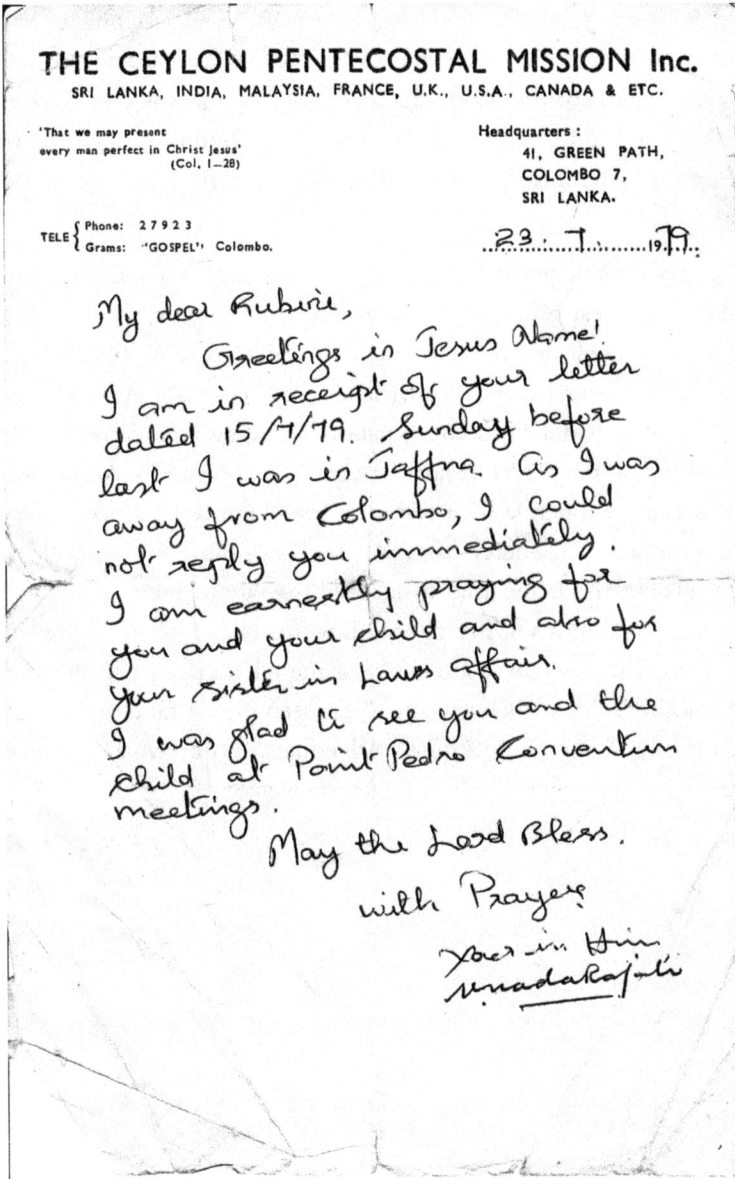

The last letter my uncle wrote

My second brother Bala recollected another incident. One day a man appeared at our door step claiming that while he was working as a clerk in the plantation in the hill station, he had a vision to preach about Christ, and from then onwards he was travelling to various places. When he came to our area, he had a vision to come to my parents. My parents gave him food and a place to sleep.

He stayed for some time. He used to go out to do his preaching. One day my second brother and mother were travelling and he was also in the bus. At a particular place some of the Hindu devotees got into the bus returning from the temple. He started to preach them. The provoked Hindu devotees tried to beat him. Then my mother intervened and released him from the beating. Afterwards he was never seen.

My brother Bala got acquainted with the Bahi Ulla mission and they visited our house. Then my eldest brother introduced the Tent mission people. There were two people, who came home and preached Christianity. At first it was at our house. My eldest sister had a piece of land a few blocks away. They erected a tent there and they had a small congregation attending their meetings. Beautiful music and different people from Jaffna came as speakers. They were not Tamils but Burgers. The two gentle men stayed at my eldest sister's house for quite a long time. One was Mr. Sherer from Australia and the other was Mr. Dorman from Newzeland. The latter used to talk with us about his country when they came for occasional meals. Once he told how his home town was destroyed by tidal waves. At that time it was a fantasy for me till we really saw the tsunami in 2006. My mother's friend belonged to the Assembly of God and we also had occasional visits from the 7th day Adventists. Nobody in the name of Christianity was ever rejected, in fact they were welcomed.

Chapter 56

Tornado in Point Pedro

In 1962 we had the experience of a Tornado in our town. My mother had gone on a visit to the capital to see her friends and relatives. My two brothers, my second sister, I and my father were at home. The boys slept in one room near the dining room and I, my father and my sister were in the bed room. It was almost bed time. My father finished his dinner and went out to the front yard to have a small walk. We were all in bed. Suddenly there was a big noise as though many army trucks were coming. My father rushed inside and then the strong force of the tornado attacked our house. And there came a sudden wind of hammering fists against the door and the old hinges strained and squealed as my father set his shoulder to the panels again and again. My father struggled to close the door but could not. He was almost fighting with the wind not to allow the wind to enter the house. We also heard a big noise of a metal clang. The electricity went off. We were in total darkness. It lasted only about ten minutes and then everything was quiet.

My father closed the door and came in. I stirred in the valley of my pillow. Then we heard a bang on the door between our room and my brothers' room. My second brother came in with a solemn face. He said "I felt the bed of Chelva (my third brother) and it is wet. I think it is blood. Something has happened to him." We were about to go but we had to find the candle and the match box. My father shoved away a sheet of metal, lifted a wooden beam stepped over the rubble but saw no blood. While we were in the process of searching we heard a movement. And in the dark we could see another figure emerging through the kitchen door. It was my third brother. He said "I thought I was the only one who survived because I could not find Bala in his bed". We kept awake for some time and soon it was dawn. It was the December season. The Hindus have a ritual of singing religious songs and walking through all the streets. They were shocked to see our street because the other parts of the town were not affected and they did not even hear anything.

My father was the first person to go out and he came back running to say "Come and see this miracle" We all ran out to find the whole aluminium roof of the Rotary Club about five hundred meters away from our house, lying on the space at our back yard, between the well and the house just fitting the space. It had flown over the house and had fallen into the space. What we could not understand was, how was it possible it just fitted the space without damaging our house. My father said it was simply a miracle. The tornado touched our town in a haphazard way. Some houses were damaged but the houses next were not. The girls' school and the church were damaged but not much damage for the Boys' College. For weeks we did not have classes but we all went and cleared the rubbles in the school premises. Mostly the broken pieces of tiles scattered all over.

Chapter 57

Mother's illness and second sister's marriage

My mother was a very active woman. Attending meetings, weddings or at least visiting her friends, not only locally but also in other parts of the country. Once, when she was getting down from a taxi near my aunt's house, she fell on a heap of pebbles. She did not take much care about it but had some pain, and later, it became acute. She was taken to the capital and was in a paying ward where special care was taken. My aunt, that is my mother's third brother's wife, was the principal of the nurses training college in the city. So there was a lot of care for my mother and finally they found out that it was a slip disc and gradually she would be bedridden. At the hospital ward her neighbour was the wife of a very rich Sinhalese business man from Kurunagala, whose brother was a minister in the cabinet at that time. My mother could make friends easily. So this lady Sita, and my mother became friends. She was there for a heart problem, quite young and beautiful. From the north every weekend my father, my second sister and I took turns to visit my mother in the capital which was about 280 kilometres from our town. We had to take the famous Yaaldevi, an express train which went quickly to the city, in 6 hours. Sometimes we took the Friday mail train. My father used to take the Ayurvedic medicine, with gold as the chief component, to my mother for her heart condition. Somehow or the other the topic cropped up between Sita and my mother, and when my mother returned home bedridden, Sita and her husband decided to come and stay in Point Pedro and take this native medicine made of gold. They rented a house and stayed with us for a month, they brought their own servants and maids to look after Sita. And they had a young son called Srinath.

My mother was bedridden for two years. We tried all the medicine but it did not work. Then one day a friend of my father told that there was special oil made out of the fat deposit on peacock's legs and this would make the disc supple. So we got this medicine, the oil was applied on a plantain leaf and my mother was laid down there.

That was the time when my father insisted and my mother wanted that my second sister got married. She was teaching at the Girls' School at that time. There were some outside proposals that did not come through. Then my parents decided our cousin Thavaratnam, my father's sister's son, would be the best match. Things started to work out quicker than expected. My aunt agreed and the arrangements for the wedding were quickly made. That was a wedding within the family and had fewer formalities. Decisions were made by my father and mother. The staff of the girls 'school, and her friends cooperated. It was a pink and blue wedding. We had pink and blue curtains at home. Bride's maids' sari blouses were made in Jaffna and the flower girls had long dresses. I and my cousin, the sister of my brother in law, were the bride's maids. Two days before the wedding my sister's new gold wrist watch was lost but the staff of the girls' school immediately bought a wrist watch as a wedding present and brought it the day before the wedding as a surprise. My uncle conducted the wedding ceremony. Because of my mother's illness, we could not have the reception at our house, as we did for my eldest sister.

Soon after the church ceremony, there was a big reception at the school hall. My mother could not come for the wedding because she scarcely could walk, and stayed at home. It was sad but we tried our best to make our sister's wedding a success. Her wedding was totally different from my elder sister's wedding, grand in its own way, and was organized by the staff of the Methodist girls' school, especially by a very close friend of my sister, Mangalam Arulnanthy, who was also my English teacher. My father was happy that it went on well and when the bride and the bridegroom arrived home after the reception, to their surprise they saw my mother, walking to the entrance with the garland. That was the first step of my mother's recovery. We were overwhelmed to see her walking. Seeing that my father said "God moves in a mysterious way, which cannot be understood by us" with tears in his eyes.

My second sister as a bride with mother standing for the first time after two years in bed

Of course the traditional dinner was held at home, according to the modern style. My sister continued to live with us, while my brother in law worked in the capital and came for the weekends. Slowly my mother recovered her health and was able to go to the church. To reduce the strain of walking a long distance, we had to move to my sister's second house which was closer to the church.

Chapter 58

The final stages of my parents

This last chapter has nothing to do with my golden days of my childhood but I felt the book should end with the "Good Bye" I said to my wonderful parents, whose good deeds follow us like a shadow in our lives.

My third brother Chelva became a member of the APEX club, while he was at the University. One day, he informed my parents that he had a chance to go to different countries, and he would like to go on this trip. It sounded quite exciting and he convinced my mother first and since he was an adult my father thought he knew what he was doing. He said it would be only three months. Well, adults were treated like adults in our house. I was in India doing my degree in Madras. My brother was in Turkey, where he was supposed to take the flight back to Sri Lanka via India. One of the planes from Turkey crashed in India and all the passengers died, and my brother's name was listed. My parents received a telegram about my brother's misfortune. In the mean time he visited my college one day before, asking the Director, for permission to see me at the college. Because he had a beard and did not look good in the eyes of the director she sent him out telling him to meet me at the hostel later. He went to Paris Corner and stayed at the YMCA. Due to the pressure of time he left Madras without seeing me. So when the next day I received a telegram saying "Chelva died in India make the funeral arrangements" I rushed to my College seeking help. When my director heard that she was so upset, repeatedly telling "It was my fault that I did not allow him to see you." My English lecturers Miss. Ratna Papa (The famous Kutchupuddy dancer) and Miss Renuka, were quite sympathetic and immediately took action to find out, what had happened. Miss Renuka's father was a high official in the Madras Police Department. Since my brother came the day before, and the telegram said he died before, there was confusion about the contradictory messages. Miss Ratnapapa was so kind that she took me to her house, not leaving me to mourn alone in the hostel. One night I was in agony, but the next day the Police confirmed that my brother had crossed to *Mannar* (A port in Sri Lanka where ships carried passengers from India) from Rameswaram (a port you board the ship in India to go to Sri Lanka). Although all ended well, Miss RatnaPapa kept me at her house for the weekend, and took me for a wedding of a film producer's granddaughter, where I met a lot of film stars and upcoming playback singers like Malaysia Vasudeven and SB Balasubramaniam, who later topped the list.

Bad news always seemed to come in twos and threes. The story of my brother did not finish there. Soon after my parents heard the message about my brother's death, people visited them and they had a service at home for his life. Unaware of any of those things, three days later, my brother, who returned to the country, knocked on the door in the middle of the night. It was my mother who, opened the door. There stood my brother with unshaven face. She actually thought it was his ghost. Then the others joined and were overwhelmed by the safe return of my brother. He forgot that my mother was a heart patient. Two extreme shocks were too much for her. Some weeks later my mother passed away peacefully in her sleep. When the news reached me they all thought it was a joke again. As for me a cold tickle went down my bones. But there was one friend Geetha, in the hostel, who helped me, to book the flight to go home for my mother's funeral, as I always had an open return ticket. That was the most difficult time for my father, because he had to bare the loss of my mother and at the same time, supportive to my brothers and me at the university. My father sat on the sofa and cried when he lost my mother, who was his life partner for 45 years. I remember him saying just before the funeral, "My Mani is gone, what that is in the coffin is only a body. I don't want to see that. I would like to have a living memory of her and not this body". Soon after that, my father had a sudden acutely unpleasant feeling of loneliness but continued to live with my second sister.

The most difficult time my father had was, when both my brothers had problems at the medical college. They did not pass their compulsory examination, mainly because of their fault and partly because they had big problems with the professors, resulting in their leaving the medical college and trying other studies, one in theology and the other in law. They were twisted in a depravity from which, it would be unimaginable to redeem them. A moral vacillation, when a decision jeopardised their own career. Both had the open selection of other fields of studies. My father was devastated. There cannot be much experience in human existence, more harrowing than witnessing your own child, the bearer of your name heritage, treading downwards, after all the efforts to bring them to that level. My father had a Muslim student and his name was Sheik Thamby. After studying at the Boys' College he started his own business in a textile shop. His shop was called the Corner shop in Tamil because it was at the corner. He had great respect for my father. One day, when my second brother was travelling in the bus, he met him and was really sorry about our brothers' situation, and advised them to appeal against the decision. He said to ask the popular minister and politician, who was a friend of my father to get the help. When my third brother approached him, he sent my brother to another expert, an old student of my father and a well known legal adviser. He found a legal loophole in the constitution of the university. My brother Chelva underwent a 5 hour operation in the maxillary region, as a research student, and that was enough ground to be admitted again. The surgeon, who operated him was fully supportive and he had the chance again to continue his medical career. My second brother Bala, followed suit and was readmitted and both finished as medical doctors, before my father passed away. When my brothers were readmitted his happiness increased with laughter and a rich chortle of pure joy escaped his lips. Opportunity seldom knocked twice but in my brothers' cases it did. My father's good nature played a big role in his old students helping my brothers. I think that was the most difficult period in my father's life.

12 years later, when my eldest daughter was born, my father visited me at the hospital and named her Sophia after my mother. 16 days after that, he visited all of us, including his sister and two days after that, he developed a chest pain and the next day, he passed away. I said the same thing he said after my mother died. He was a blessed man, who saw the grand child of his youngest daughter. I refused to look at the coffin carrying his body saying, "I want to have a living memory of my father", which I still have.

I was an adult when my mother died and a mother when my father passed away thereby those memories should not be included as my childhood memory. The genuine purpose of including this chapter was to show not only how they lived with their Christian principles but left the same message for us, their children. Again I could only quote a verse from the bible which is appropriate for my parents.

"I have fought a good fight; I have finished my course I have kept the faith"

2nd Timothy 4.11

One last word

An extract from my thesis

Some theorists emphasize the conflict resolution model focus on how people weigh the forces in adjusting their attitudes. Some theorists say such departure stress the intellectual aspects of persuasion while the others point out as emotional considerations. But they tend to neglect the process of persuasion and thus serve to supplement rather than supplant.

A humorous passage from the children's classics Charlotte's Web could be the best illustration. "The young lamb had refused to play with Wilbur the pig because 'pigs mean less than nothing to me'. This was an unreasonable refusal. So Wilber gives this angry answer. 'What do you mean less than nothing?... I don't think there is any such thing as less than nothing. Nothing is absolutely the limit of nothingness. It is the lowest you can go. It's the end of the line. How can something be less than nothing, it would be something – even though it's just a very little bit of something. But if nothing is nothing, then nothing has nothing that is less than it is'. 'Oh, be quiet', said the lamb. 'Go play by yourself'

(Courtesy from: E.C.White. Charlotte's Web Page 28)

It is confrontational direct with a short philosophical argument on the exact meaning of the word 'nothing', instead of humbly understanding the loose every day use of the word. I expect the later from my readers.

Author

Thank you Professor

With Professor Dr.Kavin Pickering at the post graduation in London.

Epilogue

I have written the life I had with my parents and nothing beyond that. When I was allowed to take decisions independently I made many blunders which I regret now. That was because father was not there to advice me. Those independent decisions should not reflect on my parents. But one should accept that life cannot be always guided and to err is human.

When I sit with my children and my grand-daughter I had an urge to share the best part of my childhood with them. I had five childhood dreams, which appeared to be impossible to achieve, when I was a child. But to my surprise, I achieved all my goals and fulfilled my dreams.

Professionally none of my siblings or I failed my parents. If they were to be alive they would be proud of their children. It is a pity they did not live long to see the success of all their children. The upbringing, the love, the understanding, the tolerance and guidance they gave us were remarkable. The result is, now we have a reasonable balance in human affairs. The grief, the disgust and regret are replaced by bliss and peace only when I think about those golden days of my childhood. It woke memories of scores of old quarrels I could only laugh at. Sometimes I struggled to compose myself and felt my sense of humor coming to my rescue. Again that was the influence of my father.

As I started to write this book memories came flooding back together with people who played significant and insignificant role in my childhood. There are sometimes in your life when you are asked a question and you know the answer well but you cannot find the words to fit. They do sound so dull and silly you feel shame. But that did not happen here. Within my own territory I am safe and comfortable. When I wrote the book I perceived in myself the existence of a darker motive infinitely more obscure one which my rational mind continue to reject.

Many friends and relatives of my parents scattered all over the world are Perhaps interested to know where and what their children are doing.

I like to acknowledge about their children for those people who would like to know about them.

Late Mrs. Cecilia Gunamani Rajaratnam nee Gunanayagam
(retired Deputy Principal Methodist Girls' high School Point Pedro)

Late Edward Gunaseelan Gunanayagam
(Accountant, Upali group of companies, Sri Lanka)

Mrs. Mary Gunaratha Thavaratnam nee Gunanayagam
(retired Principal, Methodist Girls' High School, Point Pedro)

Dr.Soloman Gunapalan Gunanayagam
(retired Surgeon Commander of the Sri Lanka Navy
and now a Baptist pastor of BOCQ in Canada)

Dr. James Gunachelvam Gunanayagam
(Formally missionary doctor in South Africa and now in Sri Lanka)

Dr.Gloriana Gunarubini Selvanathan nee Gunanayagam
(International Coordinator for International Film Festivals and Jury for the same in Germany,
France, Norway and India, Founder TISERS English school in Berlin)

Childhood dreams are not always impossible and could be fulfilled: determination that matters. On the whole I am satisfied with my life. Whenever I said this, my friends would say, 'very few could say that'. For the young people, who complain about the stress they have in their childhood, I could only say 'a stress is a stress only when you think it is, you can always turn it into a bliss without doubt.'

Gloriana Selvanathan

Berlin, 2014

Acknowledgements

I would like to say a big thank you for the following for helping me to complete this book.

1. My daughters Sofia Binias, Irene Selvanathan and her fiancée Timo Hahn for their help in computer technology

2. My son Thilak Selvanathan, My son in law Phillip Binias, My daughter in law Daniela Selvanathan and my loving grand-daughter Mina Selvanathan for their inspiration

3. Mrs. Josephine Bienert-Köhler for the unique cartoon back cover

4. Miss Sandra Hoff for her support

5. My Brother in law Mr. J.S. Rajaratnam for those rare photographs

6. My sister Gunarathy Thavaratnam for photographs and information

7. My brother Dr. Solomen Gunapalan for sharing his memories

8. My brother Dr. James Gunachelvam for his graceful permission

9. Mrs. Gowry Shanmuganathan for the wedding lunch photo

10. A special thank you for all my teachers, friends, neighbours, and all the others involved in this book.

11. My Publishers - Arima pulishing, UK

12. E.C. White – author Charlotte web

13. Courtesy. Jena film festival for the Photos

14. Courtesy: Sehsüchte film festival Potsdam for press photos

15. Courtesy: Seventh Channel communicaton for the festival photos

16. Courtesy: EMF catalogue 1996, Berlinale.

17. Courtesy: Norway film Festival for the photo

Gloriana Selvanathan

www.ingramcontent.com/pod-product-compliance
Lightning Source LLC
Chambersburg PA
CBHW070943150426
42812CB00066B/3250/J